PERFORMING PRC

Curious Intimacies

'This book makes a series of important theoretical, aesthetic and pedagogical moves. It is an absolutely original and generative contribution to the study of performance.' – **Michael Peterson**, *Associate Professor and Director of Instruction, Department of Theatre and Drama, University of Wisconsin-Madison, USA.*

How does proximity between audiences and performers change the nature of live performance? How does it feel? How long can it last? How close is too close?

Exploring the rise of close encounter, immersive productions that shine a light on performer-audience relationships, this book considers the impact of space and proximity in live performance.

Drawing on their experience as internationally acclaimed performance artists, Leslie Hill and Helen Paris richly document their creative processes, performances and audience's responses in a series of illuminating case studies. Relating their practice to wider issues in contemporary performance and detailing workshop exercises that aid performance making, this unique fusion of artistic and academic reflection is crucial reading for students, scholars and practitioners alike.

Leslie Hill and **Helen Paris** are Associate Professors of Performance Making at Stanford University, USA. They are co-editors of *Performance and Place*, and writers, performers, filmmakers and co-directors of Curious, the award winning London-based theatre company, produced by Artsadmin.

Performing Proximity

Curious Intimacies

Leslie Hill and Helen Paris

palgrave
macmillan

First published 2014 by
PALGRAVE MACMILLAN

Palgrave Macmillan in the UK is an imprint of Macmillan Publishers Limited, registered in England, company number 785998, of Houndmills, Basingstoke, Hampshire RG21 6XS.

Palgrave Macmillan in the US is a division of St Martin's Press LLC, 175 Fifth Avenue, New York, NY 10010.

Palgrave Macmillan is the global academic imprint of the above companies and has companies and representatives throughout the world.

Palgrave® and Macmillan® are registered trademarks in the United States, the United Kingdom, Europe and other countries.

ISBN 978–1–137–32829–8   hardback
ISBN 978–1–137–32828–1   paperback

This book is printed on paper suitable for recycling and made from fully managed and sustained forest sources. Logging, pulping and manufacturing processes are expected to conform to the environmental regulations of the country of origin.

A catalogue record for this book is available from the British Library.

A catalog record for this book is available from the Library of Congress.

Typeset by MPS Limited, Chennai, India.

Printed in China

This book is dedicated to Christine,
always close despite the distance

and to our friends and collaborators Alex, Emmy and Claudia, who have
shared many proximate performances and processes with us.

Contents

Contents

List of Illustrations

Acknowledgements

This book and the performance work described within it would not have been possible without the contributions of many talented people for whose support we are hugely grateful.

Our love and thanks to our extraordinary families and friends who make our lives richer by their proximity. Deep thanks to our wonderful collaborators: Claudia Barton, Hugo Glendinning, Alex Hyde, Andrew Kötting, Graeme Miller, Emmy Minton, Gretchen Schiller, Lois Weaver and Caroline Wright. Thanks to Julie Tolentino, Geoff McGarry, Rene Newby and Joseph Young for your performances and to production managers Nao Nagai and Steve Wald for making everything work. Thanks to Upinder Bhalla and all at the National Center for Biological Sciences, Bangalore, and to Quasim Aziz and all at the Wingate Institute for Neurogastroenterology, London.

Our huge gratitude to all at Artsadmin, especially Cheryl Pierce, Judith Knight and Gill Lloyd for their indefatigable support of all the projects detailed within this book and to our brilliant and generous Curious board: Theresa Beattie, C. J. Mitchell, Jennifer Parker Starbuck, our champion chair Philippa Barr.

Thanks to our funders, particularly Arts Council England, the British Council and Wellcome Trust and to Salette Gresset for years as our company's ACE officer. Thanks to all the producers who have supported the work of Curious over the years, especially Mark Ball, Francis Alexander, Anthony Roberts, Helen Cole and Nikki Millican. Thanks also to Wellcome Trust arts producers Clare Thornton and Shognah Manson, and to Ophelia Huang and Simon Kirby in Shanghai. Thanks to Lyn Gardener for her support and her work in highlighting Live Art in the United Kingdom.

As ever, thanks to Lois Keidan and the Live Art Development Agency for their support of Curious through the years and for supporting the artists communities which nourish us all. When we were embarking on our performance careers in the 1990s so many of our touchstones and reference points were the artists whose work we saw via Lois's Live

Art programming at the ICA in London. Some icons of our coming of age were Ron Vawter, Karen Finley, Nao Bustamante, Penny Arcade, Robbie McCauley, Nigel Charnock, Annie Sprinkle, Lois Weaver, Peggy Shaw, Ron Athey, Lawrence Steger, Bobby Baker, Tim Miller, Forced Entertainment, DV8, Goat Island, Guillermo Gómez-Peña, the Wooster Group, Maria La Ribot, Laurie Anderson and Marina Abramović. This was 'the cannon' in which we first became literate in performance and performance making. These were our progenitors.

Thank you to Peggy Phelan and Jill Dolan for the inspiration of your writing over the years and to fellow artists for the inspiration of your work.

Thank you to each of our readers who somehow made time in their own hectic schedules to give us insightful and generous feedback on draft chapters: Josh Abrams, Ann Carlson, Laurie Beth Clark, Jennifer Parker Starbuck, Jisha Menon and Michael Peterson. Thanks to Christine Paris Johnstone for her precision proofing and rapid-fire turn around despite the eight-hour time difference between San Francisco and Cheltenham. Thanks to all at Palgrave Macmillan, in particular Paula Kennedy, Jenna Steventon, Jenni Burnell, and to Emily Rosser who commissioned our first book with Palgrave in 2006. Special thanks to our brilliant copy editor Penny Simmons.

Thanks to all our wonderful colleagues in the Department of Theatre and Performance Studies at Stanford and to all our students over the years for keeping us curious.

Thank you to all the audience members, performers and workshop participants who have so generously shared insightful feedback of their experiences and whose voices are an integral part of this book.

1 Introduction

From the inside out

This book considers the relationship between proximity and intimacy in live performance. It looks, quite literally, at the distance in physical space between performers and audiences and how that distance or proximity impacts our encounters with one another. In the chapters that follow we write about close encounters between performers and audience members from our unique vantage point as performers of works for small audiences. This project, like our years of work as performance makers, is about paying close attention to people in the moment. We write at length about creating, sharing and witnessing small, delicate encounters and exploring the various alchemies created in works and processes that feature face-to-face encounters. Writing this book is our way of synthesizing and sharing our experiences of performing to audiences in close physical proximity, sometimes close enough to reach out and touch each other, sometimes close enough to see the patterns in each other's irises.

In writing to you now we can't see your eyes, let alone the patterns in your irises, nor do we know anything about your age or gender, if you are inside or outside, if it is late at night or early in the morning, what season it is, what country you are in or any of the individual details we would appreciate about our audience members through shared proximity. In this regard you, dear reader, are much farther from us than our audiences. Still, through writing we hope to convey some of our most acquired thoughts and reflections on performance, offering a different kind of intimacy, one that shares a longer story, a life's work, a series of contemplations rather than a face-to-face encounter.

This book traces the artistic trajectory of our personal quest as makers for meaningful exchanges between audience and performer, for different ways of creating and performing up close. We discuss processes by which we attempt to create experiences that are carefully authored and performed, yet remain open to some level of two-way communication with the audience. In a nutshell, this book is about why we, as makers, value close proximity to audiences and what we have learned through performing to intimate audiences over many years.

This book is performer-oriented in its approach to ideas and experiences. It's about the impact of space and proximity in relation to actual performances rather than abstract or virtual notions of proximity and spectatorship. It deals with specific performers, specific performances and sometimes specific audience members. While this is not exactly a collection of writing that adds up to a methodology for 'proximate performance making', we hope it will provide food for thought for scholars and inspiration for makers in terms of the ways in which they think about audiences and space. The performance works we describe and analyse in this book are not the product of a set form or method. We don't consciously follow formal axioms or rules, nonetheless patterns emerge that we think will be of value to scholars of immersive, participatory and small audience work as well as to performance makers interested in thinking deeply about spatial relationships to audiences. One of our early readers, Michael Peterson, said that he found reading the 'Interior' section useful in relation to a performance he was making at the time. This was a dream readership moment for us, to hear that the writing about specific projects (ours) can be read in fruitful conversation with a host of other ongoing projects (yours).

In terms of situating the work in an artistic, geographical and temporal landscape, the productions described in this book can most comfortably be seen as part of a UK-based Live Art milieu of what is often called small audience or 'one-to-one' performance. Personally, we tend to use the words 'experiential', 'sensuous' and 'intimate' to describe our works for small audiences. In this collection the word 'proximity' is central in talking about the expanding and contracting distances between audience and performer, which we are so interested in exploring.

This book draws from what can be described as 'practice-based research' or 'practice-led research', though we think it important to clarify that the performance works we write about here were not conceived of as research projects. We are artists first and scholars second in terms of chronology – the order in which we approach ideas. We usually work from the 'inside' of our performance-making practice 'out' into investigations of what other artists and scholars have written about related topics and how their work connects (or not) with our ideas and our experiences. Admittedly there may be more two-way exchange between theory and our artistic practice than we are conscious of when we are creating work. Having said that, what was most important to us in making the performance work discussed in this book was the contact and communication between the audience and the performer. In other words, in making these works we weren't trying to prove a theory about proximity and performance; we were trying to make good performances. What is important to us now, in writing this book, is connecting insights from an art practice to the ideas and insights of others in the field and putting them into conversation with each other. After creating many works since 1997 that explore the possibilities of audience-performer dynamics, our collective experience of performing in close proximity to audiences leads us to writing this book as a way of sharing some of our insights and experiences from the performer's point of view.

Although the performance work discussed in this book was not under-taken as 'research' per se, recurring questions run through it which lend themselves, dozens of projects later, to discussion within the context of practice-based research. All of our projects start with a question or a series of questions. We are curious about the world we live in – thus the company name: Curious. Many questions we delve into are project-specific, such as 'What is the relationship between the sense of smell and memory?' (*On the Scent*) or 'What are "gut feelings"?' (*the moment I saw you I knew I could love you*), but the questions we find ourselves returning to time and time again over the years, across multiple projects are:

- What forms of contact and communication are uniquely possible between audience and performer in the live moment?
- What types of experience are only possible in the live moment? What are the textures and temperatures of these moments? How do they feel? How long can they last?
- How can we as performers incorporate the intimacy of 'one-to-one' moments within performance works for larger audiences without rupturing delicate connections between audience and performer?

In this book we muse on what years of performing intimate works has taught us about audience-performer relationships and the value of close physical proximity. We reflect on the intense labour of small audience performance and how this labour impacts directly on the quality of experiences for audiences and performers. We think of this type of performance labour as 'shift work' in that we perform about eight hours a day, repeating performances several times in order to keep the performer-audience ratio intimate while making the work available to larger numbers of people. 'One-to-one' or small audience performance pays attention to the audience in a very particular way and this effort is rewarded in the quality of the experience, both for audience and performer.

Some of the questions explored in this book are:

- How does proximity enable different modes of performance?
- How close is too close for the performer... for the audience?
- Are there 'ideal' densities of audience for particular performances and how do we as makers find the friction points?
- How might we bring the 'intimate senses', the haptic, thermal, taste and olfactory, into more performance experiences and how might this change the nature of the art form?
- What are some of the ways technology enables proximity in live performance?
- How does the extension of our social distance as a species (through communication technologies) diminish or increase our appetite for situations that occur in personal space?

This book also contributes to the current surge in publication about immersive, participatory, intimate and interactive performance, such as Josephine Machon's *Immersive Theatres: Intimacy and Immediacy in Contemporary Performance* (2013), Maria Chatzichristodoulou and Rachel Zerihan's edited collection, *Intimacy Across Visceral and Digital Performance* (2012) and Gareth White's *Audience Participation in Theatre: Aesthetics of the Invitation* (2013). As autoethnographers of theatre practice, we offer insights and analyses as well as our passion and hope for the future of performance. We offer these insights from either side of the performance, from before, after and from within. We offer these reflections as a duet, as individual remembrances and experiences.

In *Utopia in Performance*, Jill Dolan considers, from a critic's point of view, the performative nature of writing about performance:

> Writing, like performance, is always only an experiment, an audition, always only another place to practice what might be an unreachable goal that's imperative to imagine nonetheless. Writing, like performance,

lets me try on, try out, experiment with another site of anticipation, which is the moment of intersubjective relation between word and eye, between writer and reader, all based on the exchange of empathy, respect, and desire [...] Trying to capture something of performance itself – even if it's those inarticulate, ineffable, affective exchanges that are felt and gone even as we reach out to save them – is also a 'doing,' a kind of performative that attempts to fill the 'aporia between logos and the body,' the gap in which performance inevitably, spectrally swirls.

(Dolan, 2005, p. 168)

To us, the project of experimenting through writing with alternative sites of anticipation and encounters, of trying to capture something of the performances themselves, to attempt to fill the aporia, is a project that performance makers should contribute to. In writing this book we see our roles as front-line correspondents, reporting from the scene of audience-performer encounters and offering our reflections. The writing, however, isn't just a reporting after the fact on the project; the writing is part of the project. We take inspiration from our intimate encounters with audiences. Over and over, our audiences teach us how precious shared spatial-temporal experiences are, today more than ever. Dolan searches for utopia in performance; we search for utopia in audiences. In Dolan's utopian spirit, we wish to share the inspiration of our experiences with you.

Performing proximity

Not so many years ago, the word 'space' had a strictly geometrical meaning: the idea it evoked was simply that of an empty area. In scholarly use it was generally accompanied by some such epithet as 'Euclidean', 'isotropic', or 'infinite', and the general feeling was that the concept of space was ultimately a mathematical one. To speak of 'social space', therefore, would have sounded strange.

(Lefebvre, 1991, p. 1)

Notions of proximity are central to this project, so it seems useful to begin by thinking about different ways of measuring and sensing distance or closeness between people. As part of this project on performance and proximity, we would like to reconsider some of the concepts of proxemics within the context of contemporary performance studies. In 1966 anthropologist Edward T. Hall published *The Hidden Dimension*, a landmark work introducing the 'science of proxemics', still widely quoted across many disciplines in relation to the norms of the physical proximity between people in different cultural interpersonal contexts. Hall's model of human proxemics, which draws upon Heini Hediger's work on territorial behaviours in animals, looks at the distances between people in terms of public, social, personal and intimate space. Part of Hall's contribution to anthropology, applied in many other cognate fields, lay in recognizing the central importance of sensory factors beyond the visual in the human perception of space and spacing. He explains that:

> Man's sense of space is closely related to his sense of self, which is in an intimate transaction with his environment. Man can be viewed as having visual, kinesthetic, tactile, and thermal aspects of his self which may be either inhibited or encouraged to develop by his environment.
>
> (Hall, 1966, p. 63)

Hall's humans have much in common with Hediger's animals in their use of multisensory cues to negotiate territory and maintain 'personal space'. Personal space is Hediger's term for the normal spacing patterns that members of a like species maintain between themselves. This personal space exists as an invisible bubble around each organism, with dominant animals having larger 'bubbles' than submissive ones. Likewise, dominant humans, such as public figures, are accorded larger bubbles, so that the more important a person is in your culture, the less chance you have of being physically near them. For Hall, '[...] the realization of the self as we know it is intimately associated with the process of making boundaries explicit' (1966, p. 12). These boundaries are defined by both somatic sensory information and by psychologically and physiologically internalized, but often unconscious, cultural norms.

Hall's work was also significant in terms of his interest in uniquely human cross-cultural and inter-cultural patterns and codes (though some of his examples make slightly jarring reading decades after it was the norm to talk about husbands spotting arrowheads in the desert while wives spot cheese in the refrigerator, or to write broad-stroke chapter subheadings such as 'Germans and Intrusions'). Despite the presence of these 1960s race and gender 'time bombs', Hall's basic concepts of proxemic zones divided into public space, social space, personal space and intimate space have remained current in many fields (Illustration 1.1). Hall's work can be seen as related in spirit to some of the philosophical projects gaining currency in the 1960s, such as Merleau-Ponty's work on the primacy of perception in human experience and cognition and Lefebvre's work examining the cultural production of social space.

Let's work from the outside in, starting at the outside edge of 'public space' and zooming in towards 'intimate space' as we go. 'Public Distance – Far Phase' for Hall is a distance of 25 feet or more, with a perimeter of 30 feet being the distance automatically set around important public figures. Hall illustrates the concept of this zone with two examples. The first example looks at space from the outside in – the force field that developed overnight around John F. Kennedy when he became the Democratic Party nominee, and therefore possibly the next President

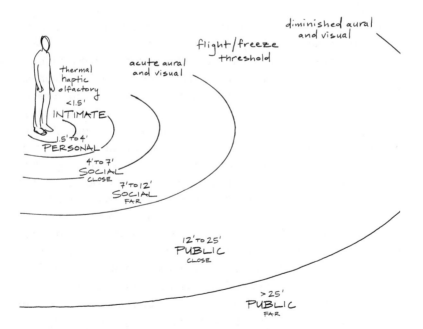

Illustration 1.1   Proxemic zones
[Sketch by Angrette McCloskey]

of the United States. From this moment, others were no longer free to approach Kennedy for a handshake or a few words, but had to wait at the edges of an invisible 30-foot perimeter to be invited into his now public-sized personal space. Interestingly, Hall's other example of the far phase of public distance is from the inside out, looking at the distance divide from the perspective of an actor who, by virtue of their training, knows that 'at thirty foot or more the subtle shades of meaning conveyed by the normal voice are lost as are the details of facial expression and movement' (Hall, 1966, p. 125). In the first example it is the responsibility of those around Kennedy to respect and perpetuate his stature by keeping their distance. In the second example, it is the actor's job to exaggerate or amplify expression, movement and voice in order to bridge the perceptual gulf between performer and audience. The example from the outside in is one of social deference; the example from the inside out is one of specialist training and skill. Actors have a unique cultural role in relation to space in that they must frequently adjust for distance by modifying behaviour in order to create the illusion of being closer than they really are.

To continue a bit further with the Kennedy and actor pairing, let's take the theatre at the Kennedy Center in Washington DC as an example of the kind of distance an actor might expect to work with in performing a play. The 'Ike' theatre is the smallest building in the Kennedy complex, with a seating capacity of 1100. Even in this mid-sized venue, an audience member would be very hard-pressed to get a seat within 25 feet of the actors and so would experience the play far outside the rings of Hall's proxemics zones – in fact they may well be ten times that distance from the stage. So the actor's job of bringing intimate moments to life for the audience involves a learned ability to connect with people across the physical chasms of theatre architecture. Most of the actor's work is done in the no-man's-land of what Hall, with almost humorous simplicity, calls 'not close'. Beyond the 25-foot threshold of the public distance far phase, 'not close' isn't so much a zone in Hall's proxemic model, as it is everything that lies outside the zones, from 30–40 feet to outer space. Outside the radius of Hall's proxemics zones, naturalistic expressions, voice and movement are impossible for audiences to interpret with anything like the precision with which humans can read each other at closer distances. Much of what we think of as theatre acting, in fact, can be seen as an art form developed in response to a type of architecture in the 'fixed feature space' of theatres. As artists, the theatre shapes us as much as we shape the theatre.

The cavernous size of theatre buildings has always been a challenge for actors, many of whom prefer smaller houses, but also for writers and directors who aim to convey situations and emotions in their work in closer-focus modes. Artists and producers a hundred years ago felt many of the same push-pull conflicts experienced today between the artistic and financial demands of theatre. August Strindberg, a leading figure in the Naturalism movement, longed to escape from grandiose Victorian theatre architecture: 'If first and foremost, we could have a small stage and small house, then perhaps a new dramatic art might arise' (Strindberg, 1955, p. 73). The Royal Court, managed by Harley Granville-Barker at the turn of the century and with a reputation for producing innovative new writing (including Henrik Ibsen, George Bernard Shaw, Maurice Maeterlink and Granville-Barker's own work), had a smallish capacity at 841 in comparison to Henry Irving's 2000-seat Royal Lyceum Theatre. The Royal Court was later redesigned to seat only 380 in the downstairs theatre with a smaller 85-person theatre upstairs for even more intimate or experimental possibilities. The remodelled Royal Court kept its reputation for cutting-edge new writing, producing the 'angry young men' John Osborne, Edward Bond and Arnold Wesker and later works by authors such as Caryl Churchill, Martin Crimp and Sarah Kane. As in everything, size is relative: for a London theatre, the Royal Court is pretty small; for a theatre producing experimental contemporary work, the Royal Court is fairly large. In spaces such as the Royal Court's proscenium theatre much of the audience remain in 'not close' space, but a critical mass of spectators have seats within Hall's 25-feet radius, enabling them to pick up on complexities and subtleties in the performances, as well as allowing the performers to have a closer sense of the audience.

In London today the large Victorian theatres tend to be used for long runs of distinctly non-naturalistic forms such as blockbuster musicals, while writers, actors and directors looking to create more intense psychological dramas may seek out smaller spaces like the 250-seat, publicly subsidized Donmar Warehouse. The thrust stage design of the Donmar means that audience members and actors are not forced into the proxemic badlands of 'not close' endured by audience and performers in larger venues. Instead, they encounter each other in what Hall would call 'Social Space' (4–12 feet) and 'Public Space' (12–25 feet). Although working in a small venue isn't a guarantee of producing exemplary theatre, it's probably not coincidental that in its short history, Donmar productions have received an unprecedented number of awards.[1] The opportunity to be closer to the audience is obviously a huge draw for the many talented writers, directors and performers who could easily be earning much more and playing to larger houses elsewhere.

For Hall 'Social Distance' occurs in its close phase at between 4 and 7 feet and in its far phase at between 7 and 12 feet. Both close and far phase social distance is frequently used in the workplace, with close phase more common in social gatherings. At this distance people can use a normal rather than a raised speaking tone and people's faces still appear round whereas in 'public space' people's features flatten out and appear less expressive. In social space people are just out of reach of each other, but can pass an object if they stretch towards each other. In more intimate theatres like the Donmar or the black box spaces of many experimental theatres, some members of the audience will be seated within a 'social' distance from the performers, enabling them to receive more finely tuned aural and visual stimuli without feeling vulnerable in their proximity to the actors – they are still at a 'safe' distance. Depending on the production, one might argue that a 'social' distance from the performers makes for a very good, if not the best, audiencing position.

'Personal space' in Hall's classification system, is 1.5 feet in its close phase and 4 feet in its far phase. Within personal space the aural and visual powers of perception are further heightened; we can hear a whisper or see fine facial details such as eyelashes or freckles. We are able to read much finer distinctions of emotion in each other's faces and body language. Olfaction comes into play in this range as well as kinaesthesia; we can smell someone's perfume or breath, we can reach out and touch someone or be touched. Our vision is acute at the far edge of this zone, beginning to distort at the near edge.

It is relatively rare for theatre audiences to share personal space with performers, especially for a significant length of time. The most common experience of this kind of proximity between audience and performer is when the performer enters the audience and singles out one or more people for a brief exchange or some kind of special attention. This is the type of attention so many audience members dread – an attention that turns the focus of the rest of the audience onto them. In this situation an audience member may not experience a particularly 'personal' moment with the performer because they are too hyper-aware of being watched by the rest of the audience. Some performers, perhaps by virtue of sheer charisma, seem to be able to create less angst-ridden or self-conscious personal moments for audience members within larger shows by engulfing or shielding them within their own personal space 'bubble'. We have seen Peggy Shaw move into an audience in the middle of a show and serenade audience members one by one, taking their hands in hers as she sings. The recipients of her serenades didn't appear worried about the rest of the audience; Shaw's aura seemed to encircle them, offering a kind of magical protection. This type of moment can, of course, go horribly wrong in the hands of a less skilful or charismatic performer, and a truly panic-stricken audience member can sink the most seasoned performer. Either scenario is ghastly to witness and surely collective memories of such incidents are the source of much fear and loathing of audience participation.

Within the close phase of 'personal space', between 1.5 and 2.5 feet, Hall notes:

> The kinesthetic sense of closeness derives in part from the possibilities present in regard to what each participant can do to the other with his extremities. At this distance, one can hold or grasp the other person.
>
> (Hall, 1966, p. 119)

Interestingly, it is the possibility rather than the actuality of closeness that defines the close phase of personal space; the frisson of the almost but not quite intimate. The flipside of this frisson is, of course, tension and anxiety, a mutual fear. Performers and audiences have long been wary of each other if not outright afraid, even from 'not close' distances, so of course with increased proximity comes the risk of an elevation in fear. Hall defines 12 feet as the amount of space needed for an alert subject to 'take evasive or defensive action if threatened. The distance may even cue a vestigial but subliminal form of flight reaction [...]' (Hall, 1966, p. 123). If a performer crosses this 12-foot threshold, the nearest point of public distance, the audience are more likely to freeze than flee if approached further. Perhaps this is why some audience members prefer the back row and the aisles, which offer the greatest possibility of escape. A performer who comes into the social or personal space of the audience may engender feelings of closeness and contact, but their nearness may also cause fear and/or a feeling that there is 'no way out'. Different types of venues and festivals, of course, have their own unwritten codes and expectations about relationships between performers and audience members, so a Donmar audience member, for example, might appreciate being close enough to see Jude Law's dirty fingernails in Anna Christie, without feeling any particular anxiety that the performers will try and interact with them.

The centre of Hall's proxemic model is the radius of 'intimate space' that starts with our skin and extends 18 inches outward all around our bodies. In this zone the visual is often overloaded or distorted, as it becomes hard or impossible to see someone this close, sometimes creating a 'cross-eyed' look; hearing is acutely focused on breathing or other low-level sounds that are inaudible from a distance; the olfactory stimulation is at its peak; haptic and thermal receptors come into play as we feel the heat from each other's bodies, the moisture from each other's breath or direct physical contact. In Hall's words, 'This is the distance of love-making and wrestling, comforting and protecting. Physical contact or the high possibility of physical involvement is uppermost in the awareness of both persons' (Hall, 1966, p. 117).

It is very rare that theatre audiences share intimate space with performers, though, as many theatre scholars have pointed out, it is interesting that the audience members in a conventional theatre are seated within personal and even intimate distances from each other. If seated next to a stranger, however, this distance isn't normally perceived as 'intimate' or 'personal', but instead simply as close or crowded. Hall explains how humans have special defensive devices for taking the intimacy out of proximity in public situations like the theatre or the subway that force people closer together than they would naturally arrange themselves. Strategies include being as immobile as possible, withdrawing upon accidental contact (if possible), and keeping eyes fixed on infinity to avoid eye contact beyond a passing glance (Hall, 1966, p. 118).

Large theatres, in particular, are challenged both in the crowded distance between spectators and each other and in the remote distance from stage to auditorium. Long distances between performers and audience can be a negative in terms of appreciating nuance or details, but within the auditorium, the acute lack of distance between hundreds of audience members can be claustrophobic, obstructive and distracting.

In their psychological study of theatre, Lenelis Kruse and Carl Graumann point out that conventional theatre spaces are actually designed to stifle or mute audience responses with rigid seating, all facing in a uniform direction, where audience members are expected to sit silently in the dark without moving. For audience members, then, there is a distinct challenge in zoning out everything around you, making yourself as still, invisible and inaudible as possible, and focusing in on a performance that is occurring at a distance.

For audience members seated in orthodox seats, cultural conventions serve to safeguard us from unwanted intimacy. But if a performer approaches an audience member within 18 inches, there is no convention to shield either party from an acute awareness that they are in the intimate zone of 'love-making and wrestling'.

> At intimate distance, the presence of the other person is unmistakable and may at times be overwhelming because of the greatly stepped-up sensory inputs. Sight (often distorted), olfaction, heat from the other person's body, sound, smell, and feel of the breath all combine to signal unmistakable involvement with another body.
>
> (Hall, 1966, p. 116)

I (Leslie) remember seeing Tim Miller's *My Queer Body* at the CCA in Glasgow in the 1990s and really being taken by surprise when Miller, stark bollock naked, came and sat on my lap and talked directly to me for a few minutes of the show. In those few minutes the audience shifted from watching him talk to them from on stage to watching him talk to me on my lap. I shifted from listening to a plural address (to us) to a singular one (to me) that triggered a personal response, a feeling of closeness, but was still essentially plural in that it was intended to be witnessed by the rest of the audience. I don't remember feeling terribly self-conscious of the rest of the audience in the moment, as Miller's body more or less shielded me from them. I do remember a sense of balancing and fine-tuning in the eye-contact communication as Miller approached me – I would paraphrase the eye-contact conversation as something along these lines: Tim, 'I know this is strange, but if it isn't going to panic you I'm going to sit in your lap now...' Me, '... okay.' Although my participation was unplanned and unknown to me in terms of what it might entail, I did feel as though the encounter was consensual; in a moment of eye contact I felt that he asked and I gave permission.

What does it mean to be so close to a performer or an audience member inside a piece? Thinking back to Hall's rule of 30 feet being the distance automatically set around public figures raises the question of whether or not a performer is a public figure during a performance. I'm thinking here of a 'public figure' status that resides in the moment of performance, rather than the 'public figure' status attached to celebrity. If we take it as an anthropological 'given' that a performer in a piece is usually accorded a certain 'public figure' status by the audience, though this will vary in degree, how does this status change (or not) when performers collapse the normal proxemic boundaries between themselves and members of the audience? Does coming nearer to the audience decrease the status of the performer? Does it burst their 'public figure' space bubble, rendering them more ordinary? Conversely, does it decrease the status of the audience members? Do audience members have more spatial status when they remain at a distance that serves to underscore the financial relationship between the performer (worker/entertainer) and the audience (customer/patron)? Does moving out of public space into social, personal and/or intimate space humble the status of the performer or the audience or both? Or can coming closer reinforce and magnify the status of the performer or the audience or both? We believe any and all of these power shifts are possible as the distance between audience and performer contracts.

As performers, we have experienced doing shows for small audiences as humbling, which is a different issue than experiencing humility through actually being close to them; an issue of quantity (audience numbers) in the service of a type of quality (audience proximity). To perform a show for one person at a time, for four people at a time or for 20 people at a time rather than playing to one large full house is humbling. Performing multiple times a day in order to keep the audience close is definitely a labour-intensive experience rather than a 'star turn'. For the audience, a small audience-to-performer ratio may have the effect of elevating or promoting them to VIP status, having a performance given 'just for them'. It may also, consciously or subconsciously, result in the audience downsizing their idea of the performer's status, for aren't traditional theatre audiences conditioned to think that commanding an audience of 2000 is more impressive than telling a story to four people? If an audience is allowed within four feet of the performer, the performer's status is hardly dominant by proxemic standards.

As a performer, sharing personal or intimate space with the audience feels like entering each other's gravitational fields. If the audience members are close enough to touch if we both reach towards each other, then we experience their reactions, their witnessing as exerting a kind of pull over our performances. If they maintain eye contact, then they exert a stronger force and we can feel ourselves calibrating to the type of energy or mood they are giving off, making a performance slightly more humorous, more reflective or darker in relation to their responses. Normally we experience this as a positive interplay of influences, one which gives a vibrancy to performances, making them feel less rehearsed, more authentic, more conversational. The relativity of such encounters also makes them less predictable, edgier and more fallible. Very occasionally an audience member exerts a strong negative influence, which can make getting through a performance in close proximity feel like riding out a turbulent air-pocket, never knowing quite how long it will last or if, perhaps, you are all going down. In a small audience group, a negative audience response also clouds the experience for the other audience members to a much greater extent than it would in an orthodox theatre setting, where fixed seating and lighting states encourage the audience to tune each other out. In our experiences this is rare; close audiencing generally begets greater inter-subjectivity and communitas than 'not close' audiencing.

We'd like to draw a parallel for a moment with these close encounters in live performance and the close-up in film. Film theorist Mary Ann Doane points out that whilst in Russian and in French the term for close-up denotes largeness or large scale, in English it is nearness or proximity that is at stake (Doane, 2003, p. 92). The close-up in film created new performative geographies, surfaces and texts, zooming in on fragments of human life, fragments that become full body worlds in their own right. Although not enabling a magnified or disembodied image, nonetheless the performative close-up elevates the intimacy of the encounter. French filmmaker and theorist Jean Epstein writes, 'The close-up modifies the drama by the impact of proximity. Pain is within reach. If I stretch out my arm I touch you, and that is intimacy. I can count the eyelashes of this suffering. I would be able to taste the tears' (Epstein from 'Magnification', as cited in Doane, 2003, p. 109)

What are the qualities of the performative close-up? What are the qualities inherent in the nearness and in the quality of the encounter, in the pitch and shift of it? What are the textures of proximity? In writing for our performances our desire is to present clear images that move us close to our sensate condition, to what it is to be human. There is a desire in that moment to elicit a sense of making the absent body (following Drew Leder) present. Writing is part of the performance of proximity, imbuing works with physicality and agency. In tandem with this there is a desire as performers to enact a poetic presencing of sorts through the delivery of the text, such as through eye contact, timbre of voice. In this way the delivery enacts a 'getting closer' through how we pace, pause, hold the text and give it to the audience as if we were talking not at them, but to and for each of them individually.

As performers we have noticed an interesting phenomenon in terms of the way we remember traditional theatre performances versus intimate performances. (Though this book is about work in close proximity, we have made many shows for conventionally seated theatre audiences.) Over the years we gradually realized that we remember intimate performances in significantly greater detail than theatre performances. Performances on stage go by in a bit of a blur, leaving us with only general impressions of the experience from one performance to the next. In performances to small audiences, however, we retain very clear memories of the audience members, how they reacted, what they looked like, what they laughed at and when they looked thoughtful, and so we also remember ourselves and what we were doing in those moments more distinctly. We have two theories as to why this might be. The first relates to the nature of the three kinds of memory: episodic memory is remembering an event that actually happened to you; generic memory is memory of general knowledge, such as the alphabet; procedural memory is memory of skills and procedures that one has learned, like playing a musical instrument. Our personal memories (or lack thereof) suggest to us that we experience theatre performances as 'procedural' and intimate performances as 'episodic'. This implies two very different cognitive states for a performer in these two types of work: in conventional theatre we are in a skills mode, performing something we have learned in the same way the musician performs a song; in intimate performance, even though we have memorized lines and rehearsed a sequence of actions, we are engaged in an experience with the audience members and remember the event in the same cognitive manner that we process episodes in our lives. Procedural modes are by nature more automatic, a kind of autopilot made possible by rehearsal, so it doesn't seem particularly surprising that we wouldn't remember the distinct differences between performances in a run or a tour of a theatre show in great detail. (Though if you give us the first line, we could probably repeat the entire text of any of these shows, calling on our procedural memory.)

The thing that we think is significant about the contrast in how we remember the two different types of performance is that it suggests that we experience intimate performances in a cognitive manner that is much closer to a lived experience. In proximate performances we still experience what we are doing as performance – it is choreographed and scripted and composed in a way that real life isn't – and yet we remember these encounters with the audience through our episodic memory. Significantly, and this is the second part of our theory, intimate performance is multi-sensory in a way that real life generally is and performing in a theatre generally isn't. Theatres are audio-visual by nature and performers are used to operating with much less sensory information than we have in 'real life'. Theatre lights make us extremely short-sighted – on stage we are sometimes lucky if we can see our hand in front of our face. If we are amplified, we are usually behind the sound speakers, which also makes us slightly deaf to what the audience are hearing. The stage operates as something of a black hole – it swallows in order to create. In providing a blank slate for endless possibilities it erases many sensory particulars. The word 'blackout' is used for theatres and cinemas and in the process of making these spaces conducive to images that can be seen by large crowds simultaneously, it's worthy of note that we blackout a great deal of sensory stimulus. Intimate performances employ the haptic and the olfactory much more than conventional theatres, but the auditory and the visual also operate much differently in close proximity than in conventional theatre venues, giving us more information, more nuances. From the performer's point of view, there is a much richer sensory palate to work with, and a much richer field of sensory feedback for us to work from in terms of being able to 'read' the experiences of our audiences. So perhaps performing to small audiences is more experiential or 'episodic' for the performer in part because they have more sensory input, which is of course directly related to their proximity to the audience, a proximity that leads them to experience the encounter more as a lived event than a skilled recital.

An overview

Our company has produced over 40 projects since we formed in 1997, and many of them have explored expanding and collapsing audience-performer distances. We find it more helpful to the analytical concerns of this project, however, to focus in depth on a handful of specific performances rather than skimming and talking about proximity across the work generally. The first part of the book, Proximity and Performance, presents four case studies in two sections. The 'Interior' section looks at interior performance spaces as well as the interior of the body, with a focus on the 'intimate' senses of smell, taste and touch. In this section we write first, in Chapter 2, about our piece On the Scent (2003 ongoing), one of the works in which we are physically closest to the audience throughout, as the piece is performed in houses for audiences of four at a time. The audience experience is designed around sensory stimulus that relies on close proximity, particularly smell and taste, so there is also a particular physical interiority to the piece. We have performed On the Scent hundreds of times in 14 different countries and many more different cities, so we have several hundred hours of experience of performing this show, which adds depth and breadth to our reflections on performer-audience dynamics. The second case study in the 'Interior' section, Chapter 3, is *the moment I saw you I knew I could love you* (2009 ongoing), a piece performed to audiences of 24 at a time seated in three eight-person life rafts on the stages of black box theatres. The subject matter of the piece – instinct, impulse and gut feelings – as well as its intimate staging made it an obvious case study for 'Interior' where we explore proximity in relation to cognition and the senses and literally look into the interior of the body. The audience in *the moment I saw you I knew I could love you* are held within a theatre building as well as cradled in the interior of a small raft. As with On the Scent, we have hundreds of hours of performance experience with this piece, which helps us to know and reflect on the audience-performer dynamics more deeply.

In the spirit of spatial perspective, we switch in the next section of Proximity and Performance from an interior focus to an exterior or landscape perspective. In the 'Landscape' section we analyse two site-specific projects that play with shifting performer/audience proximities within urban and natural landscapes. In 'Landscape' Chapter 4 we discuss *Out of Water*, a collaboration between Helen Paris and Caroline Wright commissioned for the London 2012 Cultural Olympiad, which took place on Holkham Beach, Norfolk, and later at Fort Funston Beach, San Francisco as part of PSi19.[2] In this section we also look in Chapter 5 at *Lost & Found* (2005), a project which was set in three different urban centres of regeneration and transformation, Shanghai, the Black Country and East London. These projects encompass significant contrasts in physical distances between performer and audience, from hands touching to miles apart. The two pieces provide temporal contrasts in terms of the pace at which gaps widen and close between performer and audience, with *Out of Water* taking its rhythm from a walking pace and *Lost & Found* employing the more urban velocity of a city bus. We are also interested in looking at these works as landscape pieces, where the audience experiences a heightened sense of the world around them through being both inside the performance and outside in the natural or urban environment.

Where the first part of the book looks at proximity in performance, the second part of the book explores proximity in relation to different types of process. Chapter 6, 'In the Lab and Incognito', looks behind the scenes at some of the research processes we have undertaken in proximity to other work/research cultures exploring our subject matter through different means or methods. It includes descriptions of collaborations with olfactory scientists in the making of On the Scent, with neurogastroenterologists in the making of 'the moment', as well as a behind-the-scenes look at quite a different research process, as Helen describes her experience of working in London's Lost Property Department as part of developing her script for *Lost & Found*.

Chapter 7, 'In the Studio', discusses how we share performance-making ideas and techniques in the studio and classroom, focusing on a creative workshop series we ran called Autobiology (2008 ongoing). Throughout the months we were working on making the performance piece 'the moment' and the companion film *Sea Swallow'd* (2010), we explored working with consciously physical prompts in the rehearsal studio, such as body memory and gut feelings. In the Autobiology workshops we shared many of these generative techniques with other artists and students as 'open source' methods to use in their own practices. In this case making a show in a particular way opened up a new line of classroom exercises and methods. The workshop students weren't engaged in research for our performance, but rather our performance-making process generated new teaching methods for the workshops.

Chapter 8, 'In Situ', examines our ongoing practice of asking a project-related question across a range of people outside the frame of performance events. In asking these project-specific questions, such as 'What smell reminds you of London?' for *Essences of London* (2004), we invite a cross-section of people to consider a question that we are asking in our performance practice, such as 'What is the relationship between smell and memory?' Like people in any field, we are interested in the ways in which other people approach the same questions, what they think and how they arrive at their opinions, hunches or conclusions. For us, the invitation to consider a shared question is a way to get closer to a wider range of people than would attend a theatre or live art event. This chapter discusses projects of questioning across different communities that developed into their own short film outputs: *Essences of London*, *Lost & Found* (2005) and *(be)longing* (2007).

In writing about our own performance work and processes, we have been inspired by sociologists Phillip Vannini, Dennis Waskul and Simon Gottschalk in their use of the term 'sensuous scholarship'.

> [...] We should use a subjunctive mode to capture the uncertainty, complexity, and plasticity of interaction, to convey how sensations and their expressions unfold and produce one another rather than pinpoint what causes them, to acknowledge the tentativeness, situatedness, and ability of fieldwork and somatic work, and to evoke a sense of emergence. We believe that these four strategies of sensuous writing (indeterminacy, performativity, contingency, and emergence) are key characteristics of all forms of embodied representation.
>
> (Vannini, Waskul and Gottschalk, 2012, p. 76)

In our own field of performance studies, of course, many writers, such as Sally Banes, Jill Dolan, Barbara Kirshenblatt-Gimblett, André Lepecki, Peggy Phelan and Richard Schechner, have also advocated and practised sensuous writing, sensuous theory and/or sensuous scholarship. Our aim here is to contribute to this growing area of writing. While writing for a reader is a very different project than performing for a live audience, we hope that the 'sensuous scholarship' of our embodied experiences as performers comes through in these pages and transports you, if only for a moment, to some of the performance interiors and landscapes we have created and inhabited with audiences in our work over the years.

Our overall aim throughout the writing which follows is to make an analytical contribution to the field from the experience and intellect of performance makers engaged in different ways of creating and performing works with a keen attention to proximate relationships with audiences. We hope that this writing about our performance experiences finds resonance with artists and scholars as they continue to think about the ways in which performers and audiences can draw close to each other.

Part One

Proximity and Performance

2   Interior I: *On the Scent*

This chapter explores proximity and the senses, particularly the sense of smell, a powerful sense often neglected in comparison to the audiovisual in performance work that maintains more traditional spatial temporal modes between performers and audiences. *On the Scent* (2003) is a performance about the relationship between the sense of smell, emotion and memory (Illustration 2.1). In this chapter the sensuous proximity between audiences and performers is considered in detail, foregrounded through the immediate sensory experiences uniquely possible in situations where audiences can encounter the work through smell, taste and touch. We first give a detailed account of the performance itself before moving into analysis of the performance in terms of proximity and the senses. We then reflect on the piece from the point of view of the performers (Leslie Hill, Helen Paris and Lois Weaver) and audience members. In describing this piece we found it clearest to narrate the experience in the second person; while we don't claim to know how individual audience members feel in specific performances, this is a composite 'you' based on our observations as performers and feedback we have had from audiences.

The performance

You are given an address and a time of arrival, 3.30pm. You make your way to the place: an apartment building in Shanghai; a detached house on a leafy street in Cambridge; a gothic mansion in Porto Alegre. It is raining. You are the last to arrive. Three strangers stand at the front door. You are handed a key. You hesitate, look to the others for confirmation, they shrug, then nod. You turn the key and enter the house. You smell the strangeness of another person's home, at first recognizable more for its otherness than any specific scent but as you take a moment to hang up your coat, fold your umbrella you notice another smell, a heavy perfume, some exotic flower, maybe. 'Come in!', a woman's voice calls, urgent and not entirely welcoming. You follow the voice through

Illustration 2.1 Helen, *On the Scent*
[Photo by Hugo Glendinning]

a door and enter the sitting room. There you see a blonde woman
(Illustration 2.2), in a black cocktail dress and glamorous evening shoes
reclining on a leopard-print sofa, addressing a video camera with the red
record light flashing.

'Stay right there. I need to catch this', she commands, waving a hand in your direction but keeping her focus on the camera. She seems to be recording a memory.

[…] there was an elegance even though I know she bought it at Woolworths… but it's the dust and talcum powder that fell around its cobalt blue base and the fragrance of sweat and relief of flesh freshly released from rubber and steel that I remember best…

It seems you have interrupted something, yet at the same time that you were expected, a trespassing guest. The woman seems to have no interest in anything but the camera. You let your eyes wander. You see vases full of lilies, their yellow pollen powdering the shelves, scores of half-empty perfume bottles scattered on the floor and furniture. You cast a furtive glance at the woman, divinely glamorous, still talking to the camera. You glimpse at your fellow guests, check if they are doing something different, maybe something you should be doing, but they, like you, are gazing round the room, drinking in the scene and the scent. The woman finishes her recording with a title just before she switches off the camera, '*My Mother's Dressing Table, 1955*'.

The woman moves in close to you, 'I thought you'd never get here. I have been waiting for you and the waiting felt like… *Eternity*.' She waves a bottle of perfume. Should you apologize for being late? You were the last to arrive. You open your mouth to say something, and suddenly her nose is buried in your neck. She sniffs you and whispers in your ear, 'Mmm smooth, creamy… slight hint of vanilla… jasmine, maybe?' Before you even know how or if you are meant to respond, she offers you a box of heavily scented rich chocolates in a lilac-ribboned box. 'Would you like a chocolate?' You put out your hand and in that moment she whisks the box away, plucking a chocolate for herself and popping it whole into her mouth wickedly. 'There's violet… or if you're in another mood, rose, fresh picked on a Sunday morning and forced into cream centres', she says, her words coated with the rose cream melting in her mouth. 'Did you bring me a little something?' She stares at you. You frantically think of anything in your bag you could give her, but again she interrupts you. 'I'm sorry I had to ask… It's not that I am desperate; just obsessed.'

She picks up a cobalt blue perfume bottle and sprays a puff of its contents in the air, breathing in the heady scent. 'Ah, *Evening in Paris,*

Illustration 2.2 Lois Weaver
[Photo by Leslie Hill]

1929... Reminds me of pale-blue skies reflected in dirty river water. Makes me think of wartime romance and seamed stockings...' She leans back seductively, her eyes half closed as if suddenly transported to another place, another time. You start to wonder if indeed she is a little obsessed, a strange kind of addict. As if reading your mind, she forces herself back to the present.

I blame it on the Avon lady. What got to me was her bag. It was so compact, so organized and so full of bottles shaped just to make you want to hold them, stroke them and explore the miracles of their cures. But you couldn't have them right away. You had to order them. And she could never tell you exactly how long it would take. Then the space between that immediate craving and the possibility of satisfaction was packed up inside her bag and carried down the sidewalk to her car and driven home to a place I didn't know and couldn't imagine. What do you think she did at night with all those little bottles and jars? I just had to get my hands on that bag. But she never came back. They don't last, Avon ladies. They are temporary. Itinerant. Door-to-door...

With her 'door-to-door' she ushers you out of the sitting room and into a brightly lit kitchen. You are immediately greeted by another woman in a T-shirt, jeans and cowboy boots, who invites you to take a stool at the kitchen table. Piles of bright red chilli peppers are heaped on the table alongside a mound of green limes. There are four shot glasses lined up at the edge of the table and again you have the feeling that you are expected. She leans towards you over the kitchen table.

I want to tell you about a place called Chimayo, which is very near where I come from in the Sangre de Christo mountains of northern New Mexico. I don't know if any of you might have heard of it before, but people make pilgrimages there from all over the world and they have done for about three hundred years. And the reason that all of these people come to this place is just so that they can touch the holy... dirt. Yes, holy dirt. There's a hole in the dirt floor of the adobe church and you can reach right in and scoop out the dirt and rub it on wounded limbs or into blind eyes or over barren wombs and miraculously it cures you. So the whole church is just stuffed full of crutches and slings and glasses and pictures of miracle babies. But the best part about Chimayo, in my opinion, is that holy dirt actually grows holy chilli. So you can just buy the local chilli, take it home, and then you can enjoy miracles right in your own kitchen. Now, there is a catch, because the miracle part only works if you have true faith. But the chilli works regardless. And I have to admit, I've always been in it more for the chilli. My family are a rapidly migrating mixed breed so we don't have 'a faith' as such – we just sort of piece together rituals on the fly.

As she speaks, the woman clears a space on the table revealing a piece of mirror and from somewhere under the mound of chilli and limes produces a bag of Chimayo red chilli powder, a razor blade and a dollar bill. She pours an ounce of the chilli powder onto the mirror and with the razor carefully cuts one... two... three... four... five long thin lines of the powder. The woman rolls up the dollar bill and, before your very eyes, snorts the powder through it (Illustration 2.3). You can't quite believe what just happened. More perturbing is the awareness of the other four pristine lines of chilli in a row. You are aware of the sound

Illustration 2.3 Leslie, chilli
[Photo by Hugo Glendinning]

of your own swallow, your hands feel a little clammy, you cast a sly glance at your three neighbours. What will you do if she asks you to help yourself to a line...?

The woman gets up from the table, lights up a *Lucky Strike* cigarette and throws a pork chop on a cast-iron skillet which immediately starts sizzling. She exhales a long line of smoke into the pan over the chop.

I don't smoke, and I'm more or less a vegetarian. But sometimes I just have to light up a Lucky Strike and throw a pork chop on the grill. It's like my Granny Parker is right there in the room with me.

She takes a can of hairspray and sprays a cloud of it over the pan.

But you know, to get her just perfect, I have to add a touch of Aquanet Extra Super Hold hairspray. I used to worry that she might just go up in flames with all that hairspray and the constant flicker of the cigarette lighter around her head. Anyway, if I am missing my mother, I just pop some popcorn, because popcorn was the only food she really enjoyed cooking. I like having them around together sometimes.

She fills a popcorn popper with kernels, sits back down at the table,

I never knew my Grandpa Parker. He was a Marine Sergeant who seems to have cracked up for some reason. We never knew exactly what he did because it was classified, but it was something to do with testing bombs by dropping them on South Pacific islands. Whatever it was, he just couldn't cope when he came home from that tropical paradise. Drank himself into an early grave. But when he died he left me his shaving lotion bottle collection. You never catch a whiff of a man like that these days, do you?

She picks up a glass bottle that is shaped like a vintage car. She unscrews the spare tyre-shaped lid and passes you the bottle to smell. The smell is musky but sweet, a little stale, the smell of another time, of a man from the past. You hand the bottle round to your fellow audience members who take a whiff. The woman starts to talk about where she comes from.

I was seven when I realized that I was living right on top of the biggest nuclear arsenal in the world. I used to lie in bed at night petrified – afraid to move. Anyway, as it turned out, when I grew up I lost my virginity to

a nuclear physicist from Los Alamos labs. And this, I have to admit, was a great success because we had sex the perfect mathematical number of times. And I've maintained a life-long interest in physics. You might have heard of Los Alamos labs – internationally famous in a quiet sort of way. That's where they invented the bomb. Einstein, Oppenheimer – they all came to New Mexico. I'll never forget one Sunday when Phil sneaked me into the labs. I couldn't believe it – it was like a whole city hidden under the mountain and there were all these racks of bikes for the scientists to peddle around from one part of the lab to another. It was a whole other world down there. So orderly, so quiet. They made the bomb in New Mexico and then, to see if it worked, they dropped it on New Mexico. That's the kind of place I come from. After they detonated it, blind birds rained down for miles all over the state. You know, there was no real military necessity for the American Government to drop the bomb on the Japanese. And the Government at the time didn't do it primarily for military reasons, but they did it for three other reasons...

You are suddenly distracted as the popcorn has now started to pop and is erupting alarmingly. It spits into the air and cascades over the kitchen counter and onto the floor. The meat is now burning and the smell of searing flesh fills your nostrils. The woman carries on talking.

The first reason was money, because more money was spent developing the bomb than the entire American car industry was worth at that time. So the Government was terrified of what the taxpayers would do when they found out they'd spent that much money on a weapon that was never even used. The second reason was, of course, revenge, for the attack on Pearl Harbor. And the third reason was basically curiosity, because thousands of scientists had been working on two different prototypes of the bomb – one bomb, Little Boy, was uranium; the other, Fat Man, was plutonium. And they really wanted to know... which one worked better.

The woman pours a glass of water into the smoking-hot skillet and a domestic mushroom cloud of steam rises. She turns off the popcorn popper and you are suddenly aware of the silence in the room. The woman returns to the table, takes up the razor and you watch whilst she hacks off a lock of her hair as she says:

Little Boy: 200,000
Fat Man: 140,000

Illustration 2.4 Leslie, burning hair
[Photo courtesy of FIERCE! Festival]

She pinches the piece of hair between her fingers and sets it on fire. She holds the burning hair until it melts (Illustration 2.4), then drops it into the ashtray with her cigarette butt. The smell of the burnt hair turns your stomach. 'White House Press Release: the greatest achievement of organized science in the history of mankind.' She pours you a shot of tequila and offers you a slice of lime, a lick of salt. The tastes collide on your tongue and hit the back of your throat. 'Here's to home...sickness.'

She stands, opens the door and ushers you back out of the room. You leave the world of the kitchen, still tasting the tequila on your lips, the odour of smoke and burnt meat on your hair and clothes, and walk up the stairs to a bedroom at the top. The door is ajar and you walk inside. You adjust your eyes to the gloom of the unlit bedroom. You are thinking of a hospital for some reason and then realize that there is a smell of disinfectant in the air. You see a woman lying in a bed under an old-fashioned pink brocade eiderdown that covers the bed, reminiscent of grandparents' houses. The Pepto-Bismol-coloured eiderdown is pulled right up to the woman's chin. There are four chairs in a row along one side of the bed. They are very close to each other and very close to the bed, especially the ones on the inside, nearest the face of the woman in the bed. You freeze for a moment and then file in, taking your seat at the top of the bed. You feel as if you are a visitor in a sickroom and you are also feeling slightly sick. Your own exit is blocked as there is not an inch of space between the four chairs in the bedroom; you are sealed in by the other audience members. The airlessness, the curtains closed, you feel a sense of claustrophobia, an awareness that in this room more than either of the others, it is hard to escape.

The woman in the bed speaks. Her voice is quiet and you find yourself leaning in, even closer, to catch her words.

I am home, sick, wading through the hours between afternoon and evening. There is nothing to eat. Food is available only in composite pieces; the steely block of fat, the bag of flour with its clothes-peg seal, torn pieces of cabbage floating in green and white flakes in the top of the cold water in the plastic bowl. Everything requiring a long process of cutting, seeping, boiling, mixing and adding to other things before they make any sense.

You also feel trapped in that limbo of late afternoon in this stuffy room, its cloying scents of sickness and disinfectant – is that Vicks VapoRub? You glance round the room, the clothes, shelves, pictures, ornaments, the hairbrush on the dressing table. You associate them with this woman yet you know at the same time they are probably not hers. That they belong to someone else, someone not present yet whose bedroom you are in. Again you feel that sense of trespass. The woman is talking about the pantry in the house and you are not sure which house she is referring to – the one you are in? Her own? Which is which? Who belongs where?

The pantry is the very smallest space in the house. There is a little window on one side with frosted baubled glass that makes the outside world look confused. Light falls from this window and lands on a pale-yellow Tupperware box. Through the opaque body of the box you see shadows, oblong, square shaped. Sometimes Custard Creams, sometimes Malted Milks, sometimes McVitie's Rich Tea biscuits. The secretiveness of slipping into the pantry, closing the door behind, the claustrophobia of being trapped, but oh – the guilty pleasure of the snack.

Suddenly the woman pulls off the covers, lifts up the pillow and reveals the pale yellow Tupperware box. Just as described you see shadows through the box, spheres of Rich Tea biscuits. Suddenly mobilized after her initial torpor, she whips the lid of the box off and flips herself upside down into a headstand in the box of biscuits (Illustration 2.5).

Illustration 2.5   Helen, headstand
[Photo courtesy of FIERCE! Festival]

The energy has shifted. The bed becomes her performance space as the woman plays out stories of death, disease and deception:

My Uncle had heart disease. He had slowly poisoned himself over the years with mouthful upon mouthful of finest malt. Despite his doctor's strictest orders he did not stop drinking. His bottle of whisky hidden in the back of his pick-up truck – under some sacks. The sly smell of whisky on his breath gave him away when he kissed me hello, 'Hey sweetheart'. But. My Aunt could not smell it. She had extreme asthma, which had completely wiped out her sense of smell. She walked around the house, followed by an oxygen machine on wheels, which trailed behind her like a small dog, hissing softly. He told the doctor that what he was really afraid of was dying in his sleep. The doctor said, 'Well, yes that could happen.' So my Uncle would sit in his La-Z-Boy recliner – the furniture built and designed specifically for ultimate relaxation – and he would be very, very straight and tall and try not to fall asleep.

The woman reveals a pink leather make-up case, like the box of biscuits hidden in the folds of the bedding. You watch her slowly unzip the bag and take out a miniature bottle of whisky and a small brush for applying lipstick.

My Aunt baked my Uncle angel-cake, light as a feather. 'He deserves a treat', she said conspiratorially as he slipped out of the room, 'he's given up drinking.' And I would think of him right outside loitering round the back of the pick-up.

She takes the top off the whisky, dips the brush in and then paints the whisky on to her lips. 'And he would come back and eat a bite of cake and kiss my aunt, 'Hey sweetheart', and she would smile and I would smell his Judas breath. But I wouldn't breathe a word. He died in his sleep. 'Hey sweetheart.' The woman makes eye contact with you as she says this final 'Hey sweetheart', seems to leans forward and blows a silent kiss from her lips, wet with the whisky.

Her mood shifts, as she tells a story about her endless search for Roget & Gallet Sandalwood Body Lotion, the fragrance her mother craved, but which could never be found.

When is the exact moment that Chanel #5 is replaced by three-for-the-price-of-two anonymous 'family' soap which no-one in the family claims ownership of? There should be signs to let you know what lies ahead. Government Health Warnings to let you know when her bags full of perfume and lipstick change and become full of safety pins and chewable Gaviscon indigestion tablets. That's why the quest of the Roget & Gallet Sandalwood Body Lotion was so important. It was asked for every year, a little jewel on the Christmas list, shining amongst other items: the elasticated surgical support tights, the deluxe hairnet. Roget & Gallet Body Lotion (Sandalwood)? A little question mark after. The challenge had been set. The impossible task heralded by that question mark.

She seems to blame herself for never finding the item which might help her mother retain a vestige of glamour and therefore halt the ageing process, the cause of a depression that has taken over the house:

I am home, sick. Sick of a concoction slowly compiled over the years of sighs and frowns and sinkings down into faded armchairs. It is the remembrances of things past which have been kept on way past their sell-by date. These things trip them up on the way into the living room and cause them to stumble on the way to bed where, caught within the folds of their sheets, the corners of their pillow cases are the germy smells of disease. I try and help. Fresh start. Spring clean. Blow away the cobwebs. But all change is resisted. 'Nothing must change, dear. We are holding on to the past – can't you see? Hold on tight. Don't ever let go.

With this, the woman collapses back into the bed, deflated, back in the torpor she was in when you entered, as if she is condemned to repeat this cycle, as if there is no escape from this bed, this house, this sickness. You, however, can leave. You walk back downstairs, aware that though you leave the room, you carry the remembrance on your skin, your clothes, breathed into your lungs. You return to the sitting room where the glamorous blonde woman greets you again.

There you are. Come over here and sit down a minute. Now I was hoping you were going to bring me something, but since you didn't, I'm going to ask you to give me something before you go. A little something to keep me going. Something personal. I want you to think of a smell that reminds you of home or makes you feel homesick... or just makes you sick. Tell me what it is, describe it and tell me what it reminds you of. I am going to capture it here, bottle it, keep it for later...

Illustration 2.6   Lois, recording smell memories

[Photo by Leslie Hill]

You sit on the sofa with your fellow guests. You realize your relationship to them has shifted though you have not spoken. They don't feel like strangers, they are more than unknown audience members. You have shared the encounter with them, taken the communion of the tequila shot. Now, when you are asked to tell your smell memory it feels possible to share. The camera is pointed at you, records what you say, 'bottles' your smell 'for later' (Illustration 2.6). As you remember and share your story you are aware you are writing that part of the performance as you speak it, that you and the other three audience members are now the scriptwriters, the performers in this last part of the encounter. You tell your story and as you recall the smell you seem to re-experience the moment, feel almost transported back to that time, to that place, that person. When you have finished the woman thanks you and moves the camera to the next person. You relax a little and listen to the other stories unfolding, glimpses into the lives of your fellow audience members.

When the woman has captured all the stories she turns off the camera. 'Thank you, that should keep me going for a while. It is just what I needed. And now that I have what I need… you can go.' You laugh, there is a release of tension but also an abruptness. You are dismissed. You meet the eyes of your fellow guests and smile. As you all get up to leave the woman stops you at the door, offering the box of chocolates once more. This time she lets you take one. You hover for a moment, rose or violet cream? You pick one and pop it into your mouth. You leave the house, close the door behind you, the sweet perfume of the chocolate coating your taste buds. You bid farewell to your fellow guests and walk down the road. You carry the heady mix of aromas from the house on your clothes, hair and skin. It will linger with you for a while into the evening. For now though, you take a deep breath. The smell of rain on grass, of wet pavement, and it reminds you of…

Olfactory performance

There is no effective way of either capturing scents or storing them over time. In the realm of olfaction, we must make do with descriptions and recollections. [...] Smell, like taste, is a sensation of the moment, it cannot be preserved. We do not know what the past smelled like, and in the future our own odor will be lost.

(Classen, Howes and Synnott, 1995, pp. 3, 204)

Performance's only life is in the present. Performance cannot be saved, recorded, documented, or otherwise participate in the circulation of representation of representations: once it does so, it becomes something other than performance. To the degree that performance attempts to enter the economy of reproduction it betrays and lessens the promise of its own ontology.

(Phelan, 1993, p. 46)

In *Smell: the Secret Seducer*, Peit Vroon writes that there are reasons to assume that a child's first sensation is in the sphere of smell. 'We begin our life, as it were, not by seeing the light of day, but by smelling a kind of "Life smell" diffused in the fluid of the womb' (Vroon, 1997, p. 21). From birth we are constantly surrounded by odour molecules yet when we want to describe them we have limited language, often using analogy as an escape route, for example: 'smells like a rose'.[1] Despite our meagre lexicon for smell we recognize about ten thousand odours and can recapture smells that instantaneously remind us of places, people and events from a long-forgotten past. Vroon gives an account of recapturing the smell of the nursery school, stating that:

Even if one does not experience the smell again for forty years, one still may recognize it in a smell test. That is a remarkable fact, since after so many years one cannot recall other essential things from that time, such as the name or even the appearance of the teacher or the number of children in the class.

(1997, p. 103)

Not only does smell so fully and comprehensively reveal memories of the past, it also re-invokes the emotion connected with that moment. As Alan Read states: 'Ask anyone to describe a place that was characterized by odour, and one is surprised at the depth of that memory, the emotion that it conveys and the very real sense of loss' (Read, 1993, p. 122).

Smell can be a hugely potent player in live performance, a pervasive, silent stalker that seeps inside us, unlocking past memories, secrets, feelings and intensities.[2] Both live performance and the olfactory share an intangibility, an ungraspability that is a defining part of the very nature of each. In *On the Scent* smell makes its presence known the moment the door opens and throughout the piece it performs a slow entering, a usurpation of the audience's olfactory bulbs and limbic systems. The smell receptor cells have tentacle-like growths called cilia which trigger neurons, 'smell messages' that are sent to parts of the brain.

> The smell receptors are found in a patch of tissue about half the size of a postage stamp on the roof of the nasal cavity. Odor molecules must travel from the entrance to the nostrils about 7 centimeters along a path that arcs upward toward the back of the skull, to a location roughly level with the eyes and behind them.
>
> (Henshaw, 2012, p. 116)

With smell, as with proximity, there can be an overpowering and rather than establishing connection, sensations become too much, people and places too close, experiences too intense. But perhaps smell can be said to engender a closeness, a 'more than closeness'. Edward T. Hall writes of creating an olfactory 'bubble' to keep a sense of distance around oneself. He describes 'personal distance' as the distance consistently separating members of non-contact species, 'a small protective sphere or bubble an organism maintains between itself and others' (Hall, 1966, p. 119). At this distance 'while olfaction is not normally present for Americans [his control group], it is for a great many other people who use colognes to create an olfactory bubble' (Hall, 1966, p. 120). Here smell is perceived as a self-imposed barrier, a smell screen offering protection. So as not to smell you, I smell only me. I retreat into my own smell as a way of escaping you/yours. But familiarity with one's own scent serves to make us less cogniscent of it; smell as a force field. When Lois greets the audience she sniffs them. In many ways a sniff can be more intimate, more proximate than a kiss. The sniff marks and unmasks them, as she deciphers their smells. In Western culture of deodorization the torrent of commercial scents enables us easy access to disguise. We are connoisseurs of the cover-up, making the insanitary seem sanitary, foul smells cloyingly fragrant. We busily concoct a camouflage; we pretend to smell other than we do and create fake aromas for non-existent items. We even pretend things don't smell at all. Classen, Howes and Synnott write:

> In our postmodern world smell is often a notable [...] absence. Odors are suppressed in public places, there are no smells on television, the world of computers is odor free, and so on. This olfactory 'silence'

notwithstanding, smell would seem to share many of the traits commonly attributed to postmodernity [...] The past irrelevant, the future uncertain, postmodernity is a culture of 'now', a pastiche of styles and genres which exists in an eternal present. Postmodernity is also a culture of imitations and simulations, where copies predominate over originals and images over substance.

(1995, p. 203)

We create personal miasmas; appropriate smells for ourselves which conceal the original scents of our bodies. Just as familiarity with the smell of our own homes decreases our knowledge and awareness of their smell we also become over familiarized with our own scent, to the extent that we can't discern it.

To smell someone is intimate; it allows access, invites particular knowledge. Proximity extends the access, intensifies the invitation. Furthermore, the knowledge that another can smell us, have a knowledge of our own scent *that we ourselves can't smell* sets up a very potent encounter. Drew Leder writes that

Opposition can arise when we identify the lived body solely with the first-person perspective, the body lived-from-within, as opposed to the 'object body' seen from without [...] There are, in fact, certain bodily profiles, aspects of one's moods and intentions, that are far more available to others than oneself.

(1990, p. 6)

Is smell one of the 'profiles' of the body that is *more available to another?* As Merleau-Ponty notes, 'as someone who smells I am in the realm of the olfactory and may be smelled by others' (1968, p. 134). If perception is knowledge (see Merleau-Ponty; also Dewey, 1932), then it could be argued that the intersubjective relationships within *On the Scent* and the combined catalyst of proximity and the olfactory engender unique connections and comprehensions between one and the other.

In conjunction with this particular access or knowledge of the other, intensified through proximity to them, we also bring a cultural, gendered, racial and personal association, reaction and response. Phillip Vannini, Dennis Waskul and Simon Gottschalk, state that 'sensations are the basis of the embodied self' (2012, p. 88) and cite Kelvin Low's statement that smell:

> Functions as a social medium employed by social actors towards formulating constructions/judgments of race-d, class-ed and gender-ed others, operating on polemic/categorical constructions (and also, other nuances between polarities) which may involve a process of *othering* in which 'an individual defines the self through a difference in odours.'
>
> (Vannini, Waskul and Gottschalk, 2012, p. 88)

Inasmuch as we are processing and collating knowledge about the other we are making associations, connections and asserting differences. Low's use of the word 'actors' situates us within the performative and it is worth noting here that the connections made concerning the olfactory in the field of sociology have strong resonance and cross-fertilization with performance. Vannini and colleagues cite key scholars from the performance field such as Richard Schechner and Erving Goffman, and also, following J. L. Austin's development of speech acts, extend this to sense acts. They describe these sense-making rituals:

> [A]cts through which we do not just note the previous existence of something, but through which we perform and generate something into existence. And one of the things – arguably the most important – that we generate is our self as a relationship between us and other in time and place.
>
> (Vannini, Waskul and Gottschalk, 2012, p. 94)

For them, like speech acts, sense acts also refer to what sensations *do*, 'Sensory acts are moves endowed with dramatic significance; that is, with the power to originate other moves in a complex ecology of communication' (Vannini, Waskul and Gottschalk, 2012, p. 129). What we are trying to get at here concerns an appreciation of an activation and a 'doingness' of smell. There is a transformation or transubstantiation, a movement from and towards that is in its very essence performative. The proximity and specific choreography of *On the Scent* creates a highly concentrated environment for this awareness to take place. Stephen Di Benedetto writes that 'if we are encouraged to use the full range of our sense perception, we become active participants rather than passive, isolated viewers detached from the artistic experience (Di Benedetto in Banes and Lepecki, 2007, p. 133).

Remembrances of things past: experiencing *On the Scent*

> To be alone, or nearly alone, in front of a performer performing, can be a horror story – even if the performer is not blatant in his need for your attention. Thankfully, the *On the Scent* performers were virtuosic in their independence [...] so we could enjoy the split-screen of their address, which went both at us, and beyond. In one room, we were given a drink, in another, the twinkle of a returned gaze. Recognition without participation, intimacy without responsibility...
>
> (Chalmers and Chaudhuri, 2004, p. 76)

We think back to the performance that Jessica Chalmers and Una Chaudhuri saw, rewinding rapidly across the years, places, performances, houses and arriving in Marvin Carlson's midtown apartment in New York City, 2004.[3] Helen is lying in the bed, a beautiful antique wooden bed, the bed Marvin Carlson was born in. Leslie is in the narrow galley kitchen the Carlsons' describe as 'perfect for reheating Chinese takeout'. Bookshelves line the sitting-room walls, like a library. Lois Weaver has left a small lipstick kiss on the white wall. We try and see again Chalmers and Chaudhuri standing in the kitchen, sitting in the bedroom, looking at us. They write of the potential horror of being 'almost alone' with the performer. Where does this fear come from? The being seen, the possibility that something will be asked of you? On one level fear is muted and the horror subsides because although the performers need you to be there for the performance to take place, they don't really need you to do anything. Lois does not need you to bring anything, Leslie does not need you to participate in her ritual, Helen does not need you to make her well. The performance and the performers are self-sufficient. And yet... *something* is being asked. A contract is set up in the eye contact that takes place in intimate, proximate performance. We are each looking directly at you, into your eyes and speaking to you and you are only a matter of inches away. This interaction is being witnessed by your fellow audience members, who sit right next to you, so close you can touch them, so close they can register every move you make. Your decision to look back at us or your decision to look away are both charged, weighted. There is no casual look or random glance here – this is the performative close-up that lays all bare. Susan Bennett writes that generally in 'conventional' theatre the spectator's mind is, 'free to wander and be inattentive to what is on stage' (Bennett, 1997, p. 140). She states that this is inevitable during the course of the performance and that some dramatists actively encourage this pause for reflection or thought (Bennett, 1997, p. 140). With the persistence of the held eye contact in small audience performance, where does this 'free' space go when non-response is a very direct, very visible response?

In the first three productions of *On the Scent,* including the New York performance that Chalmers and Chauduri attended, we performed for audiences of two at a time, rather than four. Chalmers and Chaudhuri write that 'There was barely enough room for us – we were in fact three, due to a last-minute add-on – a circumstance that intensified our immersion' (Chalmers and Chaudhuri, 2004, p. 77). It is interesting to note that Chalmers and Chaudhuri feel the expansion of the audience from two to three 'intensified the immersion'. We later made the decision to double the audience in all subsequent performances to four, based primarily on the fact that two felt 'too much', too intense an encounter for both the audience *and* the performer. This was especially apparent when, on a couple of occasions, an audience member failed to materialize on time and *On the Scent* was performed to just one person. The concentration of the interaction felt too intense to us as performers. We felt that because we created too close an encounter, the intimacy undid itself and began to operate more as detachment. Changing to audience groups of four created a more relaxed experience for performers and audience, allowing for greater immersion. When you get too close to something physically you lose sight of it, it loses its shape, its contours.

With the smaller audiences of one or two Helen found that she performed differently, rarely making eye contact. She created a separation between the edge of the bed, her performance space, and the audience. A space of separation that in reality was just a few inches became infinitely larger by sealing off the eye contact. Helen sensed the heaviness and potency of the smells in the room, alongside the narratives of sickness, death and depression, demanded more space in order for the audience to experience but not 'over experience', and she found this space by limiting the eye contact. An audience of four automatically opened up more space, so she was free to make eye contact in a way that was meaningful and increased rather than over-saturated the intensity.

Leslie's performance in the kitchen likewise changed dramatically going from two to four in the audience. In the kitchen the audience are confronted with a series of 'atomic' images from the lines of red hot chilli to the story of virginity lost to a nuclear physicist, to atomic bomb detonations and their death tolls, all within an environment filled with aerosol hairspray hovering over smoking cigarettes, exploding popcorn, burning meat, burning hair and clouds of steam. In pairs of two Leslie remembers audience members as hardly daring to move, even though sometimes they were holding back coughs in reaction to the smoke or laughs in reaction to the popcorn. In groups of four audience members ventured to taste the chilli powder, laugh at the humour, sometimes cry – either at the death statistics and the smell of burning hair or simply from the toxic assault of smells and chemicals in the room. An audience member who saw the original production in a two and saw the show a couple of years later in a group of four told Leslie she was able to listen and absorb so much more in a group of four because she wasn't constantly worried about responding 'correctly'. As one of two she experienced a hyper-awareness of being 'half the audience' and worrying that if she didn't respond in the desired manner it would spoil things; as one of four she felt she could relax into the group and watch the performance instead of feeling watched; this in turn enabled her to respond more freely.

In *On the Scent* each performer speaks a personal narrative based on lived experience, connected to the smells in the room with her. Autobiography offers its own proximity, enabling levels of access and closeness. In her edited collection *Audience Participation: Essays on Inclusion in Performance*, Susan Kattwinkel writes about how a 'manipulation of truth and fiction in work can unbalance the spectator, engaging them mentally by putting them in a position of continuous interrogation' (2003 p. 90). She cites Daphne Ben Chaim, who connects the fiction level of a performance *with* its success in decreasing distance between performers and spectators. Ben Chaim states that 'the most intense personal relationship with a minimum awareness of fictionality is "low" distance and the combination that the realist film and realistic play aspire to' (Ben Chaim in Kattwinkel, 2003 p. 90). In collating the autobiographical stories into a script there is an awareness of the emotional terrain, accessibility and possible resonances for others. They are stories that others can relate to, can identify with, stories about mothers, grandmothers, grandfathers, war, atrocity, make-up, romance, losing one's virginity, depression, death, ageing, nostalgia. Because of the almost collective associations that some smells seem to trigger, the personal narratives allowed different points of access for audience members in *On the Scent*. There are moments of sudden recognition and identification. Jim Drobnick writes, 'by conveying these smells as both a symbol discussed in the script and an actual stimulus for the audience, a represencing occurs that simultaneously recalls, relives, and actualizes the experience' (Drobnick, in press).

Part of performing *On the Scent* is our embodied experience of the smells. The smells don't just affect the audience, they also work on us as performers. Some smells have been specifically selected *because* of their emotional or traumatic connection and the very potent response we have to them (medical odours, burning hair). Others work on us through their toxicity (cigarette smoke, hairspray). Some of those smells have taken on different associations, for example the Dettol disinfectant or the Vicks VapoRub,[4] chosen because of personal connections to fear, now recall the show itself rather than autobiographical experiences. Weaver states that

> Performing the show you lose contact with the experience of your own smell – every once in a while I get a scent of the lilies and if I smell the perfume *Eternity,* which is a smell I use only in the show, I get a sensation of the show, it's in the back of my head, it's a wide feeling – a creative place. It's the place I go to be somebody else.
>
> (Lois Weaver, interview, *On the Scent*, Cambridge, UK, 2009)

As the performers inhabiting these rooms for six or eight performances (in Brazil, 12) a day, the smells affect us. In the bedroom the sickening smells that cling to Helen's bed sheets and the airlessness create a room of depression which is a gloomy space to inhabit for eight or ten hours a day. The toxic air in the kitchen (coupled with chilli snorting) gives Leslie a huge headache every day we perform the piece, so she tours with pain killers. For Lois the overpowering perfumes, not to mention the perfumed chocolates, leave her with a sickly sweet sugar buzz she remedies between performances by stealing popcorn from the kitchen. This show about 'homesickness' literally makes us sick.

As performers we find it fascinating that the butterflies of pre-performance nerves that swoop in for most performers before the show goes up are present before every performance of *On the Scent*, even before the sixth or seventh performance in a day. The moment we hear the key turn in the lock the butterflies return. There is a fearfulness and a delight in hearing four strangers making their way into the house, opening the doors, walking up the stairs, and then suddenly being so close. Each performance feels like a very unique encounter with the audience, performing the piece never enters the realm of autopilot. It always feels new because the different dynamic each audience brings is so palpable. Whether they are all friends who have come together or total strangers who met for the first time on the doorstep, each group affects the performance with a particular charge. There has been much anecdotal evidence on how actors can *feel* an audience and how a 'good' audience can bolster the performance. The experience of performing *On the Scent* several times a day, hundreds of times in more than 20 cities is proof enough for us that there is without a doubt an alchemy of some sort at play here. In the spirit of the Japanese Noh actors who study the audience just before they make their entrance and 'adjust their performances' accordingly (Banes and Lepecki, 2007, p. 16), we are able to judge an audience's nervousness, their mood, their responsiveness, their sense of humour, by listening to the ways they respond to Lois in the first few minutes of the piece and likewise adjust accordingly.[5]

Smell, like performance is ephemeral, and it is also hard to shake off; submerging beyond the proximate to the internal. You take the performance with you, not just the memory or the experience of the work but the physiology of it, it is in your bloodstream, it is directly influencing your synaptic function, bypassing the hippocampus, triggering the parts of the brain to do with memory, place, emotion. Something lingers in the cellular memory of the body. Something has been passed on, into the bloodstream, some sort of contamination. Stanton B. Garner writes that 'given that its signals involve actual molecules permeating an unlocalizeable space, smell is one of the most transgressive senses as far as illusionism is concerned' (Garner in Banes and Lepecki, 2007, p. 121). He cites a fragment of Tony Kushner's *Angels in America*:

Smell is [...] an incredibly complex and underappreciated physical phenomenon [...] We have five senses, but only two that go beyond the boundaries of ourselves. When you look at someone, it's just bouncing light, or when you hear them, it's just sound waves, vibrating air, or touch is just nerve endings tingling... [Smell is] made up of the molecules of what you're smelling.

(Garner in Banes and Lepecki, 2007, p. 121)

When Lois invites the audience into the house, it is personal from the start, already beyond the boundary, already on the inside. This sense of the personal, experiential nature of the encounter is beautifully expressed in the following audience comment:

It was a cold winter's day in Madison, Wisconsin. I arrived at a house on a snowy lake. When my small group [of four] entered the house, we were greeted by the one and only Lois Weaver in the front room of the house. Surrounded by perfume bottles, Weaver's energy filled the space and then some. I was in love with her, with the moment I was in, with my group. I could already tell how quickly the time would slip away and how many details I would desire to hold with me, but inevitably leave behind. The tequila in the kitchen, the whisky on the lips... climbing and descending the stairs. Being in such close proximity to these performers was a gift; a series of moments absolutely brimming with a lust for life. The sense of togetherness on a cold winter's night surrounded by the cast and my fellow guests comes back to me easily. When I think of *On the Scent*, I smile. I can almost smell the pork frying in the frying pan or the popcorn in the popper. I remember the way the other people in my group acted and reacted. I remember the overwhelming desire to 'go again' the minute the piece ended. The mixture of truth and fiction, of the reality of our wool socks meeting the wooden floor and the video camera prepped and ready to capture our stories mixed into another realm. Another place and another experience. The proximity between me and the performers felt charged and intimate. Completely exciting and safe.

(Audience Response, Marina Kelly, Madison, 2010)

Site-specific work comes with its own personality imbued by place and location. *On the Scent,* invested in the highly personalized private territory of the home, is saturated by its locale. Home is the form and the content of *On the Scent* which offers a bound-up-ness of smell with home and smell with self, as it questions who we are to ourselves, to our families, to our pasts. In *On the Scent* strangers are suddenly connected by their proximate relationship and become guests in a house they do not know, in a place that is unfamiliar; guests with an ever-shifting relationship to each other and to the performance.

Initial performances of *On the Scent* were more 'staged'; more of the personal artefacts, clothes, photographs, objects belonging to the owners which might distract or detract from the intended atmosphere and sense of place were removed. Chalmers and Chaudari reflect on the absence of the home owner. 'In his absence, his small and unassuming lodgings were overcoded by the sights and smells of femaleness and longing. The living room surfaces were crowded with tiny bonbons, droopy, voluptuous flowers, and heavy strings of pearls' (Chalmers and Chaudari, 2004, p. 77). Just as the framing of the stage enables particular readings, there was an awareness that certain items might cause the audience to 'read' different stories or realities for the performers. We assiduously 'made over' the house with the trappings of the show. Later, however, less of the original was disturbed, only the most necessary adjustments were made to facilitate aspects of the performance such as arranging chairs in the bedroom or the kitchen. There was something interesting for us as performers in the natural co-mingling with what was already there, letting the house present its own shapes and indentations. Audience members often reflected the particular house they had experienced *On the Scent* in was perfect, they could not imagine it in any other setting, whereas for us it became clear that in each setting, a council flat in East London, an Upper West Side apartment in New York, a country manor in Ireland, an ex-communist building in Shanghai, the performance seemed to take up residence, make itself at home.

There is a delicious feeling of trespass and curiosity, of entering someone else's home when the owners are not there. In this illicit act audience and performers are united; strangers in a stranger's house, temporary guests, momentary residents, none truly belonging, all passing through for a moment. Although the performers do not belong in this place they enact the familiar, they have taken up residence, flooded the house with their smells, claim ownership in their greetings, 'I was waiting for you', 'Sit down at the table here.' The glasses are out, the tequila is poured. And obediently the audience perform their role of guests. With the sense of being expected comes perhaps an enforced closeness; slightly proprietorial:

> You and your audience-partner put yourselves in the hands of three intent performers and let yourselves be propelled by them through a small world of smell-filled rooms. You enter through the front door of an apartment and proceed through its sights 'peristaltically,' as if urged by a thousand fingers.
>
> (Chalmers and Chaudhuri, 2004, p. 76)

In *On the Scent* the opening and subsequent scenes are a complete reversal of the usual paradigm of the spectator watching the performer make her entrance. In this show it is the audience who make their entrance into worlds that are already active. The audience create 'on stage' and 'backstage' by moving in and out of rooms. When they move out of the kitchen, the kitchen becomes backstage. In this way the spectators bring 'on stage' with them and leave 'off stage' in their wake.

By Hall's measures we are in the terrain of 'intimate distance'; the personal realm of home, yet into this private space we invite strangers. We have let them into the kitchen, the heart of the home, let them settle on the sofa in the family living room, we have opened the bedroom door and called them in. Intimate distance is turned upside down, inside out. Once inside it is hard to get out. There are none of the ubiquitous vivid green exit signs always visible in the theatre. The performers patrol the rooms, doors are closed behind you, eyes are locked with yours.

> As a device or a structure for audiences to engage with work, one-to-one or intimate encounters were completely new to me at that time and I was completely floored by the experience. I went on this bizarre internal push-me-pull-you of trying to go into myself and watch from a safe distance and being dragged back to the surface by the performances. It was really uncomfortable and totally elating at the same time. It was terrifying, exhilarating, crazy-making like having sex for the first time.
>
> (Audience Response, Emmy Minton, London 2003)

In this set up the audience are 'controlled' by the environment, and the direct and proximate contact of the performers. Audience members who are particularly claustrophobic or those who respond strongly to the smells present in the house or their own remembered smell memories were strongly affected by the experience. Some audience members describe feeling breathless, almost overwhelmed by the scents, the proximity of performance and by the emotions engendered by the smells. As mentioned above, the small size of the audience and the proximity of the performers make it hard to slip away unnoticed but even more impossible to escape are the scents themselves; our very act of breathing betrays us. There is a persistence in the proximity, a pervasiveness of both the scents at play and the performers who play with them. Yi-Fu Tuan writes that 'The olfactory sense is linked to a primitive part of the brain that controls emotions and mood and the involuntary movements of life, including breathing, heartbeat, pupil size...' (Tuan, 1993, p. 56). The proximity of the performance makes these transformations visible, olfaction makes what Drew Leder calls the 'absent body' present, palpable and, due to proximity of audience to audience, audience to performer, even visible. Jo Machon writes:

> The (syn)aesthetically styled body in performance provides the slippage and fusion between various sensual languages, such as the verbal, haptic and olfactory, which is then experienced as an equivalent sensation through the (syn)aesthetically perceiving bodies in the audience. Such a feature is exploited in the work of Curious, particularly *On the Scent* (2003) and *Autobiology* (2008–9) where the sensual workings of the human body are manipulated within the narrative and thematic experience.
>
> (Machon, 2009, p. 64)

In each of the rooms smell pervades. The molecules of scent slip silently into the lungs of the audience, caught in the very air that they breathe. The performance is inside them and with it the associations and intensities of what those smells carry. For example, the sharp menthol from the VapoRub in the bedroom carries with it the heaviness of that room, the image of the closed curtains, the matted crumpled unwashed bed-sheets, the stories of depression and death. Tuan writes:

> The senses, under the aegis and direction of the mind, give us a world. Some are 'proximate,' others 'distant.' The proximate senses

yield the world closest to us, including our own bodies. The position and movement of our bodies produce proprioception or kinesthesia, somatic awareness of the basic dimensions of space.

(Tuan, 1993, p. 35)

The audience members are implicated by their closeness, by being in the room, sitting at the bedside, trailing scents of the performance on their skin, hair, clothes, in their nasal passages.

Scents have elusive frames, but are nevertheless contained. The odors never traveled from room to room – it was only by way of our collecting them did they journey. Our small caravan seemed appropriate given the faint concentrations of odor. An audience of four is the perfect sized container for something like the smell of a fresh bundle of lilies or the sickly smell of Vicks. Much like those Russian nesting dolls, each of us nested within the group, within the room, within the performance and the house; each a container for smells, movements and memories. The contact between each container was an intimate one, murky yet felt.

(Audience Response, Ryan Tacata, San Francisco, 2011)

Emmanuel Levinas writes of the immediacy of proximity (Levinas, 2011, p. 84) and the olfactory resonates with this sense of immediacy; redolent with the very presentness of it. Trygg Engen describes the physiological design that enables this rapid processing:

The neurological impulses in the olfactory system seem to have a more direct route from the receptors to the brain. They have direct access to the limbic system and then to the cerebral hemispheres. Olfactory information may therefore be processed more quickly and with less editing than visual and auditory information. Odour memory may last longer because of a larger number of connections to different parts of the brain that may make possible more associations.

(1991, p. 109)

We witness this immediacy over and over again in the performance. We see the audience members reacting to smells, real or remembered, and in the remembering there is almost a re-smelling the odour, a re-experiencing the moment and the emotion connected to it. Lois Weaver reflects:

> In the show we did yesterday I saw someone really realize, perhaps for the first time, how powerful smell is. He remembered a smell and then his eyes lit up and he said, 'When I think about that smell all these other images come up.' In that moment he was suddenly aware of the trigger that most of us know and don't necessarily give voice to but it was his pure discovery of that moment.
>
> (Lois Weaver, interview, *On the Scent*, Cambridge, UK, 2009)

Smell is a time traveller, a nostalgic chrononaut taking us not to the future but back into the past. 'Smells resist containment in discrete units, whether physical or linguistic; they cross boundary lines' (Classen, Howes and Synnott, 1995, p. 204). And in that moment of transportation when we retrieve a smell memory often we don't just see the past, we feel we re-experience it. We remember the smell of our grandmother's kitchen and as we recount it we revisit the kitchen, seeing it from the perspective of the child-us sitting on the cold white-tiled floor. We *feel* the floor, we *smell* the cleaning fluid our grandmother used, we *hear* her talking to us, the timbre of her voice. Classen, Howes and Synnott cite a case of a woman who associates the smell of a flower with her father's death, which evokes a memory both visually and aurally vivid, 'That same kind of smell reminds me of the sadness, the helplessness, worst of all my mother's crying' (1995, p. 2) It is a fully experiential recollection, a total transportation.

We watch the audience members transported by a recollection of a smell memory, suddenly filled with the emotional charge that it brings. This 'presentness', this immediacy is augmented by the space of the performance. Within that immediacy of the olfactory, the small space of the domestic setting, and the intimate style and delivery of the performance there is something of a confrontation in this encounter. Jim Drobnick writes of *On the Scent* that

> The work achieves its visceral impact by being close-up and intimate [...] Traditional theatres tend to limit the effective use of scent, for the separation of performers from the audience and the size of most seating arrangements make the circulation of scents difficult to

control. Here, though, in an ordinary residence, the audience experiences what could be called an olfactory memory theatre, where scents appear with striking affect right in their faces.

(Drobnick, in press)

'Calling to mind' smell memories can trigger immediate emotional and physiological reactions. Engen states that 'Smell may be to emotion what sight or hearing is to cognition' (1991, p. 3). Alongside what is scripted in the performance there is also the 'unscripted performance' enacted by the smells themselves. They can trigger memories and emotions in the audience that we as performers have no real control over. We cannot second-guess the kind of associations or connections someone might have to a seemingly innocuous scent. And it is here that smell performs its own particular proximity. As Herbert Blau states: 'An Audience without a history is not an audience' (Blau in Bennett, 1997, p. 140) We cannot gauge what smell might trigger something particularly potent for an audience member due to a past experience and often in the show people have been reminded of significant and/or traumatic events provoked by a smell in the house.

One of my (Leslie) most surreal memories of *On the Scent* is of performing in an apartment in Shanghai. We had three translators, one for each of the three performers. Having someone else in the room all day was odd for me, as I'm used to spending *On the Scent* days going between being alone while the audience are in the other rooms and then being 'on' when the audience come into the kitchen. When we did the piece in Brazil one translator moved with the audience, coming and going with them, but in Shanghai our personal interpreters stayed with us all day, asking us lots of questions about London or life in the West in-between performances. The question I remember most vividly is: What is the difference between butter and cheese? It's always very strange to have performance text translated – especially when you hear what you conceive as a simple straightforward line take ages to translate, or more disconcerting when you say something quite complex and nuanced and the translation only seems to be a couple of words. And sometimes in translation you miss the laughs in the places you normally listen for them and you start anticipating laughs in surprise unfunny (to you) places. The whole notion of doing an intimate performance across a language barrier as wide as English and Mandarin is a bit surreal to begin with, but then again, translation goes on all the time in one-to-one situations.

During one of the performances of *On the Scent* in Shanghai, I was telling the story about my grandpa bequeathing me his shaving lotion bottle collection – a 1950s men's aftershave cologne series bottled in model vintage cars. In the show I tell the story and then I open the bottle and pass it round for the audience to smell. In the West people often remember this as a smell from another generation when men wore stronger spicier scents like *Bay Rum* and *Old Spice* or in my grandpa's case, *Wild Country* and *Sagebrush*. As soon as I passed the shaving lotion bottle to a man in the audience he started speaking very excitedly to the translator. The translator was in the middle of translating one of my lines when this happened and she kept talking and he kept talking at the same time. I had the feeling she was still trying to carry on with the translation, and thus encourage him to stop talking. The man kept talking – he was desperate for her to translate what he was saying to me, but the translator was strict with him. I was confused, but as soon as the two of them stopped talking simultaneously I picked up where I left off with my next line 'you rarely catch a whiff of a man like that anymore…' and carried on. There was another explosion – everyone but me was talking. The translator was talking, the man was talking and the man's wife started talking. He was holding the shaving lotion aloft, desperately shouting something at me that I couldn't understand.

By now the popcorn kernels had started popping. This often makes the audience slightly hysterical – the combination of the horrible story about the atomic bomb alongside the crazy popping – but during this performance the shaving lotion bottle man's wife saw the first piece of popcorn fall onto the floor and gasped in horror, and then I could see in her eyes a steely determination that not one more piece of popcorn was going to touch the floor. She stood up and started catching them one by one, but the popcorn really started exploding like a volcano. I was trying to finish relating the story, so I was talking. The translator was talking – I hoped she was translating but I thought she might just be yelling at the woman to sit down and stop catching the popcorn. The shaving lotion bottle man was shouting at the popcorn woman and she was shouting at him. I didn't know what to do, so I just ended my performance as usual by cutting off a lock of my hair and burning it, then gave them the customary shots of tequila. We were all exhausted and confused.

The next day I got a letter from the man, which he had got someone to translate into English. He said that when he was a little boy his greatest treasure was an identical car-shaped shaving lotion bottle that his father had been given by an American GI. He lost the bottle in the Cultural Revolution and he was so excited to see this one. He invited me to his house. He was a really fantastic political muralist. I gave him the shaving lotion bottle even though it really was an inheritance from my grandfather, so it was a bit of a wrench, but luckily my grandfather left me quite a few so it seemed like the right thing to do.

Smell bypasses the hippocampus, leading scientists to speculate that this may be why emotional connections with the sense of smell are so powerful or unfiltered. Inasmuch as *On the Scent* does not shy away from emotion or intimacy, it also invites nostalgia. Lois Weaver states that 'Nostalgia is associated with the feminine and is a way of marginalizing us for being reflective.'[6] That reflectiveness is openly courted in *On the Scent*. It is implicit in the invitation to enter the house, in the particular look and ambience of the sitting room Lois inhabits. We catch her in her reverie of the past and she invites us to share ours, to record it even. Nicola Savarese defines nostalgia as the passion for a return (Barba and Savarese, 2006, p. 185). Vannini roots nostalgia to its etymological origin as the will to 'return home' and concurs that indeed to 'return home' is a typical outcome of olfactory sensations (Vannini, Waskul and Gotschalk, 2012, p. 95). First coined by Johannes Hofer in 1688, nostalgia referred to a diagnosable disease or 'homesickness'. Both homesickness and a desire to return are fertile definitions of nostalgia when applied to *On the Scent*.[7] As well as taking place in a real domestic setting, the performance is infused with stories of the performers' own memories of home and at the end of the piece when Lois asks the audience to share their smell memories with her, it is specifically through the lens of *home*: 'What smells remind you of home, or make you feel homesick... or just make you sick?' Out of all the places we could go in these moments of borderless olfactory journeying the most common is *home*.

Vannini further develops nostalgia as an active catalyst within identity: '[T]he pragmatic relationship between sensory perception, memory, and nostalgia represents a significant form of identity' (Vannini, Waskul and Gotschalk, 2012, p. 96). Rather than nostalgia engendering a romanticized, half-remembered or 'feminine' malaise, it actively stimulates and invokes action and connectivity. Nostalgia is not consigned to immobilizing remembrances of things past, but instead to active, transformative recall.[8] In this way memory and nostalgia connect us to a sense of our past selves. In these moments of recall our selves from the past reminisce with our selves of the present, with an awareness of what is no longer present (people, places) and what is the same. In these moments smell connects past and present selves 'establishing a somatic sense of self through time – that is, nostalgically "connecting" then and "now" and thereby linking "former sensuous self" and "present sensuous self"' (Vannini, Waskul and Gotschalk, 2012, p. 98).

This activation is palpable when the audience are asked to share a smell memory, the sudden jolt from the present to the past where there is a relocation, a transformation and a reconnection of this remembered state back in to the present moment. Of course, we don't see or feel the synaptic firing – in this way Leder's absent body still retains its invisibility, but there is a vivid manifestation of physiological experience before our very eyes, or perhaps under our very noses. This moment of re-collection, of re-experience, of transubstantiation is vivid. There is no script for this moment of the show. It is embodied each and every time by the audience member who becomes performer and completes the performance. Lois becomes audience with the others and although she is focusing the camera on the person recounting their smell memory, a mirror image of how the performance started, it is evident that the real witnessing is done by the live bodies in the room.[9]

> At the end of the piece, as soon as I say, 'I want you to tell me something personal. Something that reminds you of home... or makes you feel homesick...' it is almost as if I see them leave the room for a moment. I know they are not listening anymore, they are trying to think of their smell, their memory. When I say, 'or just something that makes you feel sick', that is the moment I get them back. In the performance we give them little pathways that trigger memories or that inspire them. I think that if we asked them for a smell memory immediately when they came into the house we would get very different responses.
>
> (Lois Weaver, interview, *On the Scent*, Cambridge, UK, 2009)

Like the Avon lady who tempts Lois with a promise of the bottles and jars, we too bottle and collect the smells given by the audience members.

In several hundred performances, only two people have declined to answer. Moreover, in the contribution there is a willingness, even a need to uncork the memory and to let it pervade that particular performance. In this chosen ending they are the co-writer, co-performer and co-perfumier introducing another scent, another smell memory.

In the last segment of the performance when the audience members sit intimately together on the sofa and share their smell memories, there is a sense of *communitas*. A shared experience has been established and they have developed a sense of closeness. There is a knowledge that this closeness will be short-lived – it will dissipate as soon as the front door is opened – but for this suspended moment of the performance, it exists. They are in the sitting room, the space in the home for shared conversation, for family gatherings, for closeness. Here they share personal recollections with Lois but also with each other. Schechner asks: 'What about letting spectators see spectators and performers see spectators? Such open architecture encourages a contact that is continuous, subtle, fluid, pervasive, and unconscious. Lovely' (Schechner, 1994, p. 37). In our experience, it is indeed lovely. Audiences of *On the Scent* described telling their stories and hearing those of their fellow audience members as powerful. After experiencing the journey through the house, hearing the stories of homesickness told by the performers, they actively wanted to share their own memories triggered by the piece. Although sometimes unnerved by having to face the camera and Lois, they described a sense of relief at being invited to respond to what they had just witnessed and experienced, and remembered.

> I told a story about riding my bike past a brownie factory in Chicago, every morning, on my way to school. It was like riding into a thick cloud of chocolate batter and icing and I would always stop a block away to light a cigarette – as one might do after an incredible night of sex. This is my strongest scent memory and I gave it away willingly to a seductive woman filming me on a couch with three others by my side.
>
> (Audience Response, Ryan Tacata, San Francisco, 2011)

Through this moment in the performance an archive of smell memories and associations has formed as the work continues to tour, with each audience member contributing to the growing collection, imbuing it with something of their own essence. We could make a whole book of these smell memories, which we think would read as a kind of poetry. We uncork just a few here to leave you with.

The first bunch of rain after a long dry season, hot and dry in Zambia, which is where I'm from. And in November comes this thunder and the clouds gather and then the rain falls. And you can smell this fresh smell, the soil getting wet, basically. And it reminds me of being back home and smelling that and being young and playing out in the rain.

(London, 2003)

The memory of chlorine at the swimming baths is a strong strong smell and it's a smell that I associate with my father and going on trips as a kid to swimming baths that were so full of chlorine they'd almost knock you sideways as you entered in. And a sense of being very very skinny in slightly ill-fitting bathing trunks and shivering. And the moment I still remember in any times of fear, the moment of trying to decide to jump into the water, that was always just a little too cold. And so that's something that clicks in whenever I smell chlorine, even if it's not in a swimming bath or even if the water is actually warm.

(Birmingham, 2003)

I fondly remember the smell of bacon being cooked, because I grew up on top of a greasy spoon café and my parents used to work downstairs. And we were raised Muslim, and we weren't allowed to eat pork, but I used to always like the smell of it. And I remember as I got older, having some bacon – having it when my parents were out. And although I'm now vegetarian, I fondly remember that smell. I actually like the smell. I can't eat it, but I like the smell. And it just kind of takes me back to having to challenge my culture.

(London, 2004)

I remember the smell of a man I was in love with. And actually, we knew each other for a couple of years. And I thought I was in love with him. And I remember the first time we really were close to each other, I realized I couldn't... I couldn't smell him. And it was awful. I can't describe it because English is not my language. It's really difficult to describe a smell. But I eventually realized that this is something really important in a relationship.

(Birmingham, 2003)

My father used to use a cologne, *CD*, and I liked this perfume very much because it was the symbol of my father. But now, it smells disgusting. This is the scent of betrayal. And the scent of hurt and depression. And I hate it.

(Shanghai, 2004)

My smell is the smell of my babies' hair. They're grown up now, they're late teenagers, but I can still smell that sort of soft fragrant 'me-ness' – it was just me and them – that was so delicious. Completely delicious.

(London, 2004)

I remember rummaging in my mother's handbag as a child – for money, sweets. And being struck by her headscarf, which smelt of cigarettes and perfume. And I remember when she died, I found that scarf. And it still smelt, even after all those years. So it still brought back that memory.

(Birmingham, 2003)

And I think there's always one that, yes, is a poignant one, which is the smell of death. When my father died, he died at home, and before the undertakers came there was in the room the smell of death. And you can't... it's a sort of sweetish smell and a strange smell, but you never forget it.

(Birmingham, 2004)

In my parents' house, growing up... all the juice glasses smelled like bourbon.

(New York, 2003)

3   Interior II: *the moment I saw you I knew I could love you*

The performance *the moment I saw you I knew I could love you*[1] explores 'gut feelings', a topography of instinct and impulse, where desire, fear, anger, humiliation or panic occasionally hits us unawares like a rogue wave. Gut feelings manifest as innate awareness of physiological sensations; sudden deluges of chemicals flooding the system. The desire in making the piece was to explore these visceral experiences on a creative, textual and poetic level, mining biology, fact and fiction through a fusion of live performance and film. We aimed to work on an experiential level, engendering in the audience a sense of their own bodies, desires, instincts, and perhaps even triggering responses in their enteric nervous systems, manifested as butterflies in the stomach or perhaps just a touch of biliousness. Because it is composed of episodic moments rather than a linear narrative, performing the piece is more like leading the audience on an expedition through choppy waters than telling them one cohesive story. The overall metaphor for 'gut feelings' in the piece was, indeed, the sea.

> *They say the sea is cold, but the sea contains*
> *the hottest blood of all, and the wildest, the most urgent.*
> – D. H. Lawrence

The performance

The show is experienced with the audience sitting in three separate eight-person life-rafts (see diagram below) on the stage floor, all authentic vessels that have, at some point, been on a rescue mission at sea. The residue of the boats' working pasts can be seen in the salt incrustations on their exteriors and in the smell of rubber and the sea. As they enter the theatre, audience members are immediately swallowed up into the darkness of a black box space lit only by flashlights carried by

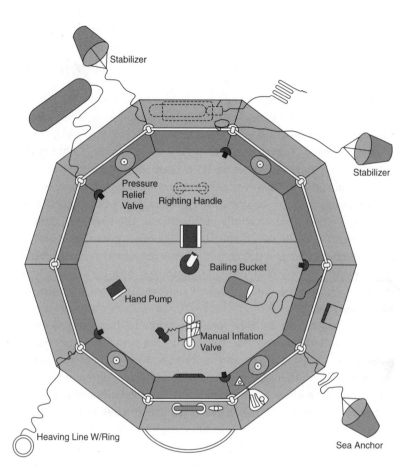

Illustration 3.1 Life-raft

the performers (Leslie Hill, Helen Paris and Claudia Barton) and small emergency bulbs atop each life-raft. They step directly onto the stage and into an ongoing performance where they are sonically engulfed in the deep bass reverberations of Graeme Miller's sound track, a piece composed to conjure the feeling of being inside the belly of a whale. In this loud, dark, destabilizing moment the audience encounters the performers who light the way to life-rafts while giving brusque warnings: 'Into the life-rafts please, quickly!' 'Please, make your way to the boats!' 'There's room for one more here.' 'Keep arms and legs inside the boat at all times.' Couples and friends lose each other or cling together as people are bundled into the small boats, amidst a mild sense of chaos and panic. When each of the life-rafts is full, the performers' torches snap off, and the voices fade, dissolving into the sound of waves slapping against the sides of the rafts.

Occasionally audience members resist getting into a life-raft, 'no thank you' or 'where is my seat'? They sometimes look around in the dark for their familiar place in the auditorium, realizing, perhaps with a surge of anxiety, that there are no seats – the only place for them is in the rafts. They have already entered the body of the performance itself.[2] They are already on the other side, beyond the safety curtain, beyond the invisible screen that protects and separates them from the performer, from the performance. Cocooned in their rafts, the space and darkness engulf them. The intent of this discombobulating start, the sense of alarm doubled with the strange undulating movements of the life-rafts was to try and cause a 'butterflies in the stomach' or seasick feeling in the bodies of the audience who sit closely together, intimate strangers, cast adrift on a midnight ocean.

Traditionally, light draws the performer close to the audience. We can see the emotions on the face, the labour, the tiny facial gestures and movements – but it also separates performer from audience – the light for the performer on the stage blanks out the audience. Here the tables are turned and the audience has entered in almost total blackness, their way lit only by the small circular lights of electric torches shining towards them. They climb cautiously into life-rafts, which are illuminated only by pinpricks of light, single tiny bulbs on the crossbeam of each life-raft. There are moments in the piece when the only illumination in the environment comes from these small safety bulbs. At first the intention is that the darkness they have entered into works to give a sense that all have been cast into an unknown environment where there is no sign of the edges, no sense of the contours. The performers appear and disappear out of this darkness in the near-invisible space surrounding the boats. The darkness in and around the boats functions both to make mini-communities in each raft and at the same time, perhaps, creates a feeling of remoteness from the performers and the other rafts, enabling both distance/privacy and proximity/vulnerability.

The soundscape is likewise designed to expand and collapse the sense of distance, resonating through the space, reverberating through the floor and engulfing the rafts and the people in them. Leslie appears out of the darkness, close to the life-rafts, making direct eye contact with audience members as she speaks to them. Despite her physical closeness to the audience, her voice is mic'd and run through the surround sound encircling the boats, allowing her to speak at an intimate, almost conspiratorial pitch – the voice is both nearby and distant.

Normally your heart and respiratory function are totally automatic and you don't really think about them too much. But every once in a while something happens that makes your heart skip a beat. And in extreme situations, instinct takes over and your body produces a fight, flight or freeze reaction. If your instinct is to flee or fight, your pulse will race and adrenaline will flood your body, your pupils will dilate and your skin will turn cold and pale as all the blood rushes to your muscles. In extreme situations your bowels may empty. If your instinct is to freeze, your body will produce the opposite reaction: your heart will slow, your breathing will become very shallow and your blood pressure will plummet.

Fight, flight and freeze – the instinctive, primitive reactions to highly emotional or dangerous situations dictated by the autonomic nervous system. Leslie situates these three physical responses in common human experiences:

It kind of makes you wonder which reaction your body would produce in an extreme situation. If, for example, you were swallowed by a whale... or found out in a terrible lie... or if someone walked in and saw you doing something you really, really didn't want them to see.

Projections fade away and the audience watch images of glistening viscera flicker over two screens to either side of the space. One of the screens is a cyclorama stretching the length and breadth of one wall, the other patched together from the unravelled innards of a life-raft, so that the images play over the rubber tubes and the emergency notices stitched into the splayed body of the raft, the screen as 'thrown-off skin' (see Jones, 2002, p. 958). The film is a confluence of 16 mm black and white footage, interwoven with archival film footage and digital video. The audience are surrounded by close-up shots of internal organs looming in the space, inescapable. The camera pans slowly over the greyish white folds of the lining of the stomach, moves across the red-brown mound of a liver, the rope-like coils of intestines. Leslie presents the audience with their own physiology:

> *This is you, in all your multiplicity. You are part reptile, part mammal, part primate, part Homo sapiens. You are twitchy amygdala; you are a dopamine fiend; you are under the spell of oxytocin. You are an unthinkably complex series of connections, of links, spun together by your genes and by your lived experience. The density of receptors in the intestines may be why we feel our emotions in that part of the anatomy, often referring to them as 'gut feelings'.*[3]

The performance locates itself inside and outside of the rafts, moving between the layers of film and live images, from the audience's bodies spilling onto each other within the rafts, to the performers' bodies without, appearing from the darkness. Helen's voice whispers across the images of the body on the screen:

> *I love you inside out. I love your bones and your blood and your bile and the shape of your organs and the dark brown of your liver and the sloosh and spill of your liquids.*

The audience has already been told 'this is you', and confronted by the topographical reality of their own insides. Huddled tightly together in the life-rafts they experience a shared bearing witness to insides outed. The audience has been cast out, surrounded by unknown strangers, swaying between personal and intimate space, the 'ocean' they are adrift in acting as a metaphor for the turbulent range of human emotions. The life-rafts perhaps work to bring their own sense of *communitas* – the bonding, the belonging together fated for the duration of the piece, displaced from the expected, much as in a real catastrophe.

Lit by only a small sphere of reflected torchlight, Helen reads out the instructions for taking 'Sea Legs' travel sickness medicine. The light bounces off the small square of paper illuminating her face and causing it to seem to float, disembodied, through the darkness (Illustration 3.2).

Helen also wears a lapel mic, enabling her to whisper the text – to be distant and yet to seem so very close as the audience pitch and shift surrounded by the sound of waves, perhaps feeling that travel sickness tablets might be an appropriate item for this journey. As Helen continues

Illustration 3.2   Helen, Sea Legs
[Photo by Hugo Glendinning]

to read, however, it becomes clear that something much more ominous than motion sickness is being discussed. This journey that is being embarked upon is one that may have no return.

> *Sea Legs Tablets may cause side effects: Drowsiness. Sickness. Homesickness. A feeling of difference. A sadness inside knowing that things will never be the same now and that there is no going back. A tight beseech in the throat, the heart racing an unsteady pulse, a trembling. In extreme cases Sea Legs might cause irreparable heartbreak. If affected, do not drive, don't operate heavy machinery. Don't go.*

These tablets, which purportedly alleviate nausea in the gut, take on a more portentous meaning.

For the first part of the performance, the performers are almost disembodied apparitions voicing fragments of stories, merging in and out of the images on the screen. Then the unthinkable happens: a performer suddenly steps into each of the three life-rafts. The occupants, already squeezed in, bundle up more closely to make room for another. They may look out across the darkness and notice another performer getting into another boat. The rafts rock and pitch further as the shift increases the physical contact (voluntary or otherwise) between audience and audience as well as bringing the performers right into the audience's personal space.

While in the rafts, each performer tells a different story to the circular huddle of their shipmates, all performed simultaneously. Miller's score, *Adrift*, which connects the atmosphere of the space across the distances of the individual boats, evokes a sense of a swirling circular movement or dance, as if each raft is caught alone in the eddies of a tide for a few minutes, aware of but apart from the other rafts. Ultra aware of the scene in their own boat, the audience can also hear slight bleeds of stories being told by other performers in other rafts. Through the magic of timing (and sharp-eared performers) three micro-performances all end together and the performers move clockwise into the next boat, starting their stories anew until each performer has been in each boat.

Claudia tells the occupants of her raft the story of a whale who watches 'the jumpers' from Beachy Head, a notorious suicide clifftop on the south-east coast of England. As she speaks she crumbles fragments of the white chalk cliffs in her hand.

The whale watches the jumpers from Beachy Head. The whale is most interested in the moment before the jump. A ray of late afternoon sun glints on a man's hair and makes it shine gold. Like a crown. Now would be a good moment to jump. A shining moment. In this particular light it would be heroic, poetic. It would look amazing. The man does not jump. The eye of the whale focuses closer, zooming in like a riflescope. He focuses on the man's trainers. They are bright white. Brand new. That will be a waste of money. The man must have had a sense of purpose when he went into the shop and bought those bright white shoes. Adidas. They have the new soles. State-of-the-art. The soles of the shoes sink their teeth into the white side of the cliff top and grip on. The whale watches a few tiny white crumbles of chalk roll down the cliff like miniature snowballs. The man still stands on top of the cliff. The sun has gone in and the sky is leaden grey. His hair no longer shines like a crown but sits like a blob on his head, slightly ridiculous. His cagoule balloons out. The day is eager to be done. He has missed his moment and looks foolish. And it is in this moment that he jumps.

In another of the rafts Helen opens a packet of Sea Legs and slides out a slim white oblong strip of tablets. She places the strip of pills onto the open palm of one of the audience members, and encourages the others to draw close. Helen projects a tiny film onto the strip of pills, transforming the audience member's palm, gently cupped around the Sea Legs, into a miniature cinema screen. An image flickers and takes shape: a woman (Helen) is floating out in the middle of the ocean on a pink lilo.[4] She wears a black dress and gazes up at a leaden sky above her. Small waves splash over her. The heavy material of her dress drapes in wet folds over her body. The lilo scuds over the water. The sea is wintry, grey-green and churning, the lilo the only thin strip of colour in the landscape, bright candyfloss pink. The woman drifts further out to sea, pulled by the current. There is no explanation for her journey. Is she following some impulse, some undefended moment, some knowledge that this day, this moment is the moment when she casts off, adrift, surrendering to the elements, to the unpredictable churning power of the sea? In the background the silhouette of Beachy Head looms, chalky-white, ghostly. When the strip of tablets becomes the projection screen for the woman on the lilo we are aware of its significance. This is perhaps a journey with no return. The small oblong screen, the small oblong inflatable, both promise help yet simultaneously reveal their vulnerability. As the film of the woman at sea plays on the tiny screen, Helen speaks in a near whisper, looking back and forth between her own projected image and the audience member who holds that image.

This is how I dream it. This is how it feels. And I am not a sailor. I cannot steer a craft. I cannot tie a reef knot. I cannot swim. But still this is how it ends. I am out here with the lost mariners, the castaways, the shipwrecked and the sea-swallowed. In the moment you swallow you can't breathe. It's a moment of give and take. The very last swallow sits caught in the throat. A crucible. A never-ending pause. It is cold out here – much colder than it looks. I have such a sense of being alone. There is the movement of the water. Tiny waves come in from the side. I stare up into the sky and time goes by in uneven chords. The lilo is full of my breath. It gives me a sense of achievement, floating out here on my own breath, on hundreds and hundreds of exhales. As long as my breath lasts I will be able to float. An inhale is full of possibility; an exhale is autumn between the leaves. It is the temperature of the body slowly cooling in the air. It is a long whistle of the farmer across the fields. An aria. A word.

Helen speaks the final words as the image on the screen fades on the woman drifting further out to sea – 'she' is gone and then she too is gone, as Helen leaves the raft.

In another raft Leslie offers the audience members a 'gut reading' using a portable ultrasound device.

> *I've got time to give just one of you a gut reading with this portable ultrasound device, so is there anyone here who would like a gut reading? Great. I'm just going to ask you to apply a bit of this gel. It's a bit cold, sorry. Now hold this just over your stomach and press. I'm going to ask you to press a little bit harder if that's okay... Ah, here comes something... well, your gimbals are working a little bit more busily than I would have guessed, but everything's looking good. Hang on, I'm getting an image. It's a bit grainy but bear with it... can you see?*

Most commonly associated with pregnancy, here the ultrasound device functions more as an oracle's reading of entrails or a fortune-teller's crystal ball. The screen is placed in the middle of the raft so that the images can be seen both by the recipient of the reading and by the others in the raft. Here the ultrasound screen offers a sonic image of a portrait in reverse; the unknown interior of the body exposed, the 'inside story'.

> *Focus is on infinity... Okay, here comes something: trees and a forest down there; it looks like trees and a forest. Looks like snow and trees. Fantastic! Little sparkly stuff... Quite a bit of it all over.*

The 'reading' is presented in a strange mix of medical/soothsayer language. As Leslie adjusts the brightness and contrast, the images on the screen gain greater clarity and are translated, with variation from person to person, into internal landscapes, trees in a forest or the outline of distant footprints.

> *Here comes something... yes, it's faint but it's there – see just there? There is a dark area here. This is very interesting. I think we can all see clearly that this is... land. And it seems to be covered with very fine grey almost like a powder – plaster-of-Paris grey. Let's magnify the image. Now, if you look just here, see those faint impressions? Footprints. From what I can see, this looks like a place where you used to feel very at home, very happy. And even*

though you haven't been there in a long time, we can see that you are still carrying it inside you. Beautiful. Is that what you expected? Is that what you were hoping for?

For the audience member there is, perhaps, a desire to concur with the interpretation – to see the faint impression of footprints or snow on trees, the magic 'sparkly stuff' that crackles and dances on the screen. Alternatively, as in a real medical reading or fortune-telling, they may experience the disappointment of an image that is not quite what they wanted to see, a story that is not quite what they hoped to hear.

As silently as the performers entered the boats they slip away, and reappear once more outside the rafts. They tell a series of stories of trauma, of foreboding, of love at first sight, of humiliation, panic, fighting, fleeing and freezing. Suddenly a film fills the large screens to either side of the stage and for the first time there is no overlap of a live performer narrating or blending with the image. In the film a very old man in a dark suit is dancing alone on a Victorian promenade by the sea. His grey hair is combed smooth to his head, thinning slightly on top. His arms are outstretched as if holding an absent partner. He dances an elegant, careful waltz. The film cuts to an old woman also dancing alone by the sea.[5] She wears a black jewelled top and bright red silk trousers. She is thin and looks frail but is engrossed in her dance, moving her hips, clicking her fingers to music playing in her head – something racier than the man's waltz – could it be *Blue Suede Shoes*? Cut to the man and woman standing together, looking out to sea. The camera pans across their faces, extreme close-ups showing deep lines of age, the roses in his cheeks, the dash of lipstick on her mouth.

The scene shifts and the couple have come off the prom onto the pebble beach. The woman places an apple between their foreheads; they both put their hands behind their backs and start to dance (Illustration 3.3), attempting the impossible task of balancing the apple as they stumble on the uneven stones. For a while they manage, moving together, bending, leaning to preserve the apple between their foreheads.

And then the apple falls and they are separated. The film abruptly ends. Claudia is suddenly lit by a bright spotlight, which seems to catch her, and perhaps the audience, off guard. Armed with a comically large boom mic, Leslie asks, 'How did you feel? How did you feel when you were watching them dance?'

Illustration 3.3   Apple dance, film
[Photo by Leslie Hill]

As Claudia struggles to answer, a single pearl falls from her mouth and rolls to the floor. It is followed by another and still another. Throughout her speech, she spits a seemingly endless number of pearls from her mouth (Illustration 3.4).

> *I felt really choked up. I actually got tears in my eyes and the back of my throat ached. I had to struggle not to cry. I don't know why they affected me like that... I couldn't stop looking at them. I think in a way I wanted to be them. There was something that made me think that if I was them I wouldn't be so stressed. I wouldn't worry so much about all the stuff that normally goes round and round in my head. And I could just be. And especially when I was looking at the lady, looking at her dancing in those red trousers, such fantastic trousers, just dancing and not caring what anybody thought, I actually thought I wish I was you.*

Illustration 3.4 Claudia, pearls
[Photo by Hugo Glendinning]

The silhouette of a man appears, again directly opposite the place the audience have been watching. A single beam of light from a torch catches him. His arms are outstretched as if he is holding an absent partner. He wears a dark suit, his grey hair is combed smooth to his head, thinning slightly on top. He dances an elegant, careful waltz. He is the man from the film (Geoff). There is a ripple of recognition from the life-rafts – it's *him*. A recording crackles faintly, then more clearly and we hear the 1969 recording of the transmission between Michael

Collins and Neil Armstrong describing the surface of the moon. Like the ultrasound image, the quality of the sound recording is ghostly.

Focus is on infinity... Okay, here comes something: trees and a forest down there; it looks like trees and a forest. Looks like snow and trees. Fantastic! Little sparkly stuff... Quite a bit of it all over.

The audience might recognize snatches of this text from the 'gut reading'. The inner landscape of the audience member becomes epic, cosmic, layered with the wonder, excitement and mystery of the moon landing. The verbatim lines from the Apollo 11 transcript hold in them a yearning, a desire to imagine and see what Armstrong sees as described to Collins, the man who went on a half a million miles round trip to the moon but never landed, never set foot. (He had to keep the ship in orbit for the other two.) The plaster of Paris 'footprints' visible on the ultrasound screen take on a different resonance as a connection is made from biology to cosmology. The quality of the ultrasound image is reminiscent of iconic grainy pictures from the first moon landing. They are also, of course, synonymous with the first black and white signs of the new life in the womb. In an age of high definition it is interesting how poignant this obscure, almost ghostly image quality is – as if it speaks to some sort of authenticity or mortality.

Throughout the moon landing transmission, Geoff continues to dance his solo waltz, slowly orbiting the life-rafts. The projection screen is filled with the image of Helen on the pink lilo, floating out to sea. The story about the woman 'floating on her breath' previously heard in the rafts now becomes lyrics to a song sung by Claudia. As Claudia sings, Helen pulls down a rope which hangs in front of the cyclorama and lowers herself into the image, into herself, into the ocean, finally disappearing with the image into darkness as Claudia sings the last lines of the song:

I am out here
with the castaways
the shipwrecked and sea-swallowed
I cannot tie a knot,
I cannot swim,
but this is how it ends.

Swallow
swallow
swallow

Just after the lights fade to black, signalling the end of the performance, a song begins which is soon recognized as Elvis singing '*I can't help falling in love with you*'. A spotlight reveals a woman in a black jewelled top and bright red silk trousers. It is the woman from the film (Rene). She walks to Geoff who comes towards her, his arms open as if to dance a waltz. When she draws near, Rene hands Geoff an apple and the couple performs the precarious apple dance from the film in the centre of the stage amidst the rafts. Audience members look up at them, often with tears in their eyes. Halfway through the song, as Geoff and Rene continue their dance, the performers help each of the audience members out of the life-rafts and partner them up, giving each duo an apple to balance between their foreheads and the performance ends with everyone paired up in an apple dance as Elvis sings '*I can't help falling in love with you*'.

Making 'the moment' – the inside story

> Both scientists and artists are exploring the nature of personhood, the meanings embedded in the corporeal body. Both aspire to comprehend nature's secrets... Artists' visualizations [...] challenge familiar and unquestioned assumptions by extending beyond the constraints of the present to imagine alternative possibilities.
>
> (Anker and Nelkin, 2004, p. 4)

On an anecdotal level, gut feelings are widely recognized as a significant phenomenon of human experience, but often undervalued in comparison to the rational or the cognitive. Biology offers a scientific explanation: the body's one and only 'second brain' resides in the gut in the form of the enteric nervous system which responds to sensory perception and regulates body function on a millisecond-by-millisecond basis. Part of our research for *the moment I saw you I knew I could love you* was undertaken with neurogastroenterologists at the Wingate Institute of Neurogastroenterology, exploring 'gut feelings'. The scientific terrain of the research was the autonomic nervous system (ANS), specifically the enteric nervous system (ENS) and the almost instantaneous communication between the 'big brain' and the 'little brain' (ENS) via the vagus nerve and how this communication informs and modulates human behaviour. The artistic terrain of the project was the wider phenomenological notion of 'gut feelings' and how far the public at large engages with notions of knowing things 'in their gut' and experience fight, flight and freeze instincts. The research at the Wingate Institute is discussed in detail in Part Two, Chapter 6, 'In the Lab and Incognito'.

Our curiosity in making *the moment I saw you I knew I could love you* came from both an interest in the anecdotal and scientific aspects of 'gut feelings' and a desire to know if working from 'gut feelings' could provide a creative trigger for artists, rooted in a sense of self and connectivity through sensory perception, embodied knowledge and empirical observation. This desire later led to developing a creative workshop which we call 'Autobiology', an intensive performance-making course for practitioners that came from the work on gut feelings. We have led several 'Autobiology' workshops and courses in the United Kingdom, Taiwan and in the United States, and this work is detailed in Part Two in Chapter 7, 'In The Studio.'

In developing both the live performance and the filmic elements within it, we tried to write 'from the gut', through automatic writing techniques. With Andrew Kötting, our filmmaker collaborator, we exchanged 'gut swaps', unfiltered tangles of writing and images which we sent each other weekly as part of collating and storyboarding the film. Here is an excerpt from a 'Gut Swap' exchange between Hill, Paris and Kötting:

```
It might be nice to have a floor scattered with lilos and
a loop of 16 mm B&W playing on the ceiling (a nonlinear
loop with some of the more abstract images, the more
abstract parts of the soundtrack - different edit from
same material)
OR
During performance/installation a performer gives
audience members ultrasounds and the image that comes
up is some of the B&W footage superimposed with the
live ultrasound image, soundtrack of guts mixed with
soundtrack of 'Once I Had a Secret Love' Ry Cooder,
slide guitar.
```

16 mm bolex black and white
fishing boats that are sinking
sea forts that are wobbling
land fissures in the chalk down at Beachy Head that are
consuming people into their void
black and white archive of old stainless steel hospital
equipment
helen wearing a sheep's stomach as a swimming hat
helen with an inflated cow's stomach as rubber ring
and buoyancy aid
inflated spiky pufferfish
X-rays of helen's stomach
a school classroom with chalk drawings of Beuysian
nonsensical scrawlings
the inside of a grand piano alive with the sounds of
jellyfish making their way across sandpaper
trees in winter

How about the idea of hand-cranked 16 mm bolex b/w
and faded colour? something that might have been found
floating in the sea – watermarks – flares – scratches
and glitches?

Fish gutting opening scene.
The name of a boat: 'Gut Feelings'
Spitting pearls
Offal being poured – dribbled into a GUTTER – we watch
it ooze/squeeze out of a drainpipe – the building is
old and ramshackle – we are high up.

A sense of constant dampness – damp patches when people
get up to leave – under the arms or on the seat of the
pants – walls of buildings sweat – water – leaking –
damp in the hotel room, rain, saliva, viscera.

Gut feelings compulsion out of mind out of body love lust
desire, impulse following dreams following nightmares,
rash not safe dangerous. Strength of persuasion of

another. Storms the gut feelings of the sea. Instinct.
Love. Passion. Following gut or not following it. No
second chances. Taking a plunge a risk. Being compelled
by some one else to take a risk - falling in love.
Suicide bombers, war, how you are sold things. Trust
in someone (you barely know) Leap of faith. - collage
of sound bites meandering throughout connecting and not
connecting with imagery?

In short, we worked as much as possible from the gut to make a work
about the gut, creating a piece about impulse, fight, flight and freeze
reactions by working from those states and places.

In *the moment* – audience reactions

Although sometimes at first confused or alarmed, audiences seemed to
settle in and enjoy the experience of being in the life-rafts with their
groups.

> It was a little unnerving at first, but then it felt really lovely because you
> felt a connection with the other people, you were part of something
> together, rather than the usual individualized audience format.
>
> (Audience Response, Salette Gressett, London, 2009)

> As for 'the moment', I loved the concept of the boats, and it
> encouraged the small group of audience members in each boat to be
> aware of and to some extent to interact with other audience members
> in the boats, which I thought was very nice. The unexpected little
> moments in the boats were very nice and kept a feeling of surprise
> and liveness about the production that I much enjoyed.
>
> (Audience Response, Marvin Carlson, New York, 2011)[6]

Many audience members responded particularly strongly to the small
Sea Legs-sized projection cupped in the hands of an audience member –
themselves or someone near them.

> I felt a sense of responsibility for the image, which seemed to be about
> vulnerability and loss. Also it connected me to the person holding

the projector, because together we were sustaining the image. Finally, I felt differently about my hand after it was over – it was strange to be made over into the surface for projection and it was nice feeling like I was inside the performance and also offering the image to the others in the boat with me.

(Audience Response, Heather Love, Palo Alto, CA, 2011)

It was so poignant – a piece of cinema in my hand. I loved it. It was such a novel way of looking at film – it felt quite a perfect digital moment, the intimacy. It was small and bright and magical in my hand and in a way I felt very protective of the image.

(Audience Response, Lisa Gornick, London, 2009)

Audience members who experienced the moment of holding the strip of tablets spoke of the responsibility they felt in holding and sustaining the image. Performance and projection has moved from the world outside of the rafts to within it. The audience member enables the projection of the image, holds the image of the performer in their palm.

I felt entrusted to hold her; the delicate moments as the images unfolded and a strong sense of shared experience as we huddled round to see her. The tiny size of the image and my sense of technology as unreliable made her feel fragile. When I remember that moment I have a sense of inside out – of my insides being out in the ultra-sound and of her presence almost disappearing into my hand.

(Audience Response, Theresa Beattie, London, 2009)

Margaret Morse writes: 'Since the advent of electronic media, image projections have been increasingly liberated from the need for a physical surface or support and are more and more free to haunt everyday life' (Morse, 1999, p. 2). A woman out on the ocean is suddenly a tiny projection on a pill strip held in the palm of the hand. The infinite and intimate are conflated in this moment and when the image flickers and ends, several audience members experienced it as a moment of loss. A ghosted presence remains in the hand of the audience member who feels she has been 'made over into the surface for projection', a haunting. Another audience member described experiencing the moment when the projection of the woman fades as an escape of the image from the screen, feeling the presence of the woman 'almost disappearing into my hand'.

At the end of the performance when the same footage is projected larger-than-life on the two screens, the intimate and personal is made more epic and collective:

> I was surprised and pleased when I saw the larger image projected; I had a feeling of discovery, as when you realize what you thought was a purely private experience is actually widely shared.
>
> (Audience Response, Heather Love, Palo Alto, CA, 2011)

In contrast to the tiny film, the ultrasound acts as an apparatus of magical realism, a device to enable an exploration of memories and emotions stored in the body. The screen of the ultrasound reveals sonic lines and patterns that are interpreted as some sort of patina or negative left from a momentous experience. The ultrasound is the inside outed; an extreme version of the optical unconscious, arguably revealing more than photography, through its ability to penetrate and reveal the recessive body, yet requiring much more specialized translation. Images appear from a world beyond consciousness; emotions, desires and urges still forming on a chemical level in the gut. What does it mean to see the fluid visceral underworld of the gut?

> It was strange to unexpectedly have the insides of my body exposed, although with the low lighting and in the small circle of people in the boat I felt that it was an intimate exposure. I love ultrasounds and how they translate this fantasy environment into a kind of deep-sea sonar. I am used to seeing them from the outside so it was such a strange surprise that it was actually my insides that were being projected.
>
> (Audience Response, Heather Love, Palo Alto, CA, 2011)

What is exposed when the 'gut readings' of the viscera are revealed? What does the audience member see, recognize and interpret as they are both subject and object in this moment? For the fellow occupants of the life-raft there comes a recognition of shared and separate landscapes of self and other as well as an 'intertwining'. In this moment technology engenders a particular intimacy, the ultrasound enabling the audience to see inside the living, breathing body of their fellow audience member.

I loved being reminded of the interior of the body – its private and usually silent goings-on. The ultrasound put me in a double spectatorship or maybe a triple one. It performed the opening and the reminder of the parallel presence of this complicated, wondrous, oft-mysterious world of blood and tissue and motion and fluid. I got to thinking of the almost sacred seal of the body – the unspoken agreement I have with my body not to breach that seal – not to intrude on this world unless I have to.

(Audience Response, Ann Carlson, Palo Alto, CA, 2011)

Asking the audience to focus on their own specific experience of moments in the performance, be it witnessing the ultrasound reading of another person or holding the projection of the film in the palm of their hand, feels like receiving a secret. There is a space between our own *imaginings* of what these experiences might feel like, with what we *wanted* them to feel like, and the revelation of the lived experience of that moment by the audience member.

How close can you get in performance? Face to face? Eye to eye? Beyond? What is it to look inside the body – of the performer? of the audience? It is almost forbidden territory even to ourselves. Seeing into our own bodies is normally enabled only by the surgeon or the midwife. And when we see, what do we look for? What is recognizable to us as ourselves in the ultrasound image? What is familiar or alien? How do we interpret the lines and graphs? The images are like land suddenly coming into view from a tiny aeroplane window over the ocean – unfamiliar, distant, but a place to touch down, home.

It is interesting to put Edward Hall's measurement for distance in conversation with a performance work that deals in primitive human emotion: gut feelings, the fight, flight and freeze response. In Hall's measurements, as performers we interact with each other in the zone he labels 'public', often 20 feet away from each other, but encounters with the audience unfold in personal and intimate space. Personal space is the space in everyday life where unwanted contact can feel inappropriate, 'it feels like they are inside you' (Hall, 1966, p. 118). This is the unwanted 'in-your-face' closeness of the subway in rush hour or in a tightly packed lift where 'the heat and odor of the other person's breath may be detected' (Hall, 1966, p. 118). This is 'improper' closeness from which, in everyday life, we perform escape strategies. The interaction between performer and audience member in the rafts takes place in this space of 'intimate distance'. The strategies the audience member may enact in everyday life can be brought into play here, but the contract is different; there is an entreaty, a desire and an expectation. There is something at stake. The audience is asked to meet the gaze of the performer and to allow themselves to be touched, asked to participate.

> Much Western theatre evokes desire based upon and stimulated by the inequality between performer and spectator – and by the (potential) domination of the silent spectator.
>
> (Phelan, 1993, p. 163)

There is, of course, the choice to look or move away, or not participate, but the audience is already somewhat entrapped in the small nest of the life-raft, thigh to thigh and shoulder to shoulder with their fellow 'survivors'. The moment of contact between audience and performer is made within the flow of the performance. There is a potential here for rupture and an implicit awareness of enablement. There is a recognition that something is at stake and the audience member in this moment is *responsible*.

In Samira Kawash's article entitled 'Interactivity and Vulnerability', the author cites Levinas's thesis of ethical demand being inherent in face-to-face interaction. For Levinas, something is demanded in the face-to-face interaction, even if the response is to turn away. Kawash writes:

> Interactive performance art makes a spectacle of this ethical encounter by staging a demand for mutual recognition; in the face of this demand, the spectator is positioned in advance as party to ethical relation. Refusing to interact is no less a part of the interaction than is becoming an active participant. [...] Levinas emphasizes the vulnerability inherent in this scene of face-to-face encounter: to be in an ethical relation with the other means to be open and vulnerable to the other.
>
> (1999, p. 51)

What is significant here is that the vulnerability is two-way. Inasmuch as some audience members cringe from 'participation', the encounter *demands* something from audience *and* performer; the performer initiates the invitation but is also dependent on the audience member to accept it. Both performer and spectator have something at stake. The vulnerability is shared. When the spectator enables the performer, and thus the performance, through their participation there is a connection established, one that is witnessed by the other audience members. Helen needs a volunteer to hold the projection screen of the Sea Legs tablets. The screen is tiny and people have to get close to each other to see it or sacrifice seeing in order to maintain distance. The exchange with the ultrasound is potentially the most intense encounter, though to offset this it is often also the most humorous. Leslie needs a volunteer in order perform the 'gut reading'. The request is to look inside the body and to reveal that image. In every case, in every single performance (125 thus far in 15 cities) the audience agree to participate, to hold the little projection in the palm of their hand or to have a 'gut reading' – in this way they facilitate and enable the performance for their fellow audience members.

There is a constant play of entrances and exits. As performers we move in, out and around the audience in their rafts giving us a physical sense of closeness to the audience. At the same time there is an unusual lack of connection between the performers – we operate almost independently of each other – more like a 'round' than a harmony. 'How did you feel when you were watching them dance?' is the only line in the piece that might be called dialogue. As performers in this piece, we don't talk to each other, touch each other, or even look at each other – everything is directed straight to the audience.

The moments where we, the performers, step into the life-rafts demand different levels of engagement and response.[7] Together they work almost as a dance. Each performer is involved with their moment but also aware of the shared time and spaces of this particular moment in the performance. Each micro-performance needs to finish at the same time to enable the performers to move to the next raft, completing the dance. The moment of stepping into the boat, especially for the very first time in each performance, feels like breaking through the audience's cocoon. It seems for a moment impossible, and for us as performers happens experientially in slow motion. We also see, in slow motion, the audience awareness of what we are going to do and there is a sense of incredulity to it. The life-rafts are strange unexpected places to be but by this point in the show they are the spectators' safe spaces; they redraw the lines between performance and audience – theatre in the round turned inside out. A difference between performer space and spectator space has still been maintained up to this point. Stepping across this threshold changes something; we leave the world of the performance at the same time as we step deeper in to it. We become one of them. We have stepped across more than just the side of the boat. Helen reflects:

> I know that feeling of stepping into that raft, into and among that collection of people tightly gathered. I can feel the force of it in my leg right now, my left leg. It feels simultaneously like an embarkation and disembarkation. Entering their world changes everything. There is a quietness. I am aware of what the other performers are doing, I can hear them faintly, am aware of their timing, the cadence of their voices. I can hear laughter as people respond to the ultrasound or something Claudia says. But it feels as if from far away. I feel adrift with these people on our raft. We are so close as I speak to them, as I project the image into someone's hand. In each performance I repeat the same words, the same action, demand the same proximity, the same interaction in three different rafts. In a day of four to six performances this means performing this section between 12 to 18 times, over and over, again and again. Each time I feel my foot leaving the space of the stage to step into the life-raft I feel myself exiting one world, entering another. There is another partition here, invisible but palpable. I feel it shimmer as I pass through it, the fascia between them and us, between you and me.

The moment in the life-rafts was finely balanced and timed. It marked a moment midway in the piece where a definite shift in proximity called a different attention to both the audience-performer relationship and to the audience with each other. The delicate balance of timing, proximity and audience required to make this piece work was challenged when a festival booking *the moment I saw you I knew I could love you* asked us to change the structure of the piece to accommodate more audience. We were all sympathetic to the festival – they were flying us to Australia to do the show and of course wanted as many people as possible to be able to see it. To this end, however, they pushed for changes in the format that would have, in our view, destroyed the composition of the piece – more boats, bigger boats, triple the audience and so on. The gig nearly fell through a few times over these negotiations. In the end we conceded to pressure from the festival to agree to slightly larger boats – three 16-person instead of 8-person life-rafts (originally they had pushed for four 24-person life-rafts). We weren't trying to be precious about the work and of course we also wanted as many people as possible to see the show, but we had huge reservations about increasing the size of the rafts – and we were right. Although we had some great feedback on the shows there, for us as performers the performances at that particular festival never transcended the ordinary experience of the theatrical into the more magical interpersonal encounters we were so often able to conjure for ourselves and for our audiences with this show. Instead of being eight people huddled together, everyone able to see (and touch) each other, audiences were larger, less personal groups – in some ways they became annoyances for each other instead of companions on a journey.

The three rotating scenes in the life-rafts, so enjoyed by audiences and by us as performers, were lost in the larger boats where many of the audience didn't even bother to try and move closer to see and hear – we were too close and not close enough. The three of us in the 'round' trio all started to dread the scenes in the boats, which is truly a horrible feeling for performers. We disliked climbing in the boats with the audience and couldn't wait to get out again and retreat to a more conventional distance. The proximity ratio made it difficult for all of us: they weren't close enough to click in with each other or with us and we were too close for them to be comfortable in the absence of the 'magic' of proximity. The recent and rapid surge of small audience and one-to-one performance is now being met and supported by diverse venues and festivals such as Battersea Arts Centre in the United Kingdom or PICA in Australia. Clearly, there are financial challenges in producing this kind of work and the task of finding and continuing to build sustainable models is significant.

Below the surface: skin

In the interaction with the ultrasound closeness is not only skin to skin but under the skin, as the insides of the body are made visible, pushing beyond Hall's measure of intimate space. Leslie hands the audience member the transducer, the small handheld instrument that emits sound waves. When the emitted sound encounters a border between two tissues that conduct sound differently, some of the sound waves bounce back to the transducer, creating an echo. Sound waves passing through the skin and muscles catch the echo and bounce it back to create moving pictures of organs, tissues and fluids. These images play on the small monitor that the audience carefully pass round to their fellows in the boat, staring silently into the secret world of the recessive body, theirs or another's. At the same time as the subject of the reading sees himself or herself; the performer and the rest of the audience see them too. It is a double sighting as we witness the sudden there-ness of their insides, their self, 'there'-self. Yet this moment of recognition, of 'self-sighting' can also be read as one of misrecognition. With a revelation of the body there is also concealment and a strangeness. Leder articulates notions of the 'dys–appearing body' where the prefix 'dys-' signifies 'bad', 'hard' or 'ill' (1990, p. 84) or, even more in this case, 'away, apart, asunder' (p. 87). Perhaps there is a sense of the *dysfamiliar* body, where the internal organs of the body are perceived as a separate entity; alien, unknown. Seeing this known but dysfamiliar territory of the body we are made cognisant of how we are strangers to ourselves, estranged from our bodies. Leder cites a psychological experiment that showed that nine out of ten people were unable to recognize a photograph of their own hands from a small series of such pictures:

> That organ with which I perform my labor, eat my food, caress my loved ones, yet remains a stranger to me. This strangeness is even more pronounced in the case of the internal organs. I would surely be unable to recognize the look of my own heart, though my very life depends upon its functions.

> (1990, p. 1)

Leder accounts the different possible ways of reading his 'body'; through X-ray, measuring his blood pressure from a sphygmomanometer, seeing his colon through a colonoscope, but this revelation is obfuscation:

> Yet, as with my surface body, the absences that haunt my bodily depths are not effaced by these reflective maneuvers. Through I can

visually observe my colon, its processes still elude experience from within. The magical power my body has to absorb water and electrolytes is not perceived as I gaze through the endoscope upon this furrowed, tubular space. The mystery of my body is only heightened by the very strangeness of the organ before me, its phenomenological non-coincidence with my body-as-lived.[8]

(Leder, 1990, p. 182)

There is an awareness that this 'unfamiliar familiar' has a power, an agency. The autonomic nervous system can indeed operate without us. Even in a comatose state the enteric nervous system, this 'little brain' in the body, still functions, unlike other systems that require life support. This dysfamiliar second brain is connected to our emotions and compels us to act, to flight, flee or freeze. It triggers impulses, desires, actions and repeatedly lays us bare to undefended moments.

For Leder when the body is caught up in various actions, such as hammering a nail or hanging a picture, the focus of the body is on the nail or the wall, not on the active body. 'My body, as the sensorimotor means of such surveying, yet recedes before this experiential primacy of ends' (Leder, 1990, p. 19).[9] Both *On the Scent* and *the moment I saw you I knew I could love you* proffer, if just momentarily, a physiological awareness and phenomenological perception of the body that attend to the gap in the information, the lacuna, within our sense of self-presence. Both attempt to transfer a sensory knowledge and practice to an audience through experiential theatre. In *On the Scent* this happens by direct engagement with the olfactory through the experience of smelling a range of odours. Within the piece, the audience experience the act of smelling as it happens along with the ensuing memory and emotional reactions that take place, creating moments of transformation and transubstantiation. (see Vannini, Waskul and Gotschalk, 2012, p. 96). Each of these olfactory processes call attention to the corporeal workings of the self. Likewise, in *the moment I saw you I knew I could love you* there are a range of sensorimotor triggers for the audience: sitting in the life-rafts close to others, the physiological experience of looking at visceral images of the body, the witnessing of projections in intimate space, being close to the performers, balancing an apple between their forehead and someone else's. All of these draw attention, conscious or not, to the enteric nervous system, a system that is operating in the *right now* of the performance, in the bodies of the audience next to them, in their own audiencing body. Jo Machon writes of Curious' work: 'The multisensory nature of the (syn)aesthetic style demonstrates the ways in which space, body, text and technology can be manipulated to empower the audience and communicate in a highly visceral manner' (Machon, 2013, p. 87).

The language, images and physical choreography of the piece perform a constant calling on the experience of the lived body: a monologue about choking that in its breathless performance attends to the act of breathing, the act of choking; a film of a sword-swallower whose blade gets stuck in his throat; a woman with a chronic pearl-spitting condition. Images, words and action are specifically chosen and timed so as to elicit physiological responses: a feeling of a dry mouth, of choking, of swallowing or not being able to swallow, of not being able to move, of feeling sick, of feeling seasick, of breathing and of not being able to breathe. There is a constant calling forth and attending to the body, and a sense of the body at stake.[10]

Drawing from physiology, Leder divides the body's sensory powers into three categories:

> *Interoception* refers to all sensations of the viscera, that is, the internal organs of the body. It is usually distinguished both from *extero-ception*, our five senses open to the external world, and *proprioception*, our sense of balance, position, and muscular tension, provided by receptors in muscles, joints, tendons, and the inner ear.
>
> (1990, p. 39)

In the life-rafts each of these areas is affected. There is a constant awareness of the discomfort of the body, a lack of personal space, cramped legs, the hard surface under the buttocks. There is an 'off balance' feeling with the roll and pitch of the raft as each movement of the audience, the crossing of a leg, a shift in position, causes the vessel to ripple, the air inside it shifting. The eyes constantly refocus with changes in lighting and the unpredictable movements of the performers around the space. In these ways the audience members have 'sightings' of the absent or recessive body.

Dolan writes that '[M]oments of liminal clarity and communion, fleeting, briefly transcendent bits of profound human feeling and

connection, spring from alchemy between performers and spectators...'
(2005, p. 168). In a desire to explore the complex chemical world of
human emotion, the body's impulses and instincts, we move inward,
closer. Each time we feel a nervousness, a compulsion, an anxiety, an
addiction. What is our invitation to the audience member? To be held
in their gaze, to be held in the palm of their hand? Asking them to
anchor us perhaps – to stop us floating too far out to sea? Perhaps to be
consumed, swallowed up by them, into them, '[...] her presence almost
disappearing into my hand.' Who is holding whom? We are all held
for this moment on the inside and it is on the interior recesses that the
attention is focused. The act of swallowing is an act of give and take.
When you swallow you can't breath. You can either breathe or you can
swallow; you can't do both simultaneously. If you try not to swallow
strange physiological reactions are triggered in the body. This is how
it feels:

> I (Helen) am doing this now as I write this to you: I am not swallowing.
> It starts with a tightness in the throat. A kind of longing. There is
> a fizz in the bridge of the nose like the beginning of tears. I feel a
> sense of panic in the stomach, in the heart. I feel claustrophobic,
> it becomes harder to type all I can think of is my throat, I focus on
> my breath. The saliva builds in my mouth. I feel a sense of a cavity
> inside. My tongue tip moves to the top of my mouth behind my
> teeth my mouth is more full now of saliva – I can feel its wetness.
> All my awareness is in my throat. The urge to swallow is great now.
> A pulling a drawing down and in. My eyes are tearing the whole of
> the inside of my mouth is full, wet. My throat aches, the front of it –
> my chest feels tight. Now my nose has started to run I can't hold on
> much longer. It is like being underwater, it is like being frozen, I need
> to swallow so badly now the body memory of all those moments
> when you do become unstuck and your voice goes your mouth dries
> all the heat flies to your gut to your bowels a desire to evacuate as
> you stand frozen speechless. I breathe again. The breathing helps,
> the focus on the breath. Soon I feel I won't be able to control it
> that it will happen without my control. I need to swallow now and
> (*swallows*) I do and it is like coming up for air it is like sound after
> silence, it is like coming out of the dark, it is a connecting in the
> body, to it and within it.

Swallowing is an overarching motif in the performance and appears many times in many guises. The action of swallowing has obvious connections to the intestine but also speaks to a mysterious emotional terrain. Claudia speaks of her own gut feeling, a kind of love at first sight when she first saw her husband-to-be. She stands in front of a huge X-ray film of a barium swallow, head and throat in profile, and tells her story as the audience watch ghostly black and white anatomical actions of swallowing and the real-time and then slow-motion movement of a substance from the mouth, down the throat. The whole experience takes place in this moment of swallowing. In a sense the temporal rhythm of the piece is one long swallow, an ingestion.

> At the other end of the kitchen table sat a man, who faced me as I walked in the door. Nobody said there would be a man there. I sat down at the chair opposite him. The room fell silent. So silent it was embarrassing. His voice was quiet and uncertain. I didn't know if I liked him. It didn't really matter. He was completely compelling. His voice had become irretrievably quiet, almost lost. He got up to leave and as he walked past me, I turned my head to watch him go. Like this. And I had no idea if I would ever be able to turn my head back again.

Claudia reflects that:

> The man in the kitchen story tells of two involuntary reactions of the body. The voice failing the man, the tightness in his throat, only producing faint rasping words, then his inexplicable flight from the situation. While I experience the embarrassment of all eyes on me, in a silence that could highlight an involuntary gulp. The gulp that is X-rayed, magnified and projected behind me for all to see.
>
> (Barton interview, 26 August 2013)

Like the X-ray projection in the show, Leder calls our attention to the body in the simultaneously conscious and unconscious 'self-moving' act of eating, swallowing and digesting. There is the sense here of the body as discrete, asserting an autonomy; 'an it can rather than an I can.' Leder describes the moment when the food leaves the volitional space of his mouth. He has a sense of a piece of apple sliding down his throat, but then after a certain place he can no longer feel it, the piece is gone (Leder, 1990, p. 38).

> Ordinarily that which enters the interoceptive field is simultaneously lost to the exteroceptive. Before swallowing the apple I can see, touch, smell, and taste it in all its crimson-tart vividness. Once swallowed, these possibilities are swallowed up as well. [...] The incorporation of an object into the visceral space involves its withdrawal from exteroceptive experience.
>
> (Leder, 1990, p. 39)

Like visceral sensations, the performance itself has indistinct borders.

Below the surface: screen

As well as through physical proximity, film and projection is specifically used to produce direct audience/performer engagement. This mélange of visceral and virtual can work to open up levels of embodiment and closeness, to tease identities and blur performer/spectator relationships. The performance moments inside the rafts enable interaction and intimacy above and below the surface of the projection screen which acts as a portal between audience and performer, exterior and interior. Also at play here is the precarious nature of the screen in terms of scale, materiality and distance, and questions around the ways in which the projection surface can be both a place of escape and exposure. The film adds another layer to the piece allowing a space away from the eye contact of the performers and a way to 'leave' the confines of the raft and the nearness of one's neighbours. The use of double projection screens not only serves to envelop the audience in the images but also involves them in further twisting and turning, causing the rafts to ripple and roll. In this way the audience has a constant awareness of their own bodies as well as the bodies next to them in the raft. And at times the video projections are the only source of light. Morse writes:

> The screen of cinema, video, and the computer is a threshold that divides the ordinary and the everyday from other realms that seem truer or larger than life [...] Like a semi-permeable membrane, the screen filters out some things and not others, conjuring an auratic

gleam from signs and symbols. Clearly, the alchemy of the screen is in the service of power as well as desire.

(1999, p. 2)

This membrane of the screen reveals the blood and guts of our own bodies, with close-ups of glistening organs. This is our very own topography, the visceral commonality of each of us.

I love you inside out. I love your bones and your blood and your bile and the shape of your organs and the dark brown colour of your liver and I love the sloosh and spill of your liquids.

the moment I saw you I knew I could love you is a love story told through the enteric nervous system, a love story played out in black and white film, through images of bodies and organs as well as fragments of stories like the old couple dancing. It is a love story from a performer to an audience, a love story from the moment they were seen, face to face, insides outed. As befits a love story, the ending of the piece is a slow dance. When Geoff and Rene appear on stage, moving from the world of film to real-life presence there is a sense of wonder, almost disbelief from the audience, sudden gasps and gestures ripple round the life-rafts, a nudge, a point. The screen presence elevates Geoff and Rene, they are larger than life, not quite real, as if characters in a film, dancing the last dance. But then suddenly they are present and dancing amongst us (Illustration 3.5). Herbert Blau sees a 'confusion of realms' (Blau, 1982, pp. 113–14) in the intertwining of live bodies with film. This mélange of live and mediated is one that nowadays reads as commonplace, but the audience double take at the appearance of Geoff and Rene, moving from the realm of film into realm of live performance. They belonged to another world, another realm, yet are now transported here. For Walter Benjamin presence is the pivot between the film and the live performance event (Benjamin, 1968, pp. 228–9). Here the appearance on film marks Geoff and Rene with a particular almost augmented presence when they appear live. The film of the couple plays with saturation and speed and these manipulations, alongside the obvious age and fragility of the pair at the edge of the sea, provoke a sense that this is a 'last dance'. The reappearance of Geoff and Rene in the performance space, together, is a *return*, a return that marks the moment when the

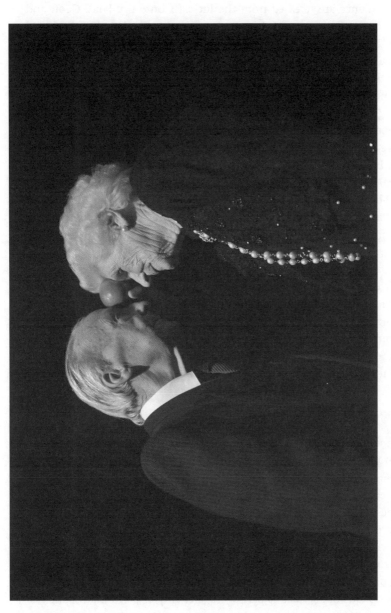

Illustration 3.5 Apple dance, theatre
[Photo by Hugo Glendinning]

darkness disappears, the murkiness of the unknown waters recede and the audience are released from the life-rafts onto dry land. Geoff and Rene are both distant and close, both present and touchable but charged with a particular aura. Many of the audience wanted to go over to them at the end of the show and physically touch them, and hear from them that their love story was really true.

The audience ends the performance with a dance, each collaborating closely with another person to balance an apple between their foreheads as they dance. They are physically responding to each other's movements, speed and tempo in the delicate act of balancing. Couples may be partners, friends or complete strangers. Each couple's proximity to each other, united in the joint task of keeping the apple balanced, establishes a connection, camaraderie. Finally given their 'landlegs' as they are released from the undulating rafts and the ocean scape of the performance, once more balance and stability is a negotiation as they work together to keep the apple pressed between them. Some speak to each other, giving instructions, some make eye contact, others close their eyes completely and surrender to the shifting equilibrium of the moment. This dance of balance, of closeness, of bodies moving and taking up all sorts of strange shapes in order to keep the apples off the ground is what brings the performance to its close. And in this closing moment of proximity who knows – perhaps even fate could play a part and for two strangers suddenly cast together it could be *the moment...*

Endings

Although some of our curiosities are sated through the making and then performing of the piece, some remain and are encountered here through this revisiting, remembering, rewriting, recreating the performance in this space on the page. There are also those other things that come out of the performance itself and reveal themselves to us in the swirl of the spectral. We maintain a curiosity and a delight in the intent and concentration experienced while creating a piece or knowing that certain elements are 'right' and how these intentions and hunches play through in the performance and its reception. The intent, no matter how opaque or abstract, is part of the alchemy of performance and the part of performance that runs free and gives voice to its own questions, its own curiosity. As mentioned previously, there was a strong desire to make the piece experiential for the audience. We fashioned a non-linear mosaic structure as a way of opening places, textures, rhythms of what gut feelings might be, using the ocean as the primary metaphor for this hidden, turbulent, powerful environment. A mosaic is particularly hard to see while you're working on it, but there is an almost blind sense of knowing what fragments are needed where. Some things only become clear in the doing. One of the earliest 'visions' of an episode for the piece was the image of an old woman in a pair of bright red trousers dancing alone, carefree and unselfconscious at the end of a pier. It was connected to a sense of abandon – letting the body lead; to just be. In the end this led us not only to Rene, an octogenarian with a stunning pair of red trousers, but also to Geoff who we took along for the film shoot and ended up working with in the live performance. The pearls Claudia spits up as she talks about watching them dance represent the paths not taken – the hunches not followed. As the oyster works and works on a grain of sand these are the manifestations of the things stored up and worried over, kept swallowed down, kept inside, agitated within the gut. Here again there is the motif of swallowing – desires, passions, wants, possibilities all gulped down. It is the very act of performance, then, that gives voice to these repressed desires, the what could have been.

> The pearls are my troubled thoughts, missed opportunities, moments that I can't let go, brooded over and rubbed into words, spat out awkwardly, mixed with saliva, at an inappropriate opportunity.
>
> (Barton, interview, 26 August 2013)

At the end of the piece Helen lowers herself into the image of the sea, into this unknown place of gut feelings, of instinct, of our volatile, vulnerable humanness.

> *It's about that moment of… surrender. Of leaving. Of letting go. About that feeling inside, that place where we know ourselves but where there is also a sense of danger or ugliness or sadness or depravity – it's about giving in to that feeling. There is a sense of darkness and a dark place and a powerful place and a churning place that is full of movement and that even if it's lying still it is a very deep stillness and anything can set it off, can set off a churning and a spilling out and a swallowing up… like the sea.*

There is an obvious reading of drowning, of death, in this image and the stage tableaux. The writing also tries to articulate what gut feelings might be, but there is no one answer or definition. We have heard scientific descriptions, 'the facts', but this attempt allows itself to be more than one thing. As Claudia sings the refrain 'swallow', Helen's live body is swallowed up in her projected one. The performance has been about a journey from the outside in, where the audience are asked to come in, to come close, to come inside, under water, under the skin.

the moment I saw you I knew I could love you explores what it is to be flesh and blood, questioning those moments when we do or do not give in to impulse, when we follow or repress gut feelings. There is a sensuous proximity through the bodies pressed close together in the life-rafts, the nearness of the performers to the audience, and a particular intimacy enabled through the very specific use of film and projection. The show does not claim to prove a validity of gut feelings, to scientifically or biologically explain what they are, instead it offers a landscape in which they are evoked, experienced and explored. It allows itself two possible endings – one being swallowed up, drawn inside by the tide, the mortality of the body. The other is unapologetically romantic, a resurrection, a constant last waltz on the prom, love at first sight, a gut feeling followed.

Dolan writes, 'We too often founder on the shoals of "what does this *do*," when how something feels in the moment might be powerful enough' (Dolan, 2005, p. 170). *the moment I saw you I knew I could love you* adheres itself barnacle-like to the possibility of what can be felt in the moment. Audience members encounter the piece from the inside, enfolded within the projection screens, subsumed in the flickering images. They bear witness to the inside stories of the performers and of their fellow life-raft members, stories of what might have been, what could be, played out in sonar waves from the gut. We see ourselves from the inside out and from the outside in, from above and below the surface. We see ourselves so extraordinary, so ordinary, we see ourselves so small, so vast.

The little raft of an image in my hand – I can't recall if it was in my hand but it might as well have been. All of us being in the life-raft blurred the boundaries of one of us and the other of us. The hand-held floating little Helen made me think of church, a campfire, a home movie – bowing our heads together in a ceremony only we understand.

(Audience Response, Ann Carlson, Palo Alto, CA, 2011)

4   Landscape I: *Out of Water*

Introduction, by way of a detour to Exotic World, Barstow, California

20 April 1997

Dixie Lee Evans, the 71-year-old Marilyn Monroe of Burlesque, personally guides us on a tour through the Exotic World Museum, housed on a former goat ranch in the middle of the Mojave Desert. With a breathy energy she switches between giving us history lessons – Aristophanes as the Father of Burlesque – and quick Marilyn impersonations singing, 'Just one more chance, dah dah dah DAH dah dah DAH', then slipping back from performance mode into reminiscence '...a song real popular at the time'. Her energy and vivacity exhilarates us, her audience, as she shares the stories of the dozens of burlesque artists pictured on the walls and immortalized in this ranch house in the middle of nowhere through their costumes and props – feather boas, ivory fans, and a mind-boggling array of nipple pasties, G-strings, garters, gowns and gloves. There is even a black velvet shoulder cape worn by Gypsy Rose Lee. We listen to tales of Blaze Star, Chesty Morgan, Sally Rand, Candy Bar, Tempest Storm – their routines, their gimmicks, their alleged encounters with the Kennedy brothers, their entanglements with the secret service, as well as Dixie's own troubled relationship with Marilyn (who was suing her) and her reaction to Marilyn's death (devastation). We are a rapt audience of two. 'That's Sheri Champagne', she says, pointing to a golden urn full of Sheri's ashes on a shelf amongst flutes and coupes, 'Now, she just wouldn't wear any costume that didn't have a picture of a champagne glass on it.' Framed in a doorway, Dixie holds out her arms dramatically and exclaims, 'We took what was real and we exaggerated it. We made it larger than life. That was Burlesque.' Dixie's was one of the many one-to-one performances we 'audienced' during the first piece of work we made together as Curious. Dixie would have probably called it a tour, rather than a 'one-to-one performance', but at any rate our road-trip project across Route 66 marked the beginning of a long series of performative encounters we sought and worked on outside theatre spaces.

Within this section of Part One we discuss two site-based performances in order to explore how moving within and across landscapes with audiences can enable shifting perspectives on distance and closeness that in turn open up levels of encounter, alongside different reciprocities of audience and performer engagement and exchange. In these performances site reveals and withholds its own narratives, simultaneously fixed and fluid, choreographed and constantly changing, as weather, environment and happenings of everyday life play their part, creating 'extra live' performance. In these external settings the audience are perhaps more aware of themselves both as individuals *and* as a defined group. There are no darkened theatre seats to settle into, no lights to dim. Outside the usual codifications of the theatre building, recognition comes with different signifiers; eye contact, nods and smiles of identification as people slowly gather at designated places: 6.30 am on top of a cliff at the ocean's edge in San Francisco, 3.15 pm at a municipal bus station in West Bromwich; unlikely rendezvous. In these performances the closeness of the encounter is often marked by and through distance, telescoping moments of near and far, as audience members are moved to and through spaces and places by performers, both seen and unseen.

The performance

Out of Water[1] (2012) is a journey from the shore to the sea. The audience starts the journey at a distance from the performers (in Holkham, Norfolk, in a wood that borders the beach, and in Fort Funston, San Francisco, on top of a cliff). They listen to a sound score of music and text on personal headphones and for the first part of their journey they cannot see the performers, the world of the performance exists purely in their experience of place and sound.

> *This is how it was when I first saw it. The tide so far out.*
> *I wanted you to come here. To travel this distance with me.*
> *I wanted you to see it like this.*
> *The sea just a thin line in the distance, like a margin in an exercise book.*

It's a long way down to the sea, I know.
There is time. I will wait for you.
You won't get left behind.
The tide is far out. Just days ago it was flooded – right where you are
walking right now.
It was at the highest tide.

This is a secret part of the day, hidden almost.
Just a few of us out here.
Sailors and lifesavers.
Singers and swimmers.

The 'just a few of us out here' refers both to the audience and to the performers who stand at the water's edge facing the sea, separated from the audience by almost a mile of beach. They too listen to the soundtrack on headphones and mentally anticipate the movement of the audience towards them by the various tracks playing: the first few lines from the BBC Shipping Forecast lets them know the audience have embarked on their journey; the overture starting marks their arrival on the beach, their feet moving through deep sand. Performers and audience are united by the soundtrack, simultaneously separated by space and time. There are points on the journey across the beach where the sand dunes rise and the audience has their sudden first glimpse of the line of performers. They point. They shield their eyes and look. At first indistinguishable from the landscape the performers are mere dots, blurs. So far away. So small. Birds? Part of the breakwater? Gradually closer images appear, forms, human shapes though gender is not clear as all wear the same voluminous blue trousers and billowing white shirts that snap in the air like sails (Illustration 4.1). Then another dip of the land and the performers disappear. The rhythm of the piece is the rhythm of the environment. It is metered out in the paces of the audience who, between the quick walkers and the slow, find a common pace as they move together down the beach.

As the audience draw near, the line of performers slowly starts to move. Mid-way down the line one of the performers slowly raises her arm and points to something in the distance. Further down the line another does the same thing. Another slowly raises her hand to shield

Illustration 4.1   Performers in the distance, Holkham

[Photo by Tony Millings]

her eyes, a slow score of movement, everyday and already enacted by the audience when they first glimpsed the performers in the distance.

Slowly the performers bend in one movement together and pick up the rope, which lies in a long curl to one side of them (Illustration 4.2). It is heavy, and over one hundred metres long it stretches the length of the line of performers. They heave ho back and forward and slowly the golden rope is pulled backwards into a coil (Illustration 4.3).

> *This line.*
> *This flight path we are in,*
> *this time line we are on,*
> *the push and pull of it, tidal.*
> *Heave ho my dears,*
> *heave ho my darling.*
>
> *I am the age my mother was when she had me.*
> *My aging pushes her backwards, older.*
> *My children aging pushes me forwards, older*
> *Heave ho my dears,*
> *heave ho my darling.*
>
> *Even when you tread water*
> *you are still moving.*
> *The push and pull of it, tidal.*
> *This timeline we are on.*
> *Heave ho my dears,*
> *heave ho my darling.*

As the rope continues its slow journey back into a huge golden coil at the end of the line of performers, a woman (Helen) suddenly breaks from the line and walks purposefully towards the audience (Illustration 4.4). She takes the hand of an audience member and leads them to the sea.

Once there she takes a handful of salt from her pocket and pours some into the palm of the audience member. They throw the salt into the sea together. The audience member is then led back up the beach and positioned purposefully. Other performers are breaking the line and taking the audience members to the sea. Slowly the performers arrange the audience members into a large V-shape, the apex pointing towards

Illustration 4.2 The rope, Holkham
[Photo by Tony Millings]

Illustration 4.3   Heave ho, San Francisco

[Photo by Jamie Lyons]

Illustration 4.4 Helen, hand extended, San Francisco
[Photo by Jamie Lyons]

the land, the ends of the lines stretching to the water's edge. This shape echoes an earlier part of the sound track:

We are here with the Pink-footed geese from Iceland, the sweet-beaked Spoonbills, slow-flying Marsh harriers. A skein of Brent geese just arrived from Siberia. They flew here from northern Russia, through the White Sea and Baltic Sea, and along the North Sea coast. They flew in V-formation. Birds flying in the V-formation can fly 70 per cent further than one bird flying alone. The bird at the front breaks the wall of air that the rest of the flock flies into, creating a wake of swirling air that gives a lift to the next bird along. Each bird gets some help from the one in front of it. If one goose becomes injured and has to land, family members will stay with it until it is ready to fly again, then they all set off and look for a new flock to join. They leave at sunset, getting their first directions from the setting sun. Then they follow the positions of the moon and stars.

As the soundtrack ends the audience and performers are all now established in this V-formation. Three performers walk slowly into the sea, sink into the water and pull armfuls of golden thread from the depths. They return to shore carrying the gold and soprano Laura Wright starts to sing, joined by a chorus of performers:

How to save a singer,
avoid the throat, keep her upright,
don't let the water spill into her lungs.
If it does you must hold her, rock her gently
so the vibrato of the water plays down the length of her larynx.

Keep her mouth open, keep her singing.
If she has forgotten the words
offer temporary replacements,
soothing vowels, soft images:
'soup'
'swoop'
'sweet'
'spoon'

Lay her down on her side to sing a sliding scale.
Stroke her gently

from her neck to her shoulder blade
Easing the notes on their way.

Weight her down, distract her,
pour red wine into the pools of her collarbones, fill them to the brim,
beseech her to hum the aromatic notes:
'burnt cherry'
'dark fruit'
'deep tannin'
'ripe berry'

At the end of the song another, smaller, V phalanx forms, comprised of seven performers, this time the apex of the V points out to sea, the direction the performers slowly head towards. The audience watches as the performers walk into the sea (Illustration 4.5).

As their bodies submerge, deeper and deeper, a soprano voice sings:

The swimmers are out of their depth
The singers are out of breath

Singing the swimmers to shore
The singers pour from their throats
a stream of notes – a golden rope of sound
Oooo

The swimmers are out of their depth
The singers are out of breath

The rasp of the surf on the land
Covers their gasps with its pounding
Sounding very much like breathing
Oooo

The swimmers are out of their depth
The singers are out of breath

Mouth to mouth the singers press last notes
On swimmers' lips, salty kisses

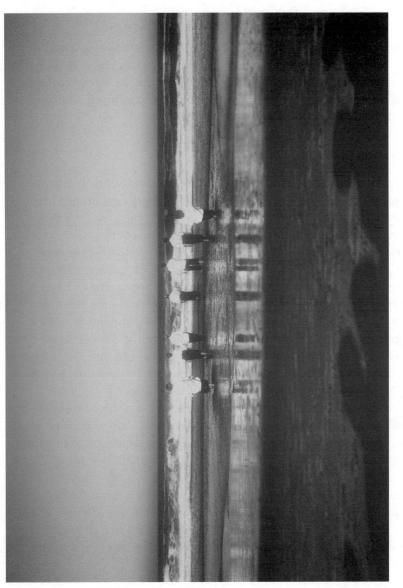

Illustration 4.5 Walking into the sea, San Francisco
[Photo by Jamie Lyons]

> *buoyed by the notes*
> *the sinking swimmers*
> *float*

The audience are slowly led away, back on the path they have come. As they walk they turn, they stop, look back. The swimmers in the water still moving forwards, they are far out now, only their heads can be seen. The audience keep looking back as they are led off the beach. This slow dance of leaving unravels and ends the performance.

Journeys of proximity

I (Helen) am writing this just days after the San Francisco performances of *Out of Water*, a pile of white shirts and blue trousers heaped on a chair in my office. A silvery trail of sand persists in the toes of my shoes. I write this account whilst the sensate experience of the world of the work still pulses in my body. I can still feel the temperature of the ocean, the particular quality of the sea air on the day of the performances. I feel the imprint of those bodies on the line. I write this in conversation with some of the audience and performers who were a part of the performances. I asked them to join me in thinking through questions of proximity. Their responses came back fast, full, and this chapter is woven through with their voices. My writing took on a different shape as I wrote in conversation with them, listened and responded – letting my thoughts and impressions intermingle with theirs.

The audience start the performance about a mile away from the performers, and slowly journey towards them until they stand hand in hand together at the edge of the ocean. This tug between the distant and the near, the long shot to close-up, is also enacted between the soundtrack and the setting. The voice the audience hear speaking to them on the personal headset is intimate, distinctly personal, in timbre as well as in what is said, sound as caress, unfolding a narrative that connects them directly to the place they are in through fact, geographical detail and personal account, 'I wanted you to come here, to travel this distance with me. I wanted you to see it like this.'

The voiceover narration opened up the geographical space through memory, music, story and sound. This took me to other places which meant I was in the beach and I was somewhere else as well... the geography unfolding before the spectator, opening up, multi-layered, both concrete and fantastical, both in the moment and as a memory. These two levels worked together to further our implication as a group, as a community of spectators in the performance.

(Sebastián Calderón, email correspondence, June 2013)

There is a strong sense of intimacy engendered by the sonic journey, a connection with the narrator alongside complicity and comradeship with the other audience members. There is a sense of both feeling a part of them and apart from them. Audience reflections dwelt on this sense of the personal and the public: 'The headphones, once the sound started, made for the anomalous experience of being alone and in a group at the same time.'[2] 'An odd combination of private and public.'[3]

The performer's voice on the headphones makes it clear she has travelled this path for and before them, navigating the route, and is now once more on it with them, leading them, asking them 'to travel this distance with me'. The soundtrack shifts from the familiar (at least to British audiences) incantation of the shipping forecast, 'Dogger, Fisher, German Bight, Humber, variable, mainly west', to life-saving techniques, 'breathe two quick shallow breaths... feel for their breath on your cheek', to factual accounts of the wildlife that inhabit the area, 'we are here with the Pink-footed geese from Iceland', to personal connections to the place, spoken directly to the audience member, 'I wanted you to see it like this. The sea just a thin line in the distance, like a margin in an exercise book.'

The soundtrack washed over me, secluded me in the midst of the crowd, and convinced me that this journey we were all taking was a journey I was to take alone. When the narrator began to speak, it was to me alone that she was speaking, to me alone that she wanted to relate her stories, her poetry, her history. She addressed us individually: 'I wanted you to see it like this', she said. She was the one with whom I connected even though she was the one who was not visible, even though there was no way of knowing whether she was on land or at sea, above or under water, speaking to us from the present, past or future. She blurred our temporalities, secluded us further within the personal inflections of our imaginations.

(Rebecca Chaleff, email correspondence, June 2013)

The audience is very much outside the codifications of the theatre building, and there is a particular bonding through proximity, through the shared experience whether it be a more prosaic union (very cold, very early, very steep) or a poetic one (the landscape, the soundtrack). In *Out of Water* the audience are connected to each other first, before they enter the world of the performance.[4] The audience develop a communal pace – a group of strangers becomes social en route; shifting proximities in a vast landscape, captured in long shot and in close-up. There is a particular charge in the black box theatre space when spatial boundaries are transgressed, such as when the performers in *the moment I saw you I knew I could love you* step into the life-rafts and suddenly there is a heightened awareness of closeness. In the home setting for *On the Scent* a different tension is at play, when the normality of intimacy which the domestic home environment elicits is suddenly at odds with the performance happening; public acts in private spaces. In *Out of Water* the relationship changes again as the landscape makes its own demands, physical, experiential. Both US and UK settings for the piece were rural, rugged, not easy to get to or, once there, to navigate, with steep steps to climb and long stretches of beach to walk. The timing of the performances added to the challenge and thus to the sense of bonding that the audience experience; meeting to board the bus at 5.45 am, encountering each other sleepy-eyed, hot coffee warming them in the cold of the early morning, intimate strangers gathered for a shared journey. Dawn and dusk are liminal, in-between space, 'this is a secret part of the day, hidden almost'. One audience member described the experience of being with the other audience members as akin to 'the feeling of after a storm or disaster, as if we were strangers who'd found each other'. There is a sense of being in it together, braving the elements, committing to the long walk and arduous climb. This increases the sense of community, and whets the appetite for the work. As one audience member commented: 'It was a longer walk than I expected, and I think that was perfect. Long enough that we "earned" some experience.'[5]

Behaviours shift in this locale as physical challenges presented by the landscape become part of the experience and alter the quality of the relationships forged with self, with others, with performer and audience and with the performance itself.

We are aware of our proximity to each other (of listening to each other) as audience members even before the performance begins.

We open up, become sensitive to each other and in that space of openness we can take in the performance at a deeper level, I feel. This is a different experience than walking to your seat in a darkened proscenium theater and then walking out once the show is done. The walk on the beach was very powerful because it built on the experience of pilgrimage and community.

(Sebastián Calderón, email correspondence, June 2013)

Artist Louise Ann Wilson writes that with her site-specific/site-sympathetic works she is interested in,

How the act of walking might engage an 'attendant' audience in the manner of a pilgrimage, where duration, immersion and the challenge of the physical journey are fundamental to the process of exploration and reflection. [...] Sometimes the auditorium lights going down means an audience can be present and not-present at the same time. In all of my site-specific work, I've taken audiences on a physical journey where they've travelled on foot or by bus, by tram, off-road buggy, pedalo or elevator. Asking people to walk, to make a journey, physically engages them.

(Wilson in Machon, 2013, p. 229)

The physical nature of the journey demands a particular type of attention and reflection, the rhythm, the ardour, being out in the elements and moving together as a group all add to the experience.[6]

The audience member simultaneously feels part of a community and has a personal connection to the sound track, 'It was sound "inside my head" in a very powerful way, and yet knowing that it was a collective experience also made me curious about what others were experiencing.' In tandem with this shifting ground between individual and collective experience the audience are constantly navigating and negotiating their relationship with the performer, the one who speaks so closely to them, the one(s) they must be moving closer to but are yet still unseen. The performer says she is with them, that she will wait for them. Physically the performers are on the beach, waiting at the ocean's edge a mile away. And yet... the performers listen to the soundtrack, hearing at the same time what the audience hears, and envisage them slowly coming toward them. In that way performer and audience travel together, unseen but pictured, and there is something in the distance between which endears. And when the initial first sightings of the performers do happen they are so slight, the performers come in and out of view as hard-to-decipher shapes on the landscape, always seeming to be in the distance, elusive, a dance of appearings and disappearings. These sightings perhaps come with a curiosity: How long have they been standing there? How long have they been waiting for me/us?

The audience stop walking when they reach the line of performers. Seemingly unaware of the presence of the audience the performers continue staring out to sea, eyes intent on the horizon rather than meeting the gaze of those who have journeyed to them. The performers start to point to something in the distance. They shield their eyes and try to make out something on the horizon – a ship? Someone in peril? Someone coming to save them? Meaning hovers between rescuers or those to be rescued and it's unclear what the audience member's own agency could be within this scenario. They are implicated, a part of 'just a few of us out here', but which ones? Sailors or lifesavers? Singers or swimmers? There to rescue or be rescued? Although the performers do not yet seem to see the audience, the words on the soundtrack become increasingly personal, emotive,

My mother taught me to swim. I was so scared out there in the water.
'Won't someone help me, can't you see I'm drowning?'
'I'll help you darling.' My mother showed me how to float, taught me how to breathe. Sometimes she would join me and I would watch her move underwater, dancing in a secret world, infinitely light.

She can't make it down to the sea now, it's too far for her. The last time I came here with her she made it halfway, further back than we have come, and then she stopped and sat on the sand, exhausted, unable to catch her breath. I realize that without her now I can't touch down, I am out of my depth, out of breath. Won't someone help me, can't you see I am drowning?

There is a distinct impassioned note in the words spoken that plays across action that is still distant, uniform, executed without eye contact. It is the disembodied voice of the woman that sustains the emotional connection, rather than the live bodies of the performers who as yet do not break their gaze out to sea (is this woman in the line? or among the audience? or here at all?). An audience member described the soundtrack feeling like touch, 'a kind of touch that at once unsettles and consoles'.[7] Intimacy has thus far been engendered by physical distance between performer and audience. The performers are anchored to each other by the long length of rope, itself a marker of time, heredity, a bloodline. Distance shifts as the rope is pulled slowly through the line of performers and those at the far end of the line are released from its tether. This release enables them to make a new connection, this time not with each other but with the audience, as one by one the performers break the line, leave behind those still connected by the rope and walk deliberately towards the audience. Here at last a sudden moment of contact, after visual and physical separation, touch, finally, after such distance, skin to skin.

> Your purposeful stride suggested a promise: 'I will,' but what? Unknown. The question (will what?) was held open for the length of your walk, which, while striding, was long enough to arouse a pleasurable tension. In my view it mattered that you held a consistent focus – that if your eyes were darting as you chose the person whose hand to take, you did not let us see this, but seemed instead to have known from before you saw each of us there.
>
> (Renu Cappelli, email correspondence, June 2013)

Much happens in this moment and an array of sensitivities register in the audience. The action of performers walking towards them elicits a sudden flurry of feelings and anxieties; about being picked, about not being picked, about doing what was expected, about the desire to 'get it right':

> Once 'taken,' participation is like a release of all that tension: oh yes, now I see, she takes me by the hand, and: I want to do it 'right', whatever it is… and then the striding toward the water raises the stakes once again: what will I be asked to do 'right,' now I've come along this far? And again your sense of purpose here seems imperative to me: your firm grip and knowing stride toward the water teaches me to trust my footing, recalls your own story about your mother teaching you how to swim.
>
> (Renu Cappelli, email correspondence, June 2013)

The crucial reminder of what is at stake in these fleeting live encounters, our human vulnerability and fragility, is reflected in the audience comment above, '*it mattered that you held a consistent focus*'. At the same time there is an intense readiness to submit to the encounter, to become part of the narrative. One audience member remembered, 'obediently waiting to be taken by the hand by a woman who might be one's mother'. This sense of ready compliance, not only to go with the performer but also to imaginatively enter the world of the performance, forms the nexus between audience and performer/performance in this moment as proximities shift, enabling a different type of encounter with and within the work.[8] The audience also experience the pull between both wanting to go and a desire to remain, to be within the performance, with the performer and also to be apart. 'I started weeping immediately when I realized she was coming to take my partner and I, and this intensified as we went to the water. Becoming (more) a part of the piece, but also losing a beautiful part of it, oddly, in that separation.'[9]

It is significant to note the intentionality and innate knowledge ascribed to the performer. Returning to the audience comment about how the performer 'seemed instead to have known from before you saw each of us there' resounds with an audience comment from Curious's 1999 one-to-one performance *Vena Amoris*. *Vena Amoris* was an intimate, experiential journey through a building (Toynbee Studios, London) for one audience member at a time that took place via a mobile phone.[10] One audience member responded to her experience of the piece as: 'Funny, shocking, humiliating, sexy, intimate, scary, touching, heartbreaking. How do you know?' It is that final rejoinder, '*How do you know?*' that demanded my attention then and again now. There is something in these four small words that speaks of a need from the audience for the performer to be invested with at least an inkling of an innate knowledge of them, of that moment, of that encounter, of what has happened and of what will happen. It is a requirement made by the audience member that the performer have an omniscience of sorts, it speaks of a desire for attention to be paid, for care to be taken. Performance interaction can be intimate, intense, intoxicating, and it can be intolerable, manifesting in a desire to escape, to ab-sent rather than be present.

Following Dolan in *Utopia in Performance* when she writes that the performer's grace, the audience's generosity and the lucid power of inter-subjective understanding is when the utopian performative happens, Bruce McConachie posits that 'grace, generosity, and the intersubjective understanding are likely to occur in the theatre when CARE is present to wrap spectators and actors together in communitas' (McConachie,

2008, p. 96). 'Is she going to walk us into the sea and away?' an audience member recounts feeling as she is led to the ocean, and with this I am reminded that much is at stake in these moments of encounter. Both performer and audience member are implicated in this action of care, to care and to give over to being cared for.[11] Doreen Massey asks, 'Why do we so often and so tightly associate care with proximity? Even those who write of care for the stranger so often figure that relationship as face-to-face' (Massey, 2005, p. 186). Care of the audience is manifested on different levels from the more pedestrian in terms of how steep, how far, how cold, pre-booking advice on disabled access, sensible shoes, extra layers to the more physiological, psychological imaginings – how will they feel when they walk here? How will it feel for them to negotiate these steep steps, feel the sand under their feet, smell salt marsh, pine trees, seaweed (Holkham), eucalyptus trees, Redwood bark, a dead seal washed up on the beach (Fort Funston, San Francisco)? How will they feel when I take their hand and lead them to the water? What actions can I do to make this feel like an invitation they want to accept?

I look for a word to describe this connection between performer and audience and settle for now on *empathy*. In her book *The Faraway Nearby*,[12] Rebecca Solnit defines empathy thus:

> Empathy means that you travel out of yourself a little or expand [...] It was the translation of the German word *Einfühlung*, or feeling into, as though the feeling itself reached out... The root word for empathy is path, from the Greek word for passion or suffering.
>
> (2013, pp. 194–5)[13]

I take this sense of travel, a moving toward, *a feeling into* and *a feeling out toward* and ascribe them all to my use of the empathy happening between audience and performer.

The movement between leading and being led, caring and being cared for, establishes a precarious rhythm of falling and catching, surrender and support, a rhythm that is sounded in the action of walking itself, as with each step the body falls and catches itself, lets go and supports. Solnit describes walking as pendulum-like, 'Where does it start? Muscles tense. One leg a pillar, holding the body upright between the earth and sky. The other a pendulum, swinging from behind... the most obvious and the most obscure thing in the world, this walking' (Solnit, 2000, p. 4).

Brian Massumi writes:

> I like the notion of 'walking as controlled falling'. It's something of a proverb, and Laurie Anderson, among others, has used it. It conveys the sense that freedom, or the ability to move forward and to transit through life, isn't necessarily about escaping from constraints. There are always constraints. When we walk, we're dealing with the constraint of gravity. There's also the constraint of balance, and a need for equilibrium. But, at the same time, to walk you need to throw off the equilibrium, you have to let yourself go into a fall, then you cut it off and regain the balance.[14]

The act of walking inherent in *Out of Water* becomes a sort of metaphor for the relationship between performer and audience. In the brief walk to the sea audience and performer journey together, hand in hand, supporting each other's fall, each other's balance. In her 2004 audio piece *Her Long Black Hair* Janet Cardiff writes: 'Walking is very calming. One step after another, one foot moving into the future and one in the past. Did you ever think about that? Our bodies are caught in the middle. The hard part is staying in the present. Really being here.'[15] Bodies meet in this moment of the present, on this timeline, twixt past and future. These connections between performer and audience, as they join hands and walk together to the water's edge, can be read as reconnections; once disconnected from the rope that binds the performers to each other they establish new bindings with each audience member. These constant connections and reconnections called to attention this moment in life that we share, *'This timeline we are on'*. This action locates each of us in this moment of time where we collide, *this* hour, *this* performance, *this* shoreline, *this* continent, we exist together in this universe, this propinquity, strange collisions of time and space wherein we are one flock.[16]

> I remember the feeling of being too far away from the performers, I wanted to walk by close to them, to look exactly where they were looking. So I was grateful when Helen took my hand, in a way, I had been waiting for it, waiting to move in closer.
>
> (Sebastián Calderón, email correspondence, June 2013)

The performers sense the audience approaching, an approach and a nearness they cannot see but which is palpable nonetheless. They also have a strong awareness of their proximity to each other, connected by the rope that measures the distance between them and binds them together.

> Everything felt like shifting time and space, shifting relations of proximity; everything seemed very near yet quite far [...] I felt like I was part of this community of performers and people I could trust and love and perhaps support, and I wanted to hug each and every one of us, yet we were standing several arm's distance from each other; I had an intense urge to merge myself with my shadow by laying myself down on the beach, fitting myself in my shadow's mould, yet I wonder where my shadow would have travelled to if I did so.
>
> (Sukanya Chakrabati, email correspondence, June 2013)

> I felt very strongly the presence of us, the performers, linked by that line of rope; a knotty chord of connections, histories, geographies that cobbled us together for a time and that seemed to stretch beyond the performance [...] When the audience came the energy, qualities of the chord shifted to become more tangible, more defined, set against this mound/muddle of shapes and felt presences [...] I haven't felt that in performance before, the approach of the audience. It was elusive.
>
> (Caroline Smith, email correspondence, June 2013)

In an interview with Machon on immersive theatre, Michael Morris of UK company Artangel states that

> In the past decade, we've seen a growing appetite for participation and interactivity. The days of passive audiences now feel numbered. There's a new audience that wants a much more visceral experience. I think that's going to be increasingly true as more and more people spend their time online. If you are going out, to something which is live, you're going to want to feel alive, and there's something very vital and very life-affirming about the experience of being immersed in a piece of art, rather than watching it from a distance.
>
> (Machon, 2013, pp. 158–9)

This desire for encounter and engagement is *reciprocal*, for performer and audience as well as between audience members. Dolan writes that 'Intersubjectivity extends beyond the binary of performer-spectator (or even performers-audience) into an affective possibility among members of the audience' (Dolan, 2005, p. 31). Performers in *Out of Water* had their own anxiety at the moment of audience contact but also a desire and openness for the encounter:

> I walked towards a couple and almost interrupted their whispery conversation to hold their hands. I was in the middle, guiding them towards the sea. Suddenly, I couldn't see them anymore, but felt their hands pressed against my grainy sand-clad palms. I was almost relieved that I didn't have to look at them, as I'm nervous to be looked at. I offered them salt from my pocket. They followed my lead and threw salt back into the sea, I led them to join the V that had been forming. I almost felt a sense of loss, as I left them there and walked away to join the choir of singers. In that ritual of holding hands, and throwing salt together, it seemed like we had already formed a bond. I felt like I owed it to them to remain by their side.
>
> (Sukanya Chakrabati, email correspondence, June 2013)

My (Helen) own feeling of the rope leaving my hands, freeing me, the first to leave the line and go to the audience, was incredibly strong. The small turn my body made away from the ocean, toward which I had been facing for so long, felt magnified and in slow motion. When I saw the audience, I remember thinking, 'Oh there you are! You came!' I felt a delight and an intense desire to move toward them. The simple ritual that then takes place; the walk to the sea, the throw of salt into the water, the congregation in the V-formation all mark the moment in the piece where the role of audience changes; no longer apart they are a part of the action. There is no separation now between audience and performers, sailors or life-savers, we are one V-formation, shoulder to chest, like the birds who migrate the thousands of miles across oceans. Within these encounters there are moments of kinship and connection moving between both audience and performer, *a feeling into* and *a feeling out toward*. 'Heave ho my dears, heave ho my darling.'

The leaving

Like the tide itself, the audience washed in upon the performance, and, later, washed away. The eventual departure was painful, as the performers had us enfolded into their quiet, seemingly fragile ceremony. They had held our hands. They had guided us. They had shaped us into a V and stood next to us. They had created uplift, and we were afloat in the mystery of their songs. 'Heave ho, my dear. Heave ho, my darling.' The earlier poem of the narrator echoed above the water, now a beautiful melody, now a shared, communal experience. The opportunity to return these gifts came soon enough. Our desire to give, to save, was challenged as we abandoned the performers in the ocean and in the sand, who stood scattered as we departed, raising their arms in a gesture that signalled both a farewell and an invitation to return. And even though we walked in silence now, the narrator's voice still resonated in the distance: 'can't you see I'm drowning?'

(Rebecca Chaleff, email correspondence, June 2013)

For a moment we are one body, one form spanning the distance from land to sea. Then seven performers break away, mirroring us in a smaller V-formation. This small flock walks to the water's edge, pauses for a moment, and then continues into the ocean. They do not look back, once again caught up in the gaze toward the horizon, this time moving inexorably towards it. We, those left behind in our truncated V, watch them leave us, watch them walk out further, deeper into the ocean. We watch until we are called by the singer's voice, her call gathers us up and leads us away from the others in the ocean; our flight path is not the same as theirs. The movements of the audience are slow, holding within them a yearning both to follow the singer, as siren like her voice compels, and an unwillingness to leave. The slow time the audience takes to leave the performers is the time the piece takes to end. Echoing the beginning in reverse the audience gradually move away from the performers, leaving them behind on the beach or out in the ocean (Illustration 4.6), letting them disappear from sight as gradually as they first appeared.

There was something notable, not to say Orphic: in not looking back, I felt sure they were still there, and would be safe and warm sooner so long as I did not stop to look... I feel the effort of each step up [the cliff], the opposite of the way down: a lifetime has passed. Only now, halfway up the hill, do I indulge and stop to look back. You, the

Illustration 4.6   The leaving, San Francisco
[Photo by Jamie Lyons]

performers, are out of sight. Only the shore and the piles jutting out of the sand remain.

(Renu Cappelli, email correspondence, June 2013)

Our feet carried us mechanically forward as our thoughts extended behind us – washed out with the tide, 'the ebb and flow of it.' We parted and we did not part: we carried the experience with us as we moved on, and as we moved on we stayed within the experience. Did we, in fact, abandon the performers in the ocean? Even now, weeks later, I feel as though a part of me is still with them.

(Rebecca Chaleff, email correspondence, June 2013)

This pull is palpable, 'as an audience member I distinctly remember I didn't want to leave, I just wanted to look back endlessly and I could also feel that vibe coming strongly from the audience when I was one of the performers.'[17] This slow wrench of leaving is also experienced by the performers who are left:

As we walked together in our already formed Vs, following the audience members this time, I felt like those sand particles and weeds that are left behind on the shore, even as the water and waves retreat into the sea. They were leaving us to go back where they came from. But they kept looking back, sometimes waving, sometimes stopping to take pictures, and sometimes just stopping and watching us freeze in our places. Did we desert them, or were we deserted? Were they one of us, or were we a part of them? When did we stop becoming 'us' and 'them'? I waited as they went farther and farther, became smaller and smaller till they disappeared completely out of sight.

(Sukanya Chakrabati, email correspondence, June 2013)

The performance has played out like a film, from long shot to close-up that then rewinds in this, the final long shot, the slow act of leaving. *Out of Water* invites encounters both epic and intimate, intimate locomotions held within the vast and the personal, out on a stretch of endless strand at the ocean's edge, guided by a voice in your ear, taken by the hand.[18]

5   Landscape II: *Lost & Found*

Lost & Found (2005) was a performance piece about change set in urban areas undergoing rapid transformations. Initial work on *Lost & Found* took place in Shanghai in 2004, where we interviewed a range of different people about the extensive regeneration of the city – this part of the project is detailed in the final chapter, 'In Situ'. The performance piece we developed as part of the *Lost & Found* project in the United Kingdom took place on a bus moving through the Black Country, a cluster of impoverished mining towns and villages in the West Midlands, and on a boat in East London travelling along the canal between Bow and Limehouse Basin. Both areas were going through immense sustained periods of upheaval and 'regeneration'. In both areas, redevelopments were far from unanimously supported by local communities as familiar streets and buildings were destroyed or repurposed, often without consultation with residents, tenants and locals. In *Lost & Found* we decided to foreground the fluctuating landscapes themselves and create a piece that literally moved through the old and new sites, giving time and space to reflect on change and loss. To that end we hired a local 1950s vintage bus for the Black Country performances and for London a 1930s canal boat dating from an era when the canal networks were major arteries of industry. Both 'native' vehicles were once familiar sights travelling through local landscapes, the roads and towns of the Black Country and the waterways of the East End. Both bus and boat invited 'intimate' audience groups (roughly 20 passengers) to a performance repeated several times a day. In this account we will focus on the Black Country performance, which is where the work premiered as part of the FIERCE! Festival.

The script of *Lost & Found* was written with Lois Weaver who also performed in the London version of the show; in the Black Country her part was performed by the artist Julie Tolentino. To write the script the three of us each researched an environment specifically associated with loss or change. Lois chose the Left Luggage repository while Leslie took on the liminal space of a Departure Lounge bar and completed a professional 'flair' bartending course as part of her research for the piece, while Helen focused on the Lost Property Department. In Chapter 6, 'In the Lab and Incognito', Helen details her experience of working in London's Lost Property Department to develop her persona and script. None of the texts written responded directly to the local changes taking place in the Black Country or London: what is 'lost' and 'found' in the performance is explored through the conceits of these more general and personal landscapes of loss and change – the left suitcase, the farewell drink, the lost glove.

The bus used for the Black Country performances had once been a regular sight around town; part of a fleet servicing the local villages that had, for many years, been retired and in storage. We also hired a 'vintage' bus driver, John. In his mid-eighties and retired, for the week of the performances John once more donned his old uniform and took the wheel, driving audience members around his old route.

The performance

Starting in the West Bromwich bus station, the bus picks up waiting audience members and embarks with them on a journey through the local villages. It makes stops along the way, picking up the performers en route. The first stop happens about ten minutes into the journey when the bus pulls up on a small side street where one solitary figure (Helen) waits. She is dressed in black and carries a black leather bag. She boards the bus, which slowly resumes its journey. The woman doesn't look like she's from around here, but she seems to know the bus, as she addresses the riders.

Who here on this bus has not lost something? Be honest. Think back. Take your time. Think carefully. Don't rush. Don't be ashamed. You are amongst friends. You are not alone. This bus has had its fair share of loss. The things I have found down the back of its seats, left hanging on the rail, propped against the emergency door! It is full of loss, this bus. Weighed down. It's amazing what people can leave behind – can just get up and walk off and let go. People leave whole lives behind. Honestly. There are even two urns down in the Lost Property in Baker Street, filed under

'Miscellaneous'. It never ends, loss. I suppose that is quite reassuring. You know where you are with loss. I know about loss. I understand it. I know its shape. I can spot it a mile off. I know its weak spots, its corners, its sharp edges. I know its appetites. I know the way of it. I have felt its coordinates, its X and Y gradients. I know its name. I have its name sewn into the back of its collar.

She opens a black briefcase and takes out a pile of white packages, cheese sandwiches, wrapped in greaseproof paper and tied with string. She makes her way down the aisle handing out the sandwiches to her fellow passengers, swaying a bit with the jerky motion of the bus. As some of the audience eat their sandwiches, she speaks compassionately yet professionally about loss for several minutes, before turning to gaze out the window in silence.

The bus starts to slow down along a scrubby field and in the distance the audience see a figure, a woman (Lois/Julie) standing in the wasteland with a large pile of mismatched suitcases. When she spots the bus she hails it frantically, and starts running towards it with her impossibly large collection of cases. The audience begin to gesture towards her, afraid she will miss the bus or lose one of her cases. She opens the emergency door at the back of the bus. She seems to be wearing a sort of bag-handling uniform and has a work ID card around her neck. She begins to slide the bags down the aisle one at a time.

Bags coming in! Heads up! Watch your back! I am Left Luggage personnel, more kept than left. You can leave your odd things with me – your sharp and flammable objects, your suspicious past – anything you don't want seen, searched or seized. I still have to ask the questions though: Is this your bag? Are you carrying any item on behalf of someone else? Does it contain any electronic or electrical items? Does it contain any firearms, explosives or ammunition? Has the bag been in your care and attention since you packed it? Not many Left Luggage left these days. They have been sealed up or closed down like litter bins, post-boxes and libraries. My motto is: 'Leave it with me and spend a little time hands-free.'

She rings the bell and the bus starts moving again. She arranges her cases on the bus, tucking them under the audience's chairs or next to them on the seat. She starts to open one of the suitcases, unpacking its contents and splaying them on the backs of the seats.

I'll hold on to them as long as I can, even if you lose your ticket or your mind or just don't come back, maybe go out on the town, have a few, forget all the things you carried with you and then forget where you left them. That happens, you know. People think it's lost when it's only left. I can keep them for a month or so. After that they become past due and get shipped down to Tooting. They hold an auction every month. Sometimes I go and buy them back. The good ones, the ones I like to keep on my shelf. You can go down too. Bid on a 'large brown pull-along case containing mainly ladies' African and small quantities of European clothing'. Going once, twice... A green/blue holdall containing a shooting cartridge belt with waistcoat, hat, waterproofs, wader boots and other clothing. Sold! What's my bid on a red Samsonite full of mystery? That's why I go. It's not the bags, it's the stories. I bid on the stories. Couldn't bear to let these go.

By now several of the suitcases have been opened, their contents sprinkled provocatively around the inside of the bus. The Left Luggage character alludes to a range of possible narratives revealed through the contents of cases until she concludes with a story that seems long ago and somehow personal, then she too falls silent and turns her gaze to the window.

The bus slows again to a more ponderous pace as it approaches another woman (Leslie) standing by the side of the road hitch-hiking. She boards the bus. Leslie takes her seat right behind the driver.

I've always been an itinerant worker. It wasn't the plan, but that's how it's worked out. There are some things you just can't go back to. But it's not so bad being itinerant, you know. You get to see a bit of the world.

Now my grandpa had a small farm and a herd of cattle, so he couldn't go anywhere. He was stuck for life on the same little patch of land out in what they used to call the Dust Bowl of Oklahoma. It was pretty rugged, but he never wanted to leave home. Bought the house right across the field from his mother. Watched the big elm tree grow all the way around his old iron basketball hoop until it disappeared altogether 50 years later. He liked to have the same thing for dinner every night too. He had absolutely no desire for change, except for getting a new pick-up truck every three years. He even used to take me on walks to the graveyard and point out his own grave quite cheerfully. I don't know if I could live with the knowledge of my own plot marked out for me. But then I'm not rooted like he was.

When I was nine, my cousin said, 'If you had to choose between never leaving home, and being able to travel anywhere in the world but never being able to come back home, which would you choose?' That question upset me because I knew right away that I was going.

Anyway, after my grandpa died and the farm was sold, my grandma got it in her head to start travelling and it was around that time that she started drinking a little too. It all began with the doctor telling her that a glass of red wine a day would be good for her heart. She said, 'At first I didn't like the taste of it, but now I can hardly get up in the morning without my Reunitti.' She didn't know that you weren't supposed to keep red wine in the fridge or drink it in the morning like juice. Later she discovered the Margarita and that became her signature drink, which was pretty cosmopolitan for a lady from a little Oklahoma farm town.

That little town couldn't under any circumstances be described as cosmopolitan. There was only one place that sold alcohol and it was called BEER. And that's all they sold. But when I went back for the funeral I saw that it has modernized, and has changed its name to BOOZE. I couldn't say if it's an improvement.

They say a place is cosmopolitan if it is composed of or containing people from different countries. But I've seen plenty of places like that – places with people from different countries – that I wouldn't call cosmopolitan, you know what I'm saying? It's all about contrasts and juxtapositions now, isn't it? They say a person is cosmopolitan if they've travelled widely. But I've met plenty of people who've put themselves about a bit who I wouldn't call cosmopolitan, you know what I'm saying?

The bus pulls into a small lay-by where a makeshift bar is set up. Leslie invites the audience to disembark and then takes up her position at the bar. She does a flashy flair routine, making Cosmopolitans for all the audience members while juggling cocktail shakers and vodka bottles. They share a drink together that is both a greeting and a farewell. After the drinks the audience re-board the bus, without the performers. The bus then begins its journey back to the bus station, ending the performance as it began with the audience once more left to their own reflections.

Locomotions at 35 mph

There were six performances of *Lost & Found* each day to the small bus-full of audience/passengers. Each performance started with John driving the romantic-looking vintage bus into the utilitarian municipal bus station in the town centre. Dwarfed by the modern double-decker buses, the elegant blue classic bus instantly became a focus of attention. Past and present collided as the ghost bus and driver returned to retrace past routes. The bus stopped and picked up the awaiting audience/passengers. The arrival of the bus, the start of the performance, is watched not just by the ticketed audience, but also by all those in the bus stop going about their local daily journeys. In this moment audience become performers of a sort as they board the bus, watched by others in the bus station. This sense of 'audience as performer' continues as none of the three performers in the piece are present on the bus at the start of the journey. The audience travel together alone, destination unknown, through a landscape of demolition and construction. The 'ownership' of *Lost & Found* belongs to them in the beginning and what happens on the bus is in their hands.

The audience are mainly locals who are impacted by the changes seen from the moving windows. The bus heralds a past that some of the audience remember and comment on, remarking on the old-fashioned handrails and design, the handsomely painted 'No Spitting' sign. As the audience look out at the changing landscape, some start to converse to each other about the changes taking place, 'that used to be the back of the factory…', 'remember how we used to sit on that wall and chat for hours after school…'. Their recollections of places and spaces, their words and gestures inscribe unique personal narratives, a choreography of pointing, nudging, moving forward, turning, and pressing noses to windows. Hands and arms draw invisible outlines of houses, streets, buildings no longer present. Each performance takes on new inscriptions in text and movement as other memories are triggered both by ghosts and remnants in this landscape of flux. The beginning of the performance is framed by and measured in the passenger windows as the riders gaze out. The screen of the window presents them with the visage of their own faces imprinted on the changing landscape, changing it, filtering it through their own image.

During the week of performances, the landscape continued to change as sections of buildings were demolished and constructed. Each new audience group formed mini travelling communities with a sense of past, present and future colliding. In some ways the 'Destination Unknown' written on the bus marque echoed the lack of control much of the community felt in the shifting fortunes of their town. Moving through it they remembered themselves within it, their echoes and shadows in the landscape, their gestures re-mapping vanished places. When the performers join them they deliver texts infused with loss, but their loss is at once more personal and more universal than the literal physical community losses traced by the bus route.

Helen: *I hate to lose things – my favourite words: Adhesive, Sellotape, Superglue, Safety pin, Pritt stick. But I have become a little lost in my life. Lost in my own small home. This morning I was lost for hours between the bathroom and the kitchen. I found myself staring out of the window wondering who I am.*

I couldn't remember who I am.

Does that ever happen to you?

Do you know who you are?

Can you remember yourself?

Did you lose the person you were, the past you had?

Can you remember all your years?

I just could not find my way back.

And I keep trying to remember the difference between being lost.

And being left.

As performers and audience travel side by side on the bus, they share a sense of contemplation on what comes with change, what is lost, what is found.

As with *Out of Water*, the collective locomotion through time and space is fundamental to the experience of performance. Moving enables a different sort of contemplation. Life is lived, relived, remembered and reconstructed at 35 mph against the heavy clanking soundtrack of the old bus engine. The bus and the journey are both integral parts of the performance as the audience experience and reflect on change and loss through movement. It is a particular kind of locomotion; slow, noisy and of another time. The journey functions as a sort of time travel, inviting reminiscences, reflections and a revisioning of what is with what was. The performers reflect a kind of temporariness, they are transitory, philosophical hitch-hikers who climb on board, appearing out of the changing landscape with their stories of loss, of travel, of change. When the performers alight and disappear, the piece comes full-circle as the audience complete their journey back to the local bus station alone, inscribing each disembarkation with their texts, spoken or unspoken. In this shared moment they form a community within a community.

In this type of piece, which looks at complex and troubled community events through a mosaic of personal narratives, real and fictional, it is not our intention to try somehow to change or implicate the audience member. Instead, we seek to find opportunities for encounter, to create moments intensified by physical closeness and shared experience where the heart of what is at stake is made more palpable. Together we turn our attention to distinctly personal and decidedly universal bereavement on the small and large scale.

Helen: *I can tell when something is about to go. When something is about to get lost. I can always tell. There is a kind of silence. I catch myself waiting for it. I can't help myself. I can predict what people are going to lose. I can. Like right now I am looking round this bus and I can see the things that people are going to lose before they lose them. Yes, you might be gripping hard on to it now but it's about to go. It is not a good idea to grip too tight, you know – that is often when things get lost. When they are held too tightly. You think that is the way to keep something, to clasp it with both hands, wrap your arms about it. Hold on tight. Hold on tight. Don't let go. Don't lose your grip. Don't let it slip. Don't get off at the wrong stop. Don't lose your place. Your head. Your heart. Don't lose sight of what you want.*

Earlier we looked at the generative role of nostalgia in our work with the olfactory. Here we want to explore nostalgia in conversation with place and memory. *Lost & Found* is a journey awash with nostalgia; the vintage bus and the old-fashioned string- and paper-wrapped sandwiches all unashamedly harking back to a remembered past. The intention here is to both give time and space to a recall of what was, whilst at the same time enable a more dynamic encounter with change and what is. In her article *Ways to Walk New York After 9/11* Marla Carlson elegantly reclaims nostalgia, enabling it to become transformative:

> Nostalgia is often enough denigrated as a preference for the unreal over the real, and by extension a denial of complexity and difference. But the word is also connected to Old English *genesan*, 'to survive', Gothic *ganisan*, 'to get well, be saved', the gap between what is known and what is imagined, nostalgia has the potential to transform the future even though it never restores the past.
>
> (Carlson in Hopkins, Orr and Solga, 2009, p. 30)

Rather than immobilizing us within a nostalgia that is conservative, a longing for a romanticized and unrepeatable past whilst trapped in a dreary monochrome present, Carlson's refiguring of nostalgia invites a malleable and transformative space. We often return to places not just in our mind's eye but physically retracing our steps, returning to the places of our past in order to remember who we were. We revisit old houses we once lived in, schools we attended and routes we took into town, in order to glimpse a trace of ourselves, a sign of who we are now, a hint of who we might become. In looking to the past we are so often trying to unearth clues to our future. We 'take a trip down memory lane' not to remain there fossilized, but in the hope that it might actually lead us somewhere else. The experience on the bus enables a revisiting by past means (the ghost bus), through the past (demolished or remodelled buildings) with a sense of a future destination, a somewhere else. Marianne Hirsch and Leo Spitzer describe nostalgic memory as 'a resistant relationship to the present, a "critical utopianism" that imagines a better future'. They suggest that a past reconstructed through the animating vision of nostalgia can serve as a creative inspiration and be 'called upon to provide what the present lacks' (Hirsch and Spitzer, 2002, pp. 258–9).

As the audience look out across the villages, so the villages look back. Within this vulnerable, shifting community, suddenly there is the unannounced arrival of a ghost bus that travels a regular route several times a day, its passengers all already on board. The bus generates its own nostalgia witnessed by those who see it from the streets, from their houses. Later, after it had been returned to storage and settled under a heavy tarpaulin, its engines quieted, many community members said that they missed the bus. One woman said she still found herself looking hopefully for a glimpse of it coming down her street. Perhaps, by taking the audience on a literal journey through the changing landscape, a space had been opened for attention and reflection. Perhaps the bus journey offered a temporary dwelling space granting momentary time travel, a slow chugging movement twixt now and then, a transitory abode in which traces can be recaptured of townscapes that are no longer present. The physical displacement of the bodies of the audience re-places memories as they journey through the present, inscribing memories redrawn and retraced through their gaze, their gestures and their language.

Byway(s) of a conclusion

We want to conclude this section by going right back to where we started. *I never go anywhere I can't drive myself* (1997) was a live-art road trip across Route 66, the first highway that linked East to West in the United States, stretching all the way from Chicago to Los Angeles. Out on the old highway the sites are more site-specific – there are no chains, no nationalized advertising logos, but the epic semiotics of roadside cafés announced by giant astronauts, flashing neon rockets, spinning rooftop hamburgers and ice-cream cones, the four-storey hot-dog man and hand-painted barn-side announcements. The places are run by mom and pop owners, not multinationals and no two places are the same. This was our first project together and everything was new, our company, our working relationship, our personal relationship, our shiny new Pontiac Grand-Am rental car, and the 'info superhighway' of the internet where we were documenting our daily encounters with people and places on the road. The thing that was old was the road itself and most of the people and places we encountered along it.

Nothing ages as fast as technology and the original website from this piece (vintage 1997 html code, still online) is in some ways as dated as the scent from an antique aftershave bottle. And yet there are many aspects of this work and the questions it asked about place, about presence, and most of all about contact and communication within shifting digital proximities that still resonate for us. *I never go anywhere I can't drive myself* laid down a road map for our creative practice that we still follow. The two questions asked time after time to travellers on Route 66, 'Where do you come from?' and 'Where are you going?' are questions we often start a workshop or a class with, asking students to give us automatic writing responses to both, responses that can be fantasy, fiction, autobiography or automythography, truth or lies.

As with *Out of Water* and *Lost & Found, I never go anywhere I can't drive myself* was a journey through a landscape. The locomotion itself was a part of the experience, a constant awareness of shifting proximities of people and place. The fluctuating audience/performer relationships were already at play in this piece even before we necessarily named them as such and the durational performance of the piece was replete with one-to-one exchanges, arrivals and departures, as we performed small acts of sharing stories, exchanging objects and leaving traces. We decided to locate the performance within the genre of the road trip, performing a time-based piece simultaneously on two-lane byways and the 'info superhighway'. The genre of the road trip is at once totally specific, totally place-orientated and yet intrinsically fluid as scenery morphs gradually from city to country, from mountain to plain. We travelled the 4456 miles from Chicago to LA and back again, both literally, via the aforementioned red Pontiac Grand-Am, and 'cyberspatially', via a daily-updated website. We, as the performers, acted as linchpins between the two venues, between place and placelessness, between real and virtual.

At the time the web was new to artists and we were interested in negotiating the performer's relationship to place and placelessness, and in exploring how artists might translate 'evidence' from the real to the virtual, how they might mark their passing in either realm. We distilled the elements of performance to the relationship between the performer and the audience based on the simple concepts of 'give' and 'take', determining that we would make these elements tangible by literally giving/leaving elements of the familiar from our own lives in the form of stories, photographs, letters and videotapes in exchange for stories, recipes, snapshots and artefacts collected en route. Before we left England we began compiling an extensive, eclectic archive including videotaped messages from site-specific English locations, such as Derek

Jarman's garden or the tomb of Karl Marx; old maps of Shropshire and Skye; family photographs and recipes; seed packets of English primroses and cowslips; souvenirs from the Tower of London; 'original' Sherlock Holmes memorabilia from Baker Street; Sainsbury's digestive biscuits and Red Label Tea; tape-recorded and written narratives; and of course, the Shipping Forecast and Gardeners' Question Time. Our idea was to leave a trail of evidence, of literal and metaphorical messages in bottles, in our wake as we travelled and conversely to replace our existing archive with a new archive collected en route from the people and places we encountered. Discovered randomly in isolation from each other by people along Route 66, our stories, objects and images were at once fragmentary narratives and links in the long thin chain of a much larger piece, linked by our physical presence as we travelled and simultaneously by the creation of the time-based website which offered accounts of both evidence left behind and evidence gathered. In 1997 we compared the site we were making to the fast Interstate 40, the super-speed highway that had made Route 66 redundant. Now our old site itself seems retro, bypassed by today's slick social network sites and blogs with their seamless vimeo. Clicking through our site feels more akin to navigating the old road, following links that no longer lead anywhere, like those parts of Route 66 that suddenly meandered into grass and wildflower.

> *Helen's Online Journal Entry: 7 May 1997*
> *Time: 3 pm*
> *Place: Route 66, somewhere in Illinois*
> *Sitting on the grassy roadside, my legs stretched out onto an overgrown fragment of the original old road itself. It lies quiet and empty, a narrow path between the grassy verges that blur its edges. Moss grows out from the cracks that split through the road in many jagged directions. I can hear the cars on the main road in the distance, but here the only noise is the birds singing and the crackle of old leaves blowing down the road.*

But what is perhaps most vivid even now are the encounters we experienced en route. The philosophical questions about places, real and virtual are perhaps subsumed by the real face-to-face meetings with the people who lived and worked along the road.

> *Leslie's Online Journal Entry: 17 April 1997*
> *Time: 4.25 pm*

Place: the Frontier Café, Albuquerque, NM

Well, I could never have guessed what was about to happen to us as I sat writing this morning. Helen got talking to one of the locals who came in, a smiley old man named Bob, who was sitting at the counter having an early lunch. The next thing we knew, we had been invited to his farm a couple of miles down the road, so we hopped in the car and followed his old green Chevy pick-up truck down a dirt track, past a tiny pink house. He took us into a barn and showed us not one, but five old aeroplanes, most of which he had built or remodelled himself over the last 30 years. He told us that when he came home to Texas after fighting in WWII in France, he became a pilot and crop duster. He says he doesn't fly anymore, but he still works on planes and his friend Jackson flies them. He was very keen that we should each have a go at sitting in the cockpit and when it was my turn to sit in the old red plane staring at the control panel, I thought – yeah, why not learn to fly. So there's my next project sorted.

At the end of our aeroplane tour, Bob decided to reveal to us a secret special hideout he called 'the hangover room', a little nook with a potbelly stove, a cast-iron kettle and a lot of bottles of Yukon Jack bourbon. He said he and Jackson used this room for drinking, lying and bragging, and hinted that they were pretty accomplished at all three. At this point I knew that there was something I wanted to leave with Bob and I went out to the car to get the pewter hip flask my friend Sarah gave me years ago. It's seen a lot of good use and I wasn't planning to part with it, but I wanted to give Bob something special. I handed it to him and told him he could keep it in the hangover room. He took a swig of the single malt Scotch, and said, 'I'll carry it over my heart always.'

In Truxton, Arizona, we met Mildred, who had run the Frontier Café and Motel together with her husband for 27 years. Since he died in 1990, she hadn't known what to do as regards the business, 'I'm 69, 70 this year, and I know I should give it up, but I always think, "you never know who you might meet tomorrow."' Mildred's philosophy became a sort of motto of our journey, the 'here and now dynamic' when potentially anything could happen on our performance-in-motion with its ever-changing audience. Which takes us right back to Dixie Lee Evans at Exotic World, Wild Road, who you met at the start of Landscape I, to a performance where we were definitely the audience, to an encounter we will always remember. So we have done a round trip, which as any traveller knows is always satisfying, but what if we don't want to stop? What if we want to keep travelling with you?

When we finally returned to Chicago at the end of the trip there was a desire to just keep on going. The sudden stillness after so much constant movement felt alien. In part, that is the lure of the road trip itself, the freedom it gives you not to be fixed in one place or another, but instead enabling a sense of abandon and anonymity in its steady propulsion forward, forward into a future that endlessly shape-shifts outside the car window. But there was something else here too, concerned with the quality of and space for reflection that comes with moving through a landscape. The shifting proximities of here and here, there and there mapped onto other projects, as did the desire for the moments of contact and communication with audiences. Tracks laid down in this project manifest again and again in myriad ways in so many projects since. This, our first project together, set us on the road of the kind of work we wanted to make; two soloists who were now a company, two people who were now a couple, and work that thrived on curiosity and sought to find the heroic in the everyday through close encounters with audiences.

Part Two

Proximity and Process

6   In the Lab and Incognito: Research in Profile

Our process on any given work often involves conversation, collaboration and/or training with and from experts from other fields such as biological scientists, musicians or bartenders. Like other performers, we sometimes learn specific skills for performances such as sign language for *The Day Don Came with the Fish*, scuba diving for *Family Hold Back*, and electric guitar for *(be)longing*. Here we talk about some of the research processes behind three of the performances detailed in the book: Helen working 'undercover' in the Lost Property Department in Baker Street for *Lost & Found*; both of us living and working at the National Centre for Biological Sciences compound in Bangalore to research smell and memory with a team of scientists; and working with a team of neurogastroenterologists at the Wingate Institute in London on 'gut feelings' and the autonomic nervous system for *the moment I saw you I knew I could love you*. In each of these field research situations we were putting ourselves in proximity with people who were dealing with the same subjects that we were working with (loss, smell, gut feelings) from completely different methodologies or processes.

Lost Property Department, London

February 2005

As part of the process for developing *Lost & Found*, I (Helen) worked for a time in London's Lost Property Department (Illustration 6.1), the biggest repository of loss in the United Kingdom, located on Baker Street, a few steps away from 221b, Holmes and Watson's famous address, now the Sherlock Holmes Museum. Perhaps whoever decided to locate the Lost Property Department here thought it seemed a hopeful location for tracking things down. Established in 1933, its cavernous basements are full of lost items individually tagged, archived and neatly labelled. The Department deals with approximately 600 items a day – things

Illustration 6.1   Lost Property exterior
[Photo by Hugo Glendinning]

found on the Underground, on buses and trains, at coach stations and in black cabs. Some of the Lost Property Department's most unusual finds include: false teeth, false eyes, replacement limbs, two-and-a-half hundredweight of sultanas/currants, lawn mower, Chinese typewriter, breast implants, four-foot teddy bear, coffin, wheelchairs, crutches, stuffed eagle, 14-foot boat, divan bed, outboard motor, water-skis, park bench, grandfather clock, Bishop's crook, garden slide, inflatable doll, jar of bull's sperm, urn of ashes, three dead bats in container, gas mask, Tibetan bell, stuffed pufferfish, vasectomy kit, harpoon gun, and two human skulls in a bag.[1]

Working at the Lost Property Department, I became fascinated by the universality of loss. What intrigued me most was the textual and gestural language around it. Every day people from all walks of life would turn up at Lost Property, queue at the counter and when their turn came, start to try and describe the items they had lost. I was struck by the detail of their descriptions, and their poetic, sometimes almost epic, language: 'I have come more in hope than in expectation.' 'It was the District line going from Embankment.' 'A shiny metallic bag, blue. *A gift bag.*' 'It was a claret from the Medoc – I can't remember the Château – 1996, I think... .' 'I don't know if you can help me. It was last Wednesday on a 23 bus going to Neasden. I took off my cap because it was raining. It is like this' (points to the one he is wearing), 'but more mottled, more tweedy – like a doctor's.' Textual descriptors were accompanied by physical gestures that gave shape and dimension to loss as their owners mimed the contours of a lost bag, the length of a mislaid umbrella, palmed the small weight of a missing wallet. A boy who had lost his NHS card, placed for safekeeping in the middle of a book which he promptly then left on a train, performed opening a newspaper in his hand and mimed the act of inserting something to make it clear what something in the middle of something might look like. Like the audience members on the bus in *Lost & Found* who expressed the contours of lost places in physical gestures, the people in the Lost Property Department gave shape to loss through words and movement. Their facial expressions were also heightened as people conveyed different mixtures of desperation, hope, anxiety, despondency and vulnerability; adults often rendered almost childlike and helpless by their loss, eager to offer any evidence or proof that might help. A woman came in who had lost her wedding shoes, 'Ivory, not like a pump, like a *shoe* shoe. Size three… It's called a 'junior shoe' on the receipt…?' Suddenly hopeful she started rootling in her bag, 'I still have the receipt!' she exclaimed, pulling it out, as if that proof of purchase might suddenly make the shoes appear. Yet she is right to be so precise, the details are crucial, the words, the descriptors, *the script*. What if they are right here standing in Lost Property and the lost item is *here too*, in the basement downstairs waiting to be claimed. What if they are not quite saying the right thing, not quite the exact adjectives and nouns and verbs that are written on the yellow Lost Property card attached to the item?

All day, every day, I audienced and performed exchanges of loss. I listened to the intricate descriptive texts, watched the lost shapes carved in the air. Separated only by the small length of the counter, I nodded, smiled, frowned, and exclaimed; I looked at faces, watched bodies, studied movements and listened carefully to texts as people performed their loss for me. I was aware of my own performances, that I was enacting several roles: as an artist researching loss; as a rapt audience to vivid one-to-one monologues of loss; as a performer 'incognito' as a lost property worker; and as an actual lost property worker, for that was my job nine to five for a time. Staff at the Lost Property Department knew that I was an artist working there temporarily to undertake research for a performance and were enormously generous with their time and help in training me so that when I interacted with clients, I assisted them as any other Lost Property Department worker would. Each day I clocked in and out, dutifully filled in claims, recorded items, made small yellow identity tag labels threaded with string that I tied to bags and bundles and parcels of loss left on buses, in taxis and on trains. I wheeled trolley-loads of lost items into the lift and took them down to the cavernous bowels of the storage rooms (Illustration 6.2), where I arranged them on endless shelves and where they then sat waiting to be claimed.

The amount of loss that passes through my hands just in a day:

A mobile phone with a green jade stone dangling from it with a screen saver picture of a frog.
An imitation Oscar statue with the inscription 'to David'.
A wooden pipe with white spots and a silver band saying DUNHILL.
A Falkland penguin mug in a British Home Stores carrier left on a train from Paddington to King's Cross.

A tub of Dulux brilliant white matt emulsion paint in a Robert Dyas plastic carrier bag.

A dark green bag containing green mid-socks, lime green fabric, bright green material and two pairs of 15 denier tights.

A shiny metallic blue gift bag containing a claret from the Medoc.

Some floral swimming shorts and a towel.

A mid-blue scarf with Institute of Physics on it, one pencil and a London A–Z.

A plastic bag containing photographs of a man's fiftieth birthday party in Jamaica and a packet of easy-cook rice.

A library book called 'Lover's Leap' and a copy of the Highway Code.

A Barbie video, a picture of a mother and her daughter in a silver frame.

A Patrizio Buanne CD and an ostrich pen.

A wedding ring, plain gold, no inscription.

During the time I worked at the Lost Property Department I was drawn to the relationships between the other lost property workers and the clients, touched by the level of care and carefulness given to the person, even over something as mundane as an umbrella, the attention paid to these lost objects. I am not just talking about people doing their jobs well, being efficient – these people seemed to understand loss. No loss was too small, each carried within its shape and description possible heartbreak for the one who had lost it. The lost property workers knew that for some, reporting the loss of a seemingly innocuous item could unlock other stories, relationships, whole worlds.

I didn't enter the job at Lost Property with a specific expectation of what it would give me. I hoped it would provide me with a landscape for exploring loss, not loss on a grand style, but small everyday loss. I found both commonplace loss and epic loss, because at the Lost Property Department I learned that they are more closely intertwined than I had imagined, the profound within the everyday. In addition, I was witness to unexpected intimacies between people over the polished wooden counter. I was audience to small confessions, to moments of care and compassion that affected me and became part of the story I wanted to tell.

An old man left a black holdall on this bus. I asked him what was inside – we have to catalogue loss. We have to give it a name. A number. He said there was a woman's purse. We have to give it a colour. A texture. It was a

Illustration 6.2 Lost Property interior

[Photo by Hugo Glendinning]

lady's purse, one of those with a silver twist opening. Inside the holdall there was also a candle and a little trowel. He was on his way to the cemetery to tend his wife's grave. She had died last year. Said they had been married 54 years. 54 years. He said there wasn't any money in the purse. He was still carrying it about with him. Still holding on. Holding it all in his holdall. All he has left. Hold on.

In such encounters I was privy to personal narratives of loss. Each day I experienced a collision of the profound and the poetic, the pedestrian and the prosaic. Some conversations were comedic, some became long narratives that took on a 'well, whilst I am here…' quality, like a visit to an attentive doctor when the patient settles and starts to air all her complaints, 'Whilst we are on the subject I may as well tell you about a couple of other bits and pieces I have lost […].' Some conversations over the counter at Lost Property took on an almost confessional air as the customer expressed anger or shame: 'How could I have been so careless, foolish, preoccupied!' Their 'sins' are heard and forgiven by the Lost Property worker: 'It's easily done, sir, you are not alone.' Attention is paid, care is given – absolution even. A woman comes in wanting directions, hoping for a map, needing to get to King's Cross. 'What part of London am I in? Is this the centre?' she demands. In Lost Property she herself is lost. 'Where is Piccadilly? Is there a nice place to have fish and chips?' She is given directions, helped to find her way.

Working at the Lost Property Department, I was constantly in close quarters with loss. I organized it, arranged it and catalogued it. I held it, carried it, lifted it, shifted it and knew the weight of it. I felt its unrelenting presence, quite literally in the sense that the business of loss in the Lost Property Department, as in life, is unending; the in-tray always full, people just keep losing things, even their lost property cards. Seasons are marked by loss; mislaid umbrellas flood in during the winter months, a sudden flurry of tennis racquets during Wimbledon. Loss is a barometer of the times, mobile phones now outrank umbrellas in 'items most lost'. I witnessed the tragedy and beauty of loss daily in the ghostly curves and contours traced in the air as well as in the solid materiality of the thousands of items spilling across the vast shelves of the basement in a kaleidoscope of shape and colour. I felt loss on a molecular level, the trace of its cells on my skin each day, the taste of it in my mouth, breathing its familiar odour. I was covered in it, contagious with it. The day-to-day encounters and conversations around loss shaped my development of *Lost & Found* in terms of my writing as well as in forming the kind of persona I wanted to develop – someone who *knew loss*, who had held it in her hands, felt its shape, someone who *cared* about loss. Below are two text extracts, one an actual exchange that took place in the Lost Property Department, followed by a section of the *Lost & Found* script that it directly inspired. I include them here as an example of the contiguity of my lived experience in Lost Property and my creative work for *Lost & Found*.

Notes from actual exchange:

Woman:	*I came from Croydon across to East Finchley.*
Lost Property Worker:	*Was it the St Pancras Cemetery you were at?*
Woman:	*Yes! I was at a funeral there – it goes on for ever, doesn't it?' (It is not clear whether she is referring to the cemetery or the funeral. She holds one lone leather glove taut in her hands and thrusts it over the counter.) I've lost the other one.*
Lost Property Worker:	*Can you be more specific?*
Woman:	*Well, it was the 18 March because that was the date of the funeral. I got the 263 to the cemetery…*
Lost Property Worker:	*(interrupts) Oh I know it well! I've spent many years running after them!*
Woman:	*It's size six-and-a-half, black…*
Lost Property Worker:	*Can you be more specific? It's just that we get so many gloves – single gloves – that is why we have to be so specific.*
Woman:	*I am not sure what someone would do with a single glove – they are no good to anyone. I mean some things are worth finding, for instance, I lost a brooch three years ago. It wasn't valuable but it was very pretty…*
Lost Property Worker:	*Did you report it to us?*
Woman:	*(apologetically) Well… no I didn't. I didn't think to.*

Lost Property Worker:	*Well, you never know. I mean I never knew we traced and covered such a vast area till I started working here. It's always worth coming in.*
Woman:	*Oh well, yes, I will in the future. So this here is the glove (hands it over the counter)...*
Lost Property Worker:	*(examines it and makes notes) Well let me see, black leather, um, size six-and-a-half... right hand...*
Woman:	*What?*
Lost Property Worker:	*It's the right one you've lost.*
Woman:	*Oh, yes, I see what you mean, I didn't think of that.*
Lost Property Worker:	*It's most common, the right glove, case of the right hand doesn't know what the left hand is doing. (chuckles)*
Woman:	*Gosh yes, I see. How interesting – but who would bother to hand a single glove in anyway? I mean you would really have to have hope, sort of a belief in human persistence that someone would come looking for something so – what's the word – so inconsequential?*
Lost Property Worker:	*You have.*
Woman:	*Yes, yes I suppose that's true. Well, leather does not come cheap these days, does it? They were Marks and Spencer, such very soft leather...*
Lost Property Worker:	*Now we know why our mums used to attach them with string!*
Woman:	*Thirty pounds they cost. Took me ages to find a pair that fit.*

My notes on the conversation above inspired this section of the script for *Lost & Found*:

People don't bother handing in single gloves because they think, 'What is the point?' 'What is the point?' they think. 'Who would bother searching for a lost single glove?' I have to deal with it when someone comes in with their single glove looking for its partner. 'I have lost my other half.' They come more in hope than expectation. They say, 'I'm not sure what someone would do with a single glove.' Then they stand there patiently and wait for me to find out if we have their glove. I mean that sort of hope needs respect.

I go through the descriptions of all the single gloves we hold: plain black small, plain black with criss-cross stitching. I wrote out that description myself. I did the criss-cross as two X Xs. I wondered if it looked like I was sending love notes. It wasn't a love note. It was the description of a glove.

Then I have to go back and I have to tell them. And there they are waiting, so hopefully, with their other glove stretched out before you – showing itself, hiding nothing. And I have to tell them there is nothing to match their description. There is no match for them. And a single glove is no use to anyone.

Working so close to loss and a myriad of dealings around it, the verbal and physical language to describe it, the filing and archiving of it, the relationships struck up around it, provided me with a rich terrain from which to write my part of the script of *Lost & Found*.

Much of the writing for our performance work comes from an autobiographical or automythological place, driven by the belief that an excavation of the personal can spark ideas and images for more universal connections. This runs parallel with the performative style of our work that is generally non-character based (we do not think of ourselves as actors) and more in the line of a live art or performance art aesthetic. The process of developing the writing and performance for *Lost & Found* was unique for me, explicitly creating a fictional character or persona, who was a composite of the real-life people and stories from Lost Property. Just as close performance can be too close, the text itself can work as a distancing tool. For *Lost & Found*, where we were working in places already redolent with loss and change, it was more powerful to create other landscapes of loss through words that were recognizable but not read as autobiographical or personal accounts. At no time did the text in the performance feign to be connected to the specific loss and change in the Black Country or London's East End. Our aim was that the fictive personas could evoke loss while leaving room for audiences to filter or fill in more personal, individual recollections and reflections for themselves.

In the lab

Relationships between the senses and cognition have been one of our primary areas of curiosity and fascination for many years, so in the course of our work we have forged a few co-investigative relationships with specialists from the biological sciences. We write here about the two most involved collaborations.

National Centre for Biological Sciences

Bangalore, July 2003

We are working with Dr Upinder Bhalla and his research team at India's National Centre for Biological Sciences, located on a lush green campus just north of Bangalore, surrounded by mango groves and jacaranda trees, where the scientists and their graduate students live and work. We are living in the guest apartment in the faculty block. The campus feels remote from the noisy, colourful city and slightly remote from 'real life', with students and faculty all living and working in this gated community. Life here seems pleasant, focused, and not without humour – all the big computers in the lab are named after different Indian sweets – Gulab Jamun, Cashew Laddu, Mysore Pak and Coconut Burfi hum in the background.

We are here because of an email correspondence we started a few months' previously with Dr Bhalla. Although we were excited about his research on the connections between smell and memory, when we first wrote to him we were hopeful, but not entirely sure, that an eminent scientist would be interested in working on an art project. As it turned out, Dr Bhalla was very open to the proposition, articulating several sound scientific motives for collaborating with artists on a performance/installation project (though later, when we knew him better, he admitted it was a bit of a shock to be contacted by performance artists from London). He sent a thoughtful, poetic reply outlining why he would indeed be interested in collaborating with us, which opened up a correspondence and later resulted in our residency at the NCBS.[2]

First, it gives a glimpse of human reactions to smell. There have been plenty of psychophysics experiments on the subject measuring things like detection thresholds and the like, but much fewer studies looking simply at what people think and how they react to smell. Although this is less quantifiable, it is in some ways more important now that the field is moving towards looking at the cognitive aspects of sensory responses. Second, humans themselves seem to be conditioned by society to ignore smell, especially in the sanitized modern world. It is interesting to see what happens when they are asked to pay specific attention to it. For myself, I am most interested in seeing how an artist approaches the topic of smell. My training has given me a particular line of thinking and this could always do with some new perspectives. I view science as an expression of creativity. It would be great to complement this with an altogether different form of expression coming from a different world of creativity.[3]

While we are resident at the NCBS, Upi generously invites us to come and watch various experiments he and his team of graduate students are running (with rats) as well as letting us film interviews with them about their work (as long as we don't film the rats). Upi explains that though scientists have long understood that smell and memory are intricately connected, it is a relatively unresearched area of biological science for the simple reason that experiments involving smell are notoriously difficult to design and execute and nearly impossible for another researcher to verify by repeating – smell stimuli are a sticky, elusive, transgressive, and extremely chemically complex bricolage of environmental elements. Vision, he explains, is a much more popular sense for scientists to work on because designing and delivering visual stimulus is easy – you simply choose your image or sequence of images and then print or project them. It's also relatively straightforward to mask unwanted visual stimuli in labs. Because smells are chemical and airborne, they pose some big problems for researchers. First, it is difficult to prepare a precise smell stimulus: you can't stop it from mingling with other compounds in the environment, which changes its nature, making it nearly impossible to produce the same smell twice. Once you have the smell, it is also incredibly difficult to deliver with any sort of accuracy or precision – you can't frame it, broadcast it or copy it like an image. Finally, once the smell is present, it is also very hard to get rid of. (These are, of course, the same reasons that smell is infrequently used in theatre.)

Much of Upi's team's time is spent on devising practical solutions to the problems of the 'purity' of the odorant and the delivery and then extraction of the odorant for any given experiment. He shows us the gargantuan vacuum system they have installed in the ceiling above the experimental chamber (for rats), which constantly sucks the air out of the room to keep it pure from unwanted smell molecules, such as the smell of a researcher's soap or the smells of the rats themselves. The vacuum is a crucial tool because without it the team would never be able to deliver a stimulus in smell-neutral environment. This is where designing olfactory experiments is almost impossibly challenging in relation to the relatively straightforward process of delivering discrete images or sounds for acoustic or visual experiments. To cease making a sound, you can just press stop or pause on a player, to finish with an image, you can turn the page or change the screen, but stopping a smell is a complex molecular process – you have to detach the molecules from any surfaces they may have attached to as well as completely refreshing the air supply in the room. In addition to the giant vacuum, the team use an 'olfac- tometer' they have developed (Illustration 6.3), which bubbles nitrogen through pure chemical odorants in glass chambers and then delivers the smell in plumes via purified air streams, where they are enjoyed (one hopes) by lab rats who may then remember sequences of behaviours and rewards based on the odorants. Some of the smells they are working with during our visit are ester 3-methylbutyl acetate, which smells like banana as well as pure chemical compounds that smell like eucalyptus and bubble gum. Some scents are comprised of 'stickier' molecules than others, which makes them harder to work with, so the team eliminate particularly sticky odorants as well as unpleasant odorants, because, well, why make your lab smell bad if you don't have to?

The flipside of the olfactory research compared to research on a sense like vision is that while visual stimuli are easy to generate, control and replicate, the way that the brain processes visual stimuli is extremely complicated, while processing for smells is a much simpler, more primitive type of brain activity located in just two areas of the brain, whereas vision is processed in about 50 different parts of the brain. The aspect of this cognitive process is particularly of interest to us as artists as it helps explain why smells operate on a more instinctual, direct, emotional level than the other senses. Smells really are a direct chemical hit, so people can literally be broadsided with a 'blast from the past'.

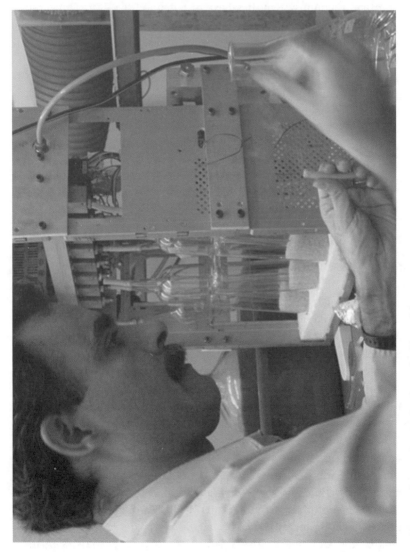

Illustration 6.3   Upinder Bhalla, olfactometer
[Photo by Leslie Hill]

Sometimes the smells are in context and create a sense of emotional wellbeing like smelling your grandmother's cooking as you walk into your grandmother's kitchen. At other times smells can sneak up on us and elicit emotional responses completely out of context, like smelling an ex-lover's perfume on an unseen stranger in a crowd on the underground at rush hour and feeling shaken. This is part of the fascination of this sense.

If it seems improbable to Upi's research team to have performance artists on site at the NCBS for a couple of weeks, they don't betray any misgivings. As well as letting us observe and interview them about their own work on mapping the connections between smell and memory, Upi and his grad students actively engage with our work, asking lots of questions about the project we are working on, but also more generally about 'daily life' in the arts. By and large they are surprised that many of the types of things we do as part of our working lives are so similar – the revelation that artists spend a significant amount of time writing grant applications and doing research, for example, comes as a big surprise to them, but the more we talk, the more they begin to draw parallels between pure/theoretical scientific research and experimental arts, contrasting them with commercial/corporate scientific research and the commercial entertainment industry. Upi sees scientific inquiry as fundamentally creative, which for him is the primary link between art and science and the team seem genuinely pleased to find an affinity between experimental science and experimental art.

At this early stage in our process, we imagine the piece that is eventually going to become *On the Scent* will take the form of a museum installation and we are discussing with Upi different methods for orchestrating smells and the ways in which people might experience them in a museum setting.[4] Upi speaks to us as an original settler, who knows how difficult the terrain is – he has made a career of finding ways to deliver and eliminate smells. He is a naturally positive person, delivering rather bad news as encouragingly as possible. Even with all his expertise available to us as a consultant, it seems that there are really no great ways he can recommend for delivering smells precisely in a museum setting (or any other setting). Upi ponders the giant vacuum employed in his lab to suck the air out of a small glass chamber (about the size of a large fish tank) and frowns at the thought of trying to replicate this method of air purification for a series of rooms in a museum.

We find the idea of spending thousands or millions of pounds on vacuums that would necessitate architectural refitting of museums extravagant, fascinating and hilarious by turns. We all pick up different occupational habits of thought and methods of practice: people tend to solve problems based on tools they are familiar with. It would never occur to us to install a giant vacuum above a gallery to stuck out all the smelly molecules, but Upi works with rats and chemical compounds in lab environments and of course his projects are experiments rather than art events. He has no particular objective to entertain the rats or give them meaningful experiences, but he does need to be able to track how odorants impact their memories in performing tasks and measure the way in which the smells are delivered. We, on the other hand, don't need to be able to 'prove' anything one way or the other based on audience behaviour, but we do want to give people an interesting, provocative experience. So our approaches to working with the connections between smell and memory are admittedly very different, as are our aims.

As part of the experience we wanted to create for *On the Scent*, we were interested in learning about connections audience members might have between the sense of smell and memory. For Upi, the question of how we might obtain this information within the context of an artwork seemed something of an impossible task. He was approaching the question in terms of measures of brain activity, biofeedback and repetitive behaviours over consecutive events with precisely controlled stimulants. In short, he was thinking like a laboratory scientist. We mulled over all the constraints and complications of biofeedback and said, hoping not to sound too simple, '[...] or we could just ask them'. It was as if we had articulated something truly radical. He thought about it for a moment, beamed and said, with the sense of wonder of a man who spends his days with rats, 'Yes, people can *talk*!'

After we went back to London we sketched our way through many different possible approaches to the piece before deciding to create a performance set in a house. The more we worked on the project, the more we became convinced that trying to create smell portraits or sequences out of context could end up being quite a flat experience for an audience member. As we talked to people about the sense of smell and their personal connections with smell and memory, we noticed that most of the stories people told us about their 'smell memories' were domestic – a grandfather's pipe tobacco, the Sunday roast, the smell of a freshly mown lawn. Working in a house, we decided, would give a context to a range of different smells (cosmetic, cooking, laundry, medical) that would enable people to free-associate with their own memories as well as allowing some measure of compartmentalizing the odours between rooms. Looking back on it, we can see that one could absolutely infer a 'lab' influence in the design of the performance – we send the audience through the experiential maze of the performance room by room and then at the end we interview them and collect their responses.

Having worked with the NCBS at the start of the project, we took a different approach to how we worked with the audience interviews after the shows than we might have otherwise, as we had an idea that they might make interesting data for Upi and his colleagues. NESTA (the National Endowment for Science and the Arts) gave Leslie a 'Dreamtime Fellowship' and as part of that fellowship she was able to have several hundred interviews databased. We then sent the database of 'smell memories' to Upi along with a video of a couple of hours of edited highlights which we pulled from some of the most common themes that emerged. One of the patterns we noticed when we databased the results was that people from urban areas frequently spoke about product smells – perfume, soap, cosmetics – while audience members who had grown up in rural areas more often talked about natural smells – the first rain after the dry season was a recurring smell memory. Our approach certainly wasn't a hard science approach. We didn't want audience members to fill out participant questionnaires; so some of the potential data we could have extracted was sacrificed to the overall concern that the experience should be one of a performance event rather than a scientific experiment. Though anecdotal rather than scientific in nature, Upi assured us that this type of information is very much of interest to scientists – stories or personal experiences and the patterns that emerge from such narratives are often what fuel a new idea or provide a hunch to follow. After working with us, Upi credited the sci-art exchange with two new lines of research in his lab:

> Their visit also inspired a new line of work in the lab. In particular, the idea of the audience as an active participant in an artistic performance, rather than an onlooker, struck a chord. This led us to think about undertaking behavioural studies in which the subject (whether

human or rat) actively responds to olfactory inputs. From this initial jog to our scientific imagination, we are now in the middle of some experiments where we ask rats not just what odour it is, but also where it comes from. This has turned out to be a very fruitful line of inquiry. We are also planning a field study among humans by taking an olfactometer to different regions of India to examine odour-sensitivity among different Indian populations. In some ways this idea reflects many of the elements of the travelling performance *On the Scent*.

(Bhalla in Arends and Slater, 2004, p. 18)

Talking to us about audiences and performances not only inspired the lab's first study with humans, but the notion of a touring show inspired the idea of taking the lab's olfactometer 'on tour' around India, a great legacy for our residency with the NCBS. In this case, working in proximity to each other's processes significantly impacted both our performance work and their scientific research.

Wingate Institute for Neurogastroenterology

London, 2008

When we embarked on a project starting with the question 'What are gut feelings?' we were generally fascinated with scientific understanding of the gut as the 'second brain' in the body. In particular we were interested in the gut as the site of 'gut instinct' and 'butterflies in the stomach' – a part of the body uniquely associated with intuition, emotion and deep truths. We loved the concept of emotions as the nexus between matter and mind in the body, and we were interested in the gut as a site where we can sometimes catch a conscious glimpse of psychosomatic connections. We wanted to learn more about how the body, specifically the second brain or the enteric nervous system, 'thinks'. We wanted to learn more about the thinking body in terms of systems, cells and chemicals. We started by reading some popular science accounts that we thought might relate to the project, such as Michael D. Gershon's book *The Second Brain* (1998), Gerd Gigerenzer's *Gut Feelings* (2007) as well as Malcolm Gladwell's *Blink: The Power of Thinking Without Thinking* (2005).

As we were doing general research, we wondered if there might be another 'Upi' out there, a scientist working on the gut who might be interested in an exchange of ideas and methodologies with artists. Everyone we consulted with in the 'sci-art' community said that Dr Qasim Aziz was absolutely *the* person we should talk to about gut feelings. We made an appointment with his receptionist via email without really noticing the address, but when it came time for the meeting we realized that the Wingate was about a three-minute walk away from our flat. We had recently moved from Islington to be nearer our studio in Whitechapel and by a twist of fate we discovered that we had moved a block from the Wingate Institute of Neurogastroenterology, the leading research centre of its kind in the world.

Like Upi, Qasim was very open to the idea of a shared dialogue with an art project and during our first meeting he kept calling in more and more of his grad students to listen to our conversation. In the first meeting we established that a point of connection between his process and ours was an engagement with autobiographical material as a method or springboard. At the Wingate autobiographical recall and writing are recognized as very powerful ways of stimulating the autonomic nervous system (ANS) in clinical tests. Autobiographical writing and recall are highly valued at the Wingate for the scientific data they produce. As part of the research we participated in clinical experiments measuring responses in the ANS and the enteric nervous system (ENS), some of which involved autobiographical writing, answering prompts such as writing a one- to two-page description of two autobiographical events, (1) a neutral routine scenario from your daily life such as getting ready for work and (2) a detailed account of an event in your life that caused extreme stress, physically experienced in the gut.

During the months when we were working on our 'hat trick' of gut feeling projects (the performance *the moment I saw you I knew I could love you*, the film *Sea Swallow'd* and the artist workshop Autobiology), we participated in research experiments at the Wingate (Illustration 6.4), taking part in their processes and giving them access to our autobiographical writing and physiological responses in order to experience for ourselves different ways of looking at and thinking about the gut. This involved several experiments such as the one that employed autobiographical writing, titled 'Influence Of Psychological Stress On Autonomic, Neuroendocrine And Gastrointestinal Physiological Responses'. A more challenging study to participate in was 'Prevalence and Stability of Psychophysiological Responses to Pain'. I (Leslie) was exposed to painful stimuli, a clinical version of thumbscrew torture,

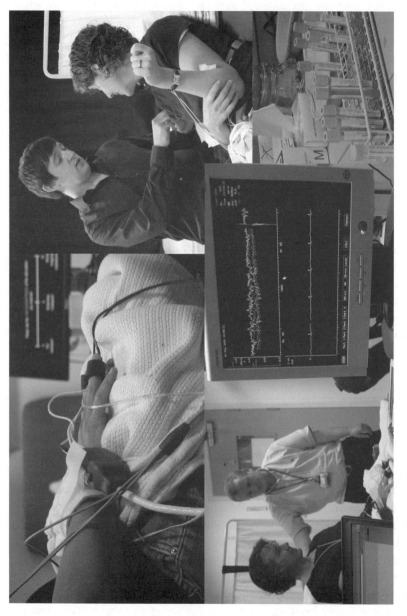

Illustration 6.4 Wingate montage

[Photo montage by Cheryl Pierce]

while having various systems monitored – heart rate, depth of breathing, skin temperature, gut motility and cortisol readings from blood drawn before and after experiments.

Unfortunately there are only three ways to obtain the data from the gut and none of them are non-invasive. The most alarming experience, pictured here, was an experiment that requires the subject to get a balloon into their stomach, either by swallowing the balloon, attached to a long tube (Illustration 6.5), or having it shoved up their nose and down the back of their nasal cavity into the throat and beyond. Participating in this experiment in particular produced a physiological 'flight' response I had to repress in order to see the experiment through. The attempted swallows caused me to gag despite the researchers' helpful encouragement to think of the tube as a strand of spaghetti, while the 'up the nose' technique created hideous internal crunching noises in my skull as the device hit the cartilage of my nasal passages which the researcher sadly noted were unusually small and therefore uncommonly tricky. (Should I feel inadequate, I wondered?) Unpleasant as the experience was, it vividly illustrated to us that not all of the tricky issues around participation are the sole property of performance.

The purpose of this particular study was to assess whether people's personality (psychological profile) had any bearing on how different parts of their bodies responded to different types of pain. I'm not sure what my psychological profile was or how I scored on the Toronto Alexithymia Scale, but I definitely responded negatively to the painful experience of having a tube pushed up my nose, as I'm sure most people would. The pay-off for taking part in these sometimes painful experiments was in getting to see the tools of the trade in action in a neurogastroenterology lab, such as a neuroscope, an instrument that can display read-outs from the autonomic nervous system in real time (pictured in Illustration 6.4). We were privileged to experience first-hand (and in other parts of the body) what processes research scientists use to discover more about the 'second brain'.

As well as wanting to know more about scientific work around the enteric nervous system, we were curious as to the relationship of what Leder calls the recessive body to writing or composition and interested

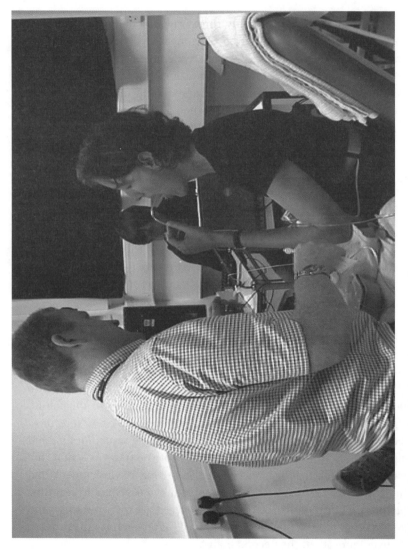

Illustration 6.5 Leslie in Wingate experiment
[Photo by Cheryl Pierce]

in asking how the physical, impulsive and the associative might be used to enhance or subvert the cognitive for creative purposes. What different kinds of 'texts', movements, images, words and sounds does the 'second brain' yield? As well as wanting to discover how synaesthetic transfer of sensory knowledge could enrich creative processes and how this could be manifested in the making of new work, central to our inquiry was how to communicate that embodied process to audiences. This desire to manifest an embodied experience led to our eventual design decision to situate the audience for our 'gut feelings' piece *the moment* in life-rafts, stimulating through sound, set, film and lighting a sense of physical discombobulation.

With brilliant clinical detachment, Qasim suggested that one of the ways to actually show the gut at work in a live performance situation would be to intubate one of us anally during the show and project the images via live feed from the gut. Although we could imagine anal intubation going down pretty well in Live Art circles, this wasn't exactly the angle on 'gut feelings' we had in mind for an immersive theatre experience. Audience members who found the ultrasound 'gut reading' we perform in the show slightly unnerving had no idea how far things could have gone.

In many ways the lab culture of the Wingate was closer to our work than that of NCBS, quite literally because it was on the same street in London, but also in terms of process, drawing on far more quantitative methods. In work at the Wingate human experiences and emotions are central, inseparable from the empirical knowledge they seek and produce. Researchers at the Wingate already worked daily with human subjects, regularly asked people about their experiences and feelings, and relied on active participation. Because of the participatory (and human) nature of the work at Wingate, it was slightly harder to see the areas where our processes may have influenced each other than at the NCBS where the radical differences between us 'jogged' each other's imagination. Our sense was that the most interesting aspect of our project to the Wingate researchers was in our Autobiology workshops with artists, a series of workshops and courses detailed in the next chapter, 'In the Studio'.

7   In the Studio: A Case Study in Performance-Making Methods

Teaching workshops and courses in performance-making to artists and students has been a sustained and vital part of our creative work. Our teaching is implicitly connected to who we are as makers, and within our workshops we share a variety of creative processes, techniques and exercises that we have conceived, refined and reinvented over the years.

As artists and as teachers one of the most valuable outcomes of the creative and scientific research work with gut feelings was the development of a generative performance-making method for artists we called Autobiology. Autobiology was a creative-workshop process that focused on the generation of autobiographical material through body-memory processes, exploring the connections between the body and the mind, biology and biography, and drawing on the impulses and associations of 'gut feelings' (Illustration 7.1). The name of the method/workshop comes from a mélange of autobiography, biology and autonomic nervous system.[1]

The aim of Autobiology was to offer workshops comprised of exercises and techniques that enhance the artist's consciousness of the relationship between their psyche and soma, biography and biology, and which combined scientific research with the practical application of techniques in the studio. These were exercises that we had been doing ourselves as part of creating the performance *the moment I saw you I knew I could love you* that we wanted to share with other practitioners. Autobiology ran as intensive week-long workshops, once in Taiwan and four times in the United Kingdom in 2008–09, presented as an 'autobiological workshop exploring the connections between the body and the mind, biology and biography, drawing on participants' "gut feelings" and generating autobiographical material "straight from the heart"'. Participants were drawn from emerging and established artists, teachers and post-graduate students. They came from a diverse range of artistic backgrounds: dance, live art, theatre, stand-up, directing, installation, sound art, visual art, and all had a sense of their own creative practice. Some, though not

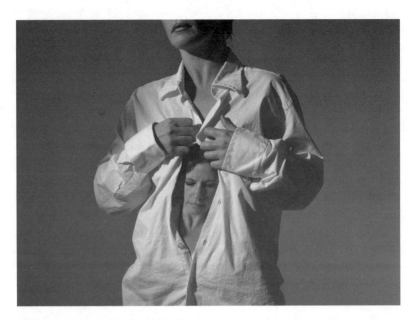

Illustration 7.1 'Gut feelings'
[Photo by Hugo Glendinning]

all, had past training in body-mind practices such as yoga or ayurvedic massage, some had previous training in psychology or art therapy, other participants were dealing with chronic illnesses and wanted to explore some of their experiences within the frame of the workshop.

The UK workshops took place in the Arnolfini in Bristol, in the Tramway, Glasgow, as part of New Territories Winter School, and twice at Toynbee Studios in London, which saw the pilot of Autobiology supported by the Live Art Development Agency's DIY scheme. Autobiology also travelled to Taipei, Taiwan, as part of the 2008 Taiwan Women's Theatre Festival. Autobiology has since been developed into a semester-long university course which we taught at the University of Wisconsin-Madison (2010), and at Stanford University (2011). Both the week-long version of Autobiology and the semester- or quarter-based university course structures provided different but equally meaningful timeframes in which to explore autobiographical and 'autobiological' work. The week-long courses allowed for an intensity and focus, which accumulated over each of the full days giving a particular immersion, force and viscerality to the work and enabling participants to take greater risks both in form and content. The longer university course timeframes of the semester and the quarter enabled thoughts and ideas to be more fully developed into more ambitious pieces and gave time for greater reading and research around the subject.

Within the Autobiology workshop explorations included: examining notions of self and authorship; investigating resemblances and mannerisms; working with body awareness and responsivity; creating maps and soundscapes of the body; experimenting with medical equipment and biofeedback; working with prompts such as 'body memory', 'parts of the body invisible to the naked eye', and 'gut feelings'. Participants generated a large and diverse body of text, gesture, image, drawings, film, live performances and installation. Because we were interested in working with impulse and engaging with the body on an instinctual responsive level, the first few days of the workshop were about generating a lot of material – written, verbal, physical – very rapidly. For some people, producing micropieces quickly from impulse is a challenging, even frightening, way of working and can take a while to feel comfortable with. To create work rapidly on the fly and then share it with a group demands that we find a way to silence the censorial voice within us that urges us to stop, cross out, cut, delete, re-do. Some of the participants who found this way of working terrifying at first, found it extremely liberating once they broke through the fear threshold. We asked people to keep a 'table of contents' of all the work they made (Illustration 7.2). At the end of the week, many participants were stunned by how prolific they had been.

After the workshop we asked participants to respond to three questions:[2]

- What was your experience of Autobiology?
- Can you briefly describe how you experienced working with gut feelings? What particular images, texts, memories or ideas were generated from the gut?
- Is this a methodology or way of working you might incorporate into your practice in the future?

Many participants commented on the impulsive, unedited nature of the work, both in terms of their own responses to exercise prompts, and in giving feedback or performative responses to other people's work. The rapid-fire provocations encouraged participants to 'go for it',

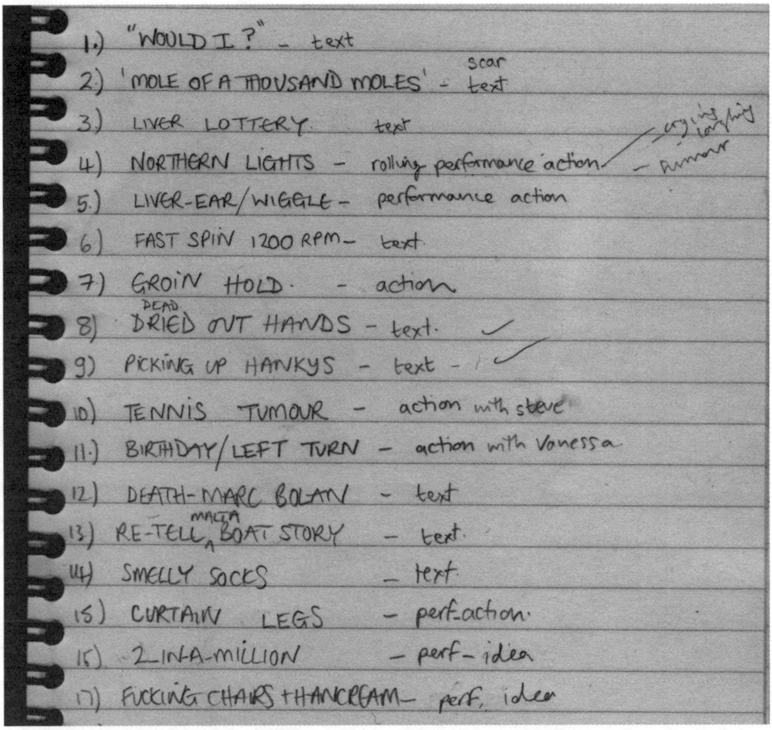

Illustration 7.2   Table of contents, Ange Taggart
[Photo by Leslie Hill]

eliminating an over-editing or 'preciousness' and enabling rather than disabling impulsive and from-the-gut responses, giving them validity.[3]

Automatic writing was particularly resonant within a workshop focused on impulse and gut feelings. Alongside daily yoga, the writing became a very fruitful way of opening mind and body, of surprising the self. As facilitators our intention, as with every creative class or workshop, was to create a safe space wherein participants gave themselves and each other permission to try, to fail, to play and to experiment. Participants expressed a pleasure in working collaboratively on autobiographic material, usually a solo journey troubled by anxieties about 'indulgence'. A great legacy from Autobiology is that many of the ideas and microperformances that surfaced through the workshops (Illustration 7.3) have been developed into fully formed

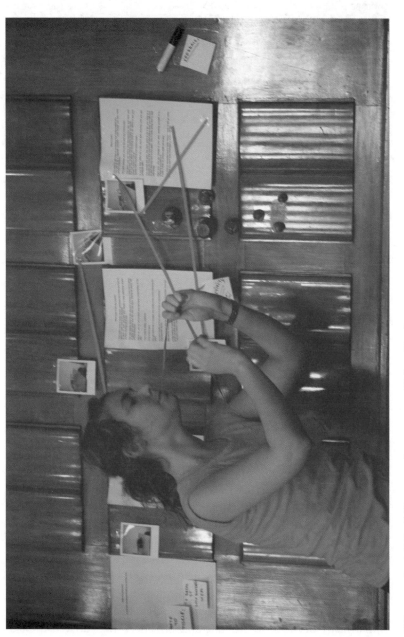

Illustration 7.3 Microperformance, Chloe Dechery

[Photo by Leslie Hill]

performances. Participants have taken, adapted and developed Autobiology exercises, integrating them into their own practice (Illustration 7.4).

First I plan to incorporate some movements/sounds/sensations from the workshop into my upcoming performance. Secondly in my lecturing work: I would like to start my teaching next year on Solo Performance Practice from the gut, rather than the mind.

Not only could I dig into my own creativity and stimulate the dialogue between my bodily experience and my thoughts but it also gave me the chance to explore new tools that I can further use to enhance my creative process, to devise further art works as well as pass them onto others in my teaching. Being formally trained as a dancer and working today as a shiatsu massage practitioner together with my artistic practice, it has helped me to draw connections between those various activities I perform in my daily life, from the sensitive perception to the release of creativity.

The inside story

The exercises in Autobiology were an amalgam of techniques we have used in Curious over the years, such as automatic writing, working with body memory, mixed with exercises specifically designed to work 'autobiologically': connecting with the autonomic nervous system; working creatively with fight, flight and freeze reactions; playing with simple forms of biofeedback to delve into the links between biology and biography. Although each week-long workshop followed a similar trajectory, we allowed ourselves to be responsive to the dynamic and make-up of each group and during the week made changes or adaptations to the exercises. What follows are some examples of activities that were part of the Autobiology workshop.

Yoga

Each day of the workshop the group were led through a series of yoga exercises. We did a mixture of dynamic and more passive poses and worked on holding postures for sustained periods of time. In her book, *Insight Yoga*, yoga practitioner and teacher Sarah Powers writes that the five organs of the kidney, liver, spleen, lung and heart:

Are connected with five basic emotions that directly affect how we experience our world. Each intense emotion we feel directly affects

Illustration 7.4 Body map, Yoko Ishiguro

[Photo by Leslie Hill]

our meridians and organs [...] When out of balance, the kidneys are linked with fear and terror, the liver with anger and envy, the spleen with obsession and worry, the lungs with sadness and grief and the heart with hatred or depression [...] Yin practice allows us the space to fully metabolize emotions we often ingest but cannot completely digest.

(2008, pp. 29–30)

Powers structure sequences around poses that stimulate meridians connected to specific organs. Whatever one's personal belief or experience in these matters, on a basic level a daily practice given over to moving through a series of specific yoga poses, focusing on breath and the body, on awareness and energy was unanimously deemed beneficial by all workshop participants. At its most basic it acted as a warm-up, facilitated group connection and bonding, and gave time to connect and focus on the body. As someone who has practised yoga for over a decade, felt its benefits physically and emotionally and who has incorporated Yin Yoga and Powers's teaching into my own practice, I (Helen) am intrigued by the possibilities this work offers a creative process in terms of exploring body and cellular memory and emotion 'held' in the body. Following Powers's sequences I designed daily yoga exercises around specific organ groupings in connection to what we would explore that day. For example, when we were working with gut feelings we did a series of exercises specifically connected to the stomach and spleen; when we worked on the autonomic nervous systems and reactions of flight, fright and freeze we did poses that focused on the lungs. For the purposes of this workshop we wanted to create conditions where people could bring emotions and memory to the surface in order to work creatively with them. We would come straight out of the physical practice directly into a creative exercise, explicitly uniting the physical with the creative.

I find the crossing of science and art an interesting and fertile area. I was very pleased to work in a focused way using different methods to generate material for performance. I found the yoga extremely effective for getting in touch with the body and accessing a flow of thoughts and feelings.

Interviews

We filmed a short interview with each Autobiology participant during which they were asked these two questions:

• Where is the body-mind connection most apparent in your creative process?
• Can you describe a time in your life you've experienced a strong 'gut feeling'?

As discussed previously, and indeed again in detail in the next chapter, 'In Situ', questioning is a very familiar method in our practice. Within this workshop we were more interested in making a deliberate, somewhat formal space for the questions and answers than working with the footage afterwards or using it for any kind of qualitative research. We wanted to give each participant time to reflect on, articulate and share within the group their specific creative ways of working with and through conscious body-mind connections. For some, working with psyche and soma was implicit rather than explicit within their practice, but in describing it they made manifest some real connections between mind and body. For others working with the body and body awareness was the mainstay of their practice. To some this way of working was completely new. The act of speaking into the camera focused the language around practice and generated a particular kind of paying attention, both of the speaker to her words and of the audience around the camera watching and listening. The camera heightens physiological awareness, both by the audience and by the speaker who might start to fiddle more, or shift from side to side, or even perspire a little, or exhibit signs of nervousness both in terms of speech pattern and physical carriage. The 'absent' body becomes very present in this moment of being looked at and recorded – a symbiotic form and content relationship in this terrain of questioning gut feelings.

Automatic writing – fight, flight, freeze

Write for five minutes on each of these words FIGHT / FLIGHT / FREEZE. In automatic writing mode, try not to take your pen off the paper. Write with your whole body engaged. If you 'freeze' keep the pen moving across the paper, whatever comes out.

Take a moment to read each of your automatic writing responses through. Underline words, fragments, sentences that you are interested in. Perhaps they surprised you, or you are curious to take them further or you are particularly pleased or shocked by them.

Consider what response is most natural to you in a traumatic or emotionally charged situation. Although individuals usually experience each of these reactions at some point – fight, flight and freeze – people tend to have predispositions to a default reaction, 'fighters' or 'freezers'. Consider which response you think is your default. Work with the text you underlined from that response. Familiarize yourself with it so you don't need to read it. Put the words in your body. Find a gesture from the words. Create a small performance moment.

I have also found a poetic written language surfacing during automatic writing, which demonstrates clearly the trust between what you instinctively create and structured ideas. I have begun to use this to generate words/text, and allowing the patterns to emerge organically. This way of creating text gives my writing an interesting rhythm, something I wasn't aware I could do.

Body memory

Lie on the floor in a state of relaxation and awareness of the body. Regulate your breathing so that you take equal-length inhales and equal-length exhales, feeling the air move in, through and out of your body. Focus on your body on the floor. Be aware of its temperature, its length, and the shape and space it takes up. Turn your attention inside. Be aware of the warmth of the blood, the density of the bones, the muscles, and the organs. Think about the part of the body where you recognize yourself, where you really know yourself. It can be internal or external. Perhaps it is where you carry your tension, or your anger or where you feel you most strongly exist emotionally. It might be a site of pain or pleasure. Try and go with your first impulse and to focus on this part of your body. Focus all your attention on this part of the body. Think about its shape, its texture, its colour, and its weight. See it up close. Now see it at a distance. Try not to censor yourself, allow yourself this moment and this task of really focusing in on one part of yourself.

Feel the impulse for movement from this part of the body. Let the movement come from the body part you have chosen, don't think what it might be, feel what it is. Don't rush. Let the movement develop slowly. It might be very small at first, it might repeat or it might extend into another movement. Keep your focus internal and allow yourself to respond to this impetus for movement. Take some time to find the movement and when you have the movement, explore its dimensions. Does it travel? Perhaps it repeats, does its tempo change? How does the movement affect the rest of the body? How does the rest of the body join in?

As you explore the movement start to be aware of the sounds generated by this movement. Again try not to think what they might be, but instead allow yourself to experience what they are. What kind of sound is it? What is the range of this sound? How does moving change or affect the sound. Try not to feel self-conscious. Give yourself permission to explore this sound. If you lose focus come back to that part of the body you chose, remind yourself of its shape, its texture, of the memories or feelings it might hold and come back to the movement, and through the movement discover what sounds come.

Keep exploring the sound and movement you have found and let them lead you to words. Be aware of any words or phrases that come from the sound and movement and start to include them. Don't over-think or pre-plan. Let yourself be surprised by what words come. Try not to censor, be surprised by yourself. If you lose concentration or become self-conscious, take your attention back to the part of the body you have chosen to work with and focus there. Don't force yourself to make sense. The text may be fragmentary, repetitive, obtuse or unfamiliar.

Now start to develop a small performance moment with this sound, movement and text you have created. Try and stay with it in your body rather than planning it out or writing it down.

The workshop exercises were provocative and presented different ways of inter-rogating the body as a source of creative material – notions of cellular memories, genetic encoding and kinetic stories were explored. Senses were examined as a source for narratives which provided a unique position to begin generating written and physical texts. The use of yoga was exceptionally interesting because as you became aware of the body it became a mnemonic – stories, memories and recollections hidden within the everyday body were stimulated to the surface through the physical exercise. There was a spaciousness that permitted the body to speak and, most importantly, be heard.

I feel these exercises particularly tapped into the gut, encouraging an instinctive way of working. In the body memory exercise in particular I experienced a particular connection between mind and body and felt my body was 'moved' rather than consciously 'moving'. I was surprised that unintended words arose vocally.

Gut manifestation

Yoga Poses prior to writing: Butterfly pose, full forward bend, Dragon pose.

Write a story about a time in your life when you felt an emotion in your gut (fear, anger, surprise, attraction). Remember the visceral experience in your body. What happened? What were the sensations you felt (heat, sweat, taste, smell, racing heart)? Record this experience as accurately as possible. Don't censor. As fully as possible write this experience down, including everything that took place before, during and after.

Find a way of manifesting this experience as fully as possible to engender a similar response for your audience. (Manifesting a gut feeling is a challenging task. For this exercise, we usually asked participants to do the writing one day and bring in the 'manifestation' one or two days later so that they had more time to let their ideas percolate.)

The workshop was uncanny in how relevant and appropriate an experience it was for me on a personal and professional level. I've dealt with sensitive guts for years so I became consciously detached from them, observing them through a filter of medical terminology and food intolerances. This proved to be a big mistake. The revelation that the stomach has its own nervous system, a rudimentary brain, is such a pivot to how I now approach my guts. It's so interesting that stomach problems are so prevalent in the modern world and I think that the potential for a workshop such as this to have an important resonance with people on a purely personal level is really huge.

I guess there is a 'calm waters' sort of feeling in the top of my stomach (diaphragm) area and also I'm sensitive to feelings in my throat and chest (even if it's quite deep down and masked by conflicting or overlaid thoughts – but it's still there underneath that – and asking gently seems to get an answer. Conversely, when something doesn't feel 'right' it's much more of a choppy sea, and a feeling of ants in my body – a twitchiness and an uncomfortability and 'things being out of place'-ness, like the feeling I get when my house is quite untidy.

The invisible body

Before coming to the workshop each participant received a letter that read:

Dear Autobiology participant,

Please bring with you some sort of 'information' about your body that is invisible to the naked eye (for example, this might be an X-ray, heart-rate printout or a secret piece of information, a text, an image...).

We had various sound and image-recording devices available including radio mics, several medical instruments including stethoscopes, thermometers, ophthalmometers and sphygmometers as well as the portable ultrasound device we were working with for '*the moment I saw you I knew I could love you*'. Participants were asked to think about and experiment with soundscapes of the body, getting various signals from the body – secrets (and lies) that the body tells and holds. After working together physically with these devices, individuals then shared their 'invisible information' (Illustrations 7.5 and 7.6) with their small group of three or four people.

The groups then created a performance in response to each person's invisible information. The person the group was responding to would wait outside for about ten minutes while the other two or three made the performance, then they would come back and be an audience of one to a piece made just for them, inspired by their invisible information.

I found it surprising how possible it was to tap into memories, both recent and past, by recollecting a particular gut feeling. And that these invoked memories were full of detail – extending into remembering sensations of touch, smell, temperature and taste. The body memory exercise on the first day I found

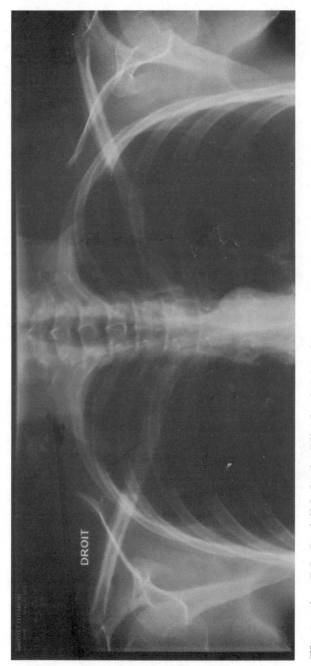

Illustration 7.5 Invisible body, Elizabeth Wautlet

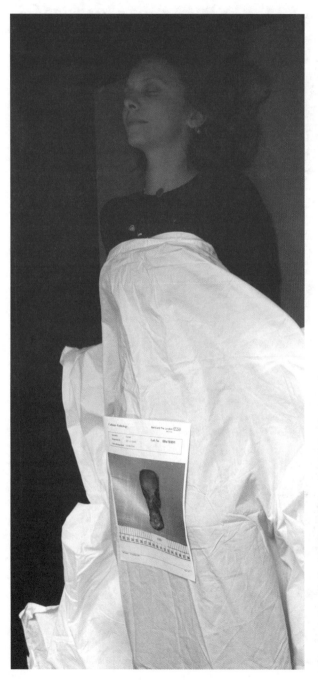

Illustration 7.6 Invisible body, Natasha Davis

[Ultrasound by Leslie Hill]

tough – trying not to self-censor but again the images, songs, words and rhythms generated/remembered seemed to come without my head being involved, which I found fascinating. Again, the automatic writing work seems to bypass your head and let you just write from somewhere else, perhaps the gut. So it was almost like spending a few days with this other bit of yourself who has a lot to say but who is usually ignored. Starting with the gut, rather than the head, put other parts of the body in focus, parts I would normally not think about so much. For example, working more with hands, fingers, arms. When working with other people's secret body information, I noticed the group came up with decisions about how to present them very fast and stayed with them, and they seemed authentic and truthful instincts to follow.

The Autobiology workshop inescapably engendered some work that could be challenging to make and to watch. Alongside the powerful, emotive and sometimes painful terrain of the work were issues around notions of self, authorship, 'universal traits', and issues of indulgence and of authenticity. Although we did make time for discussion, particularly in terms of strong reactions to performing/performances, it was also central to us to keep the work-making processes at the heart of the experience rather than lapsing into too much discussion. We worked with 'performative responses' as well as more discursive feedback in groups. Work would often be shown first in small groups and then the group would have a limited time to performatively respond to what they had experienced. As they quickly worked out a response to a person's story that person would remove themselves from the group. The groups performed the responses for each other and then shared a little time for feedback and reflection.

We found the Autobiology workshop a rich way of working creatively with and from the body, both in our experiences as artists and as workshop facilitators and teachers. We witnessed extraordinary work in each of the workshops and were moved and inspired by the performances participants created. One of the things we both like most about teaching is witnessing and celebrating the moments of genius and inspiration, the beautiful fragments of performance experienced by just a few people, suddenly, unexpectedly in the middle of the afternoon in a black box or classroom. Fleeting, unrehearsed, just-made, rough gems constitute some of our favourite memories of performance. Autobiology was full of such moments and we are so grateful to all the artists we had the opportunity to work with.

Illustration 7.7   Autobiology

[Photo by Hugo Glendinning]

8   In Situ: Extended Conversations

As Curious, our starting point for any given project is always a question; the process of making the work is a timeline of wrestling with the question; and the end result (performance, film, installation) is a distillation of the process crafted into a work that is shared with an audience. In performance works like those discussed in the previous chapters, we normally find ways of opening our central questions up to the audience either directly or indirectly within the performances so that the audience are, to some degree, co-investigators. The relationship in performance events is one of inviting people into an environment or a situation you have created or orchestrated, inviting them to consider some of the same thoughts and experiences you have been working with. The invitation in these instances comes at the end of the process where there is a piece to share, a location to gather at, a text to be performed, a film to watch, sensations to experience. This chapter, however, looks at proximity in relation to exchanges that happen in reverse order as part of the process rather than as part of the performance.

In his book *39 Microlectures: in Proximity of Performance*, Matthew Goulish quotes the MIT Physics Professor, Victor Weisskopf, as saying: 'We must always begin by asking questions, not giving answers. In this way we contribute to the joy of insight. For science is the opposite of knowledge. Science is curiosity' (Goulish, 2000, p. 55). We love the quote, but by the same token would add that art is not exactly the opposite of knowledge, as people sometimes suppose. Weisskopf's statement is powerful precisely because he knows that people generally do associate science with knowledge. Processes of inquiry, of asking questions, of approaching the same question from many different angles, is a practice of seeking knowledge common to all fields. Seeking is not the same as attaining, of course, but Weisskopf is talking about process not outcome. He is talking about a lifestyle, a practice, a mindset rather than a result, a publication or a clinical trial result. This chapter is about the practice of questioning that runs across our work and ways of sharing these questions through work in wider communities of people than theatre audiences.

We work on projects by asking questions; opening out the process of questioning is a way of working on a wider pitch than just our studio. Asking other people the same questions we ask ourselves invites other expertise, hunches, intuitions and experiences from different perspectives. We ask questions because we are genuinely curious about what people think and feel about different subjects. In some ways this process is like a very eclectic, partial and prejudiced education, in some ways it's like a holiday from our own thoughts and thought processes. Like people in any field, we are interested in the ways in which other people approach the same questions and topics – what they think and how they arrived there. We have always enjoyed the research element of working on projects, but we don't tend to think of our question-based conversations with people as 'research' per se, rather we tend to think of the people we talk to as co-investigators or fellow explorers, even if only on a small scale.

Looking back, some patterns emerge as to the types of questions we ask. We ask lots of questions about place (*I never go anywhere I can't drive myself, Seaside Towns Project, Lost & Found, (be)longing, 14 Lines* and *Out of Water*); we ask a lot of questions about bodies, the senses and cognition (*Vena Amoris, On the Scent, Essences of London* and *the moment I saw you I knew I could love you*); and we ask lots of questions about violence (*Three Semi-Automatics Just for Fun, Family Hold Back, Smoking Gun,* the *Greenham Project*). In this section we talk about some of the ways we share artistic inquiry with different communities of people by inviting them to participate in various projects.

We've spent at least as much time on Curious projects working outside theatres as inside them. Going out into different communities we often encounter a totally different range of people than we would ever meet in our audiences, through seeking them out in their own haunts and habitats, in situ. The collections of people we interact with are sometimes geographic, sometimes occupational and sometimes accidental. They are sometimes formal, such as local clubs or national associations, and sometimes informal – the people we meet in a certain place of interest or the people who answer an open call for participants. For us, the through-line of a shared question running across a group of people constitutes a series of interactions as episodes within the context of a particular project (rather than purely conversational), whether we encounter people by design or through chance. We have always considered it important to frame our questions, however briefly, within the contexts of the projects, so that people understand that they are choosing (or not) to participate in an art project. More often than not we ask permission to record people and if we think there is a possibility we might want to use recorded footage, we ask participants to make a choice about signing release forms.[1] Each person who chooses to engage with a question enters the project on some level.

Our questions are usually fairly simple and open, which probably stems back to our very first project *I never go anywhere I can't drive myself* (1997).[2] When travelling from Chicago to Los Angeles along Route 66 it was the elderly roadside inhabitants who always asked us the same two questions: 'Where do you come from?' and 'Where are you going?' Through answering those same two questions over and over again across Illinois, Oklahoma, New Mexico and California to all the different people in those little roadside towns, we began to understand how this process of asking and listening to the same question, answered by a series of different people, could become a work in and of itself. The Route 66 natives had spent long lifetimes watching people pass through their diners and gas stations and kept on asking those same two questions and listening to the answers. The process, it seemed, was part of their life's work.

Sometimes this open-ended questioning makes for fascinating conversation around a project, but doesn't necessarily leave any tangible trace on the work as seen in performance. In other projects we've produced stand-alone companion pieces, drawing directly from interview material. In this chapter we'll discuss three projects where we produced DVDs with community interview material alongside performance works: *Essences of London* (2004), *Lost & Found* (2005) and *(be)longing* (2007).

Essences of London

Essences of London (2004) was a companion project to *On the Scent*, in which we set out to create a composite portrait of London by capturing essences of the city through the sense of smell. For this project, we interviewed residents of inner and outer London boroughs (Brent, Newham, Tower Hamlets, Lambeth and Hackney). We interviewed hundreds of Londoners about their personal smell associations, including workers in 'aromatic trades' such as cobblers, fishmongers, florists, bakers and pie-and-mash shop proprietors, and rubbish collectors. We worked with groups from the Well Centre Coffee Morning in Newham to the East Ham Youth Boxing Club to the refuse collection depot in Alperton and many more clubs, small businesses, adult education classes, senior centres and youth groups, as well as working with local festivals such as the Bow Festival in East London and Brent Respect Week in West London. From this, we produced a project DVD with two hours' worth of interview material from across the city, which was distributed individually to all the people and community groups featured on the DVD (approximately 120 people). During filming, the documentary project provoked a huge amount of discussion and reflection between individuals, generating interesting and often very moving material. An interview with one market-stall owner in Dalston, for example, spread to five surrounding stalls and continued through an entire morning.

Probably the most fascinating and least anticipated outcome of recording and editing the interviews for *Essences of London* was coming to understand just what a huge role ethnicity and age play in people's sense of their olfactory environment when trying to categorize or describe a city as vast and diverse as Greater London. In the edit suite going through the clips, we could have easily edited the material into a feature-length documentary about London in relation to different influxes of immigration since the Second World War, and a viewing audience would have had no idea that the respondents were all answering questions about the sense of smell. In the East End people talked about the smell of South Asian cooking. In Brent people talked about the smell of West Indian cooking. For older Londoners in particular, the smells of ethnic cooking symbolize the dramatic changes in the city's population over the last few decades. Londoners in their eighties and nineties talked about how overpowering they found the smell of garlic when workers began immigrating from Italy and Greece in the 1940s. Most people cite the array of different cooking smells in London as a positive sign of a cosmopolitan city, but we also heard a couple of shockingly racist comments about the 'stench' of ethnic cooking. The overwhelming majority of Londoners we spoke to, however, welcome olfactory diversity. A woman in her nineties told us:

> There's an Asian family living next door to me on my estate and I don't have nothing to do with them and they don't have nothing to do with me,

but I can smell their cooking and it smells so lovely that sometimes I really wish they would invite me in!

For us, her comment typifies much of the attitude we encountered in relation to people's obviously high awareness of 'olfactory otherness' – an awareness of being simultaneously inside and outside cultures within local communities. In the Polish community in North London, Polish immigrants told us that London smells like Turkish food because of the many kebab shops. Vietnamese pensioners at An Viet House Community Centre in Hackney told us that to them London smells like hamburgers and hot dogs. West Indians in Brent said that London smells of fried chicken. People who have grown up in more culturally homogenous environments, whether native Londoners or immigrants, seem to notice ethnic differences in cooking smells much more keenly than younger generations of Londoners who have grown up in more cosmopolitan smell-surroundings.

Some of the immigrants we interviewed noted smells that stood out for them when they first arrived in London. At a women's flower arranging club, a Bangladeshi women told us of the magical experience of arriving in a strange new cold country and smelling roasting chestnuts for the first time during the Christmas season. Another Bangladeshi woman described moving into a flat near a McVitie's biscuit factory and feeling pleasantly surrounded by this strange, delicious smell. A man we met at the Kurdish Cultural Centre, who sought asylum in the United Kingdom after the chemical attack on Halabja in 1988, welled up as he told us that his most precious smell memory of London was of a chicken casserole his next-door neighbours brought his family to welcome them to the neighbourhood when they first arrived. The dish, probably a commonplace recipe to the neighbours, was strange and exotic to his family. The aroma of the dish became the smell of welcome, of safety, of home and 20 years later he says that when he catches a whiff of the chicken casserole dish, it still moves him profoundly.

As well as ethnicity, age turned out to be a major factor in people's olfactory impressions of London. One of the many groups we worked with on the project was a retirement centre in Newham, where we interviewed East Enders in their sixties to nineties, almost all of whom were white British. For this group, there were two different Londons in terms of smell-scape, the old London of 'the smokes' or 'the Big Smoke' with the factory fumes and 'pea soupers' caused by industrial smoke; and the new London which they described over and over again as smelling of 'nothing'. In the old London, houses were heated with coal fires and East London smelled like heavy industry, such as the overpowering odours from the Beckton Gas Works or the glue factories. The air was heavy and cokey. In the new homes, they complained, the central heating doesn't smell of anything. Where younger Londoners frequently cited petrol and exhaust fumes as one of the characteristic unpleasant smells of the city, the older Londoners described present-day London as either smelling clean and sanitized or simply of nothing. Although they spoke with nostalgia for coal fires in the homes, by and large these old East Enders thought it was wonderful that the air was so much cleaner, impressing upon us over and over how foul and pungent the air was a few decades ago, talking about how some days they would have to walk to work with their hands over their noses and mouths. A refuse truck driver we interviewed nostalgically remembered being a boy and going on a working holiday hop-picking in Kent for two weeks. His voice cracked slightly as he told us: 'You can't imagine what it was like to be ten years old and smell fresh air for the first time.' Again, the olfactory is uniquely linked to emotions as well as memories, and in hearing people relate their memories we could often palpably feel the emotion.

On the Scent focused on the domestic, both in the form of the performance itself and the questions we asked people around smell and memory. In *Essences of London*, by taking on the semi-impossible task of creating a smell portrait of one of the world's largest cities we discovered, sometimes to our alarm, much more about the politics of smell in terms of different communities living in close proximity as well as the politics of smell and class. Our investigations were not scientific or sociological. We were not attempting to prove a theory or produce empirical evidence. Our cross-sections of people were not assembled in relation to the census and proportional representation of different ages, incomes or ethnicities. The project was a portrait, not a quantitative study; still, we learned a lot about the city and the sense of smell.

Essences of London re-mapped our sense of the city of London as well as teaching us a lot about the sense of smell that we wouldn't have learned in Upi's lab at the National Centre for Biological Sciences or through performing *On the Scent* with its domestic focus. Through working on this project, we also encountered hundreds of people who would probably never have come to see an experimental theatre piece like *On the Scent*. Because we scheduled performances in the London boroughs where we conducted the interviews, we were able to reach out to a much less rarefied 'live art' audience. For our performances of *On the Scent* in the boroughs, 75 per cent of the audiences were local. All of these elements made the project rewarding for us – sharing an interest in the sense of smell across a diverse cross-section of people and widening our own experiences as well as bringing work to new audiences.

Lost & Found

Working in areas that were being violently regenerated, we asked residents of East London, the Black Country (United Kingdom) and Shanghai (China), 'What have you lost?' and 'What have you found?' in your own neighbourhoods. The concept of 'regeneration' is often used by government agencies and spokespeople as representing an uncomplicated positive opportunity for a community that will bring them new houses, new jobs, new wealth and new amenities. In using the term 'violently regenerated', we are recognizing that the three communities we worked in were being regenerated without much, if any, input from local residents and that the new houses, new jobs and new wealth were not for them, but for the new people who would move into the areas after the regeneration took place. In this section we'll focus on the Shanghai project, as the Black Country project is discussed in the 'Landscape' section and Helen writes about some of the work in London in the 'In the Lab and Incognito' chapter.

We started the project in Shanghai, working on site over the summer of 2004. We were living in a housing development called 'Brilliant City' near the Suzhou Creek artists' quarter of Shanghai at 50 Moganshan Road (莫干山路50号) as part of a British Council artist residency. We did a lot of filming downtown with our translator and accomplice art student Lee Xue Hue, who we asked to take us around some of the old neighbourhoods in the city. 'Better go today', she said, only half joking, as the old neighbourhoods were disappearing at a phenomenal rate. The first neighbourhood we visited had a large banner draped across the entrance to the street which Xue Hue translated as 'Cooperation with the government is important'. At the other end of the street there was a picture of the new high-rise development the area would soon become.

Along the street, life carried on as usual, people buying and selling vegetables, hanging out their washing, chatting with neighbours and so on. We stopped in a teashop and the owner told us about the neighbourhood's racy past as home to opium dens and brothels in the 1920s and 1930s. We asked him about the new development and he shrugged and said: 'Now they are employing migrant workers to pull down our houses and make apartments for foreigners.'

Asking residents in Shanghai 'What have you lost?' and 'What have you found?' didn't really elicit stories of findings or discoveries, but we were told many, many stories of loss, even by the young and successful 'A-Girls' with perfect English and good jobs. Yvonne (her English name) said she wanted us to come and meet her in town after work. She said she had something to show us. She came gliding out of a shopping centre that could have been in Beverly Hills or Monte Carlo, all Gucci and Armani and marble and gold. We wondered what could possibly be of interest here. She spun on her low heels and gestured expansively around, taking in the whole complex and said, 'I was born here. Yes. I was born here.' It turned out that her family's neighbourhood was torn down to make way for the shopping mall. She gestured, 'Here used to be a tree. It was so tall I could touch the leaves from my uncle's window on the third floor. When I lived here I could afford everything on this street – snacks, groceries, little things for the house. Now I can afford nothing.' She laughed and said it again with emphasis: 'I can afford *nothing*.' There was scaffolding all around a group of buildings across the road. She said, 'That is the last of the old being torn down. After that, nothing old. Everything is new.'

Dorina (her English name) told us that she also grew up in the old lanes in Shanghai. She said that since there was no air-conditioning, in the hot months people would just move the entire household outside, the children playing, the women gossiping and the men playing Chinese chess, people cooking and washing outdoors like a giant urban campsite. She was proud to have been taught Chinese chess by her uncle and allowed to play this serious game with the men. Now with the air-conditioning available in all the apartments, she said, 'everyone stays inside and watches TV and you can't find anyone to play chess with anymore.'

We made a short film called *Red Lantern House* over the summer in Shanghai as part of the *Lost & Found* project. The film took its name from a house we noticed when we first arrived in Shanghai. It stood at an intersection where the taxis sometimes stopped at the lights and, sitting in the back of the car, we noticed the splash of red amidst the grey rubble of a construction site. The house must have been grand once but by the time we saw it most of the exterior walls had been torn away. Just one little corner remained intact with a ceiling and four walls and over the door someone had painted a banner and strung a row of red lanterns. Xue Hue told us that the words on the banner offered a wish for a smooth journey through life. The house was the last remaining trace of a neighbourhood that had been demolished to make way for more high-rise apartment complexes, much like the Brilliant City complex where we lived on the 36th floor. Every time we went back and forth from Brilliant City into the centre of Shanghai, we saw the construction work encroaching further and further on the Red Lantern House. One day we decided to try and visit. We stood on the path in front of the house and waited to see if someone would notice us. Almost immediately a mother and her grown-up son came out. They seemed delighted to see us, perhaps because we had a conspicuously sized broadcast camera with us, and the mother asked if we would take pictures of the house for them while it was still standing (Illustration 8.1). She told us that all the neighbours had moved on, but that she wanted to stay with the house until the very end. We asked her about the lanterns and she said it was important for the house to look its best in its final weeks and days. 'There's a traffic light here', she gestured, 'people stop their cars and look: it's important.' We asked her what would happen to her when the house was knocked down. She said the government was rehousing her in an apartment that she thought was about two hours from Shanghai by bus. The new high-rises definitely weren't being built to house the people whose homes had been torn down to make room for them. We managed to get a rough edit of the film together in our makeshift edit suite the night before our flight and took a taxi over to the Red Lantern House and gave them a copy of it and a DVD player so they could take the images of the house with them when they were moved on. She and her son watched themselves on the television, fascinated and then the mother said: 'This is art.' Or at least that's how Xue Hue translated it.

In the Black Country and the East End the stories were also overwhelmingly about loss. Like Dorina's story about life in the lanes and Chinese chess, people spoke nostalgically of times in the not-so-distant past when people could leave their doors unlocked and neighbours knew

Illustration 8.1 Red Lantern House, Shanghai
[Photo by Leslie Hill]

each other and kids ran in and out of each other's houses. In the Black Country and London's East End, as in Shanghai, buildings were being torn down, but the main sense of loss here was a mourning for a past characterized by a more coherent feeling of community, of knowing the neighbours, of feeling part of a wider social group. If we hadn't known it well enough before we started, this project hammered home to us that regeneration isn't generally for locals, as well as underscoring the complex webs of relationships that must have space to grow in order to form meaningful neighbourhoods and communities.

(be)longing

In 2005 Antonia Fraser, then Director of The Women's Library in London, approached us about undertaking a commission for an exhibition on Prostitution they planned to mount in 2006 to mark the centenary of the death of Josephine Butler, the Victorian social reformer and campaigner for the rights of prostituted women. The exhibition was envisioned as a way to examine questions Butler raised about prostitution, sexual exploitation and trafficking, both in her own time and in a modern context. One of the aims was to bring together historical material from the collections of The Women's Library and other lenders alongside artist works, maps and objects to highlight the complexity of concerns around present-day prostitution and trafficking. The Women's Library wanted us to work directly with sex workers in London to produce something, perhaps a film, for the exhibition.

One of our major questions in deciding whether or not to take the commission was: why us? What could we, with our particular style and methods, offer by way of an art project to sex workers themselves and later to audiences at an exhibition on prostitution? A project of this sort, we couldn't help thinking, had the potential to go badly wrong. Our main concern was: what would be in it for the women who participated? Would they have any interest in being part of an art project or an exhibition at The Women's Library? And if so, how would they want to be represented?

We knew immediately, instinctively, that if we did accept the commission, we didn't want to engage sex workers in any kind of documentary project where we asked them questions about prostitution. Following our own particular working method of shared questioning meant that we needed to find a question that we could all engage with – us as the artists, the sex workers as the participants, as well as the audience for the exhibition. We went back to The Women's Library and said we would undertake the commission on the understanding that we would never ask the women directly about the sex trade and therefore the material we could potentially contribute to the exhibition would not be directly issue based. We proposed to call the project *(be)longing* and to ask women, 'What do you long for' and 'Where do you belong?'[3] The Women's Library agreed, and we embarked on one of the most complex projects we have ever worked on.

The biggest challenge of the entire project was simply to make contact with different populations of sex workers. We found a network of outreach groups around London – charities such as homeless groups, drug and alcohol support or sexual health clinics, which seemed to have morphed into sex-worker support groups. Our Assistant Producer, Emmy Minton, began the process of contacting the groups via emails, phone calls and meetings and discovered the huge variety of different populations of sex workers – trafficked minors from Africa, trafficked adults from Eastern Europe, women who work from flats, women who service kerb-crawler routes to support crack addictions, and women who work occasionally to support expensive frock and handbag habits – as Emmy put it: 'Women who have choice and women who emphatically do not have a choice.' As Emmy quickly identified, all of these women needed different things and all would have different reasons for participating or not participating in the project.

The groups we ended up working with formally were: Providence Row Homeless Shelter,[4] the National Health Service's Open Doors Project and the National Society for the Prevention of Cruelty to Children's support group 'There to Here' for trafficked teenagers. Informally, we also worked with prostitutes and 'maids' in Soho, London's red-light district. Each of the four groups we worked with had very different primary needs. The primary need of the NSPCC 'There to Here' group, for example, was to be granted permanent asylum in the United Kingdom. The main reason they wanted to participate in our project was to give voice to their cause as asylum seekers desperately trying to build a life for themselves in the United Kingdom and wanting to be given a chance.[5] In stark contrast, the NHS 'Open Doors' group were sex workers, working from the streets to support drug addictions. Their primary need was staying alive, staying out of prison and being able to buy enough drugs to not get sick. They participated in the project because it was something interesting to do, as we ran weekly workshops at their drop-in centre.[6] The greatest need for women in the Providence Row group was either keeping or finding a home. Providence Row agreed to participate in the project because of their mission to provide 'meaningful activity and consolidation of progress for people who are on the pathway out of homelessness', and they count art workshops as an important staple of their programme. The strongest need for women working in brothels in Soho, or perhaps more accurately the primary thing they wanted from us, was simply to have a conversation with someone who wasn't interested in talking to them about sex. More than one woman in Soho turned away clients in order to continue talking and a couple of them offered to make us tea or lunch. So the types of work we did with the different groups, by necessity, was as bespoke as we could make it to who they were and why they were participating.

Though the four groups were very different from each other, the answers the women gave were very similar across all the groups. In fact, the audio recordings we took of women answering the question 'What do you long for?' could have come from women from any class, any walk of life: they said they longed for comfortable houses, good jobs, romantic love and children. The shorthand, repeated by so many of them, was 'normal life', though the younger women sometimes also expressed grander ambitions, such as being a supermodel-brain surgeon. One teenager said: 'I long to be the wisest person on earth.' When the women from Open Doors, Providence Row or the Soho brothels spoke of belonging they often recalled landscapes from childhood – cold, majestic, windswept beaches, or nostalgic scenes with family. The NSPCC group, however, answered this question very differently: they were focused on the present, not the past and they were all adamant that England was where they belonged.

The NSPCC group had very direct political aims and they wanted to participate in something high profile, something that might make a difference, so we decided to make a film with this group, whereas work with Open Doors and Providence Row had remained 'private view' simply for members of those communities and not for the public at large. In 2007 we shot and released a short 35 mm film called *(be)longing* with five young women from the NSPCC group (Illustration 8.2). We had the film launch at the Genesis Cinema in London, around the corner from the NSPCC offices, on 'home turf' for the girls. Emmy succeeded in getting several members of the Home Office and some prominent politicians to attend the premier and meet the

Illustration 8.2 *(be)longing*

[Photo by Nick Gordon Smith]

girls. All of the girls who appear in the film were granted permanent leave to live and work in the United Kingdom and some of them were brought in as immigration and asylum consultants to the Home Office. The visibility of the project had some direct, positive outcomes in line with what the girls longed for and where they felt they belonged.

In the meantime, back in our 'normal life', the fact that we were working with women in the sex trade over a long period of time was of enormous interest to people around us. We were asked so many questions about it that we decided to start methodically collecting questions. We ordered 25 small books and distributed them to friends and colleagues. On the cover each book said: 'If you could ask a sex worker one question, what would it be?' The idea was that each person would write down one question and then pass the book on to someone else or collect a series of questions from friends or students and on a certain date all the books would be returned to us. The hundreds of questions we collected made for what we thought was an interesting piece, provoking viewers to reflect on prostitution through the lens of the perceptions and preoccupations of 'everyday people' outside – in short, our own 'identity' as a society in relation to prostitution. This piece was displayed as part of the exhibition. We never asked the women we met any of the questions.

What is it to record someone's story, someone's longing or someone's image? And what is it to then make public those stories and images beyond the context in which they were shared? As Emmy constantly asked as an ethical interrogation or moral touchstone throughout the project, 'Who is it for?' The answer turned out to be different in each group – sometimes it was just for them and sometimes it was for a wider audience. This project really brought us back again and again to questions of the currency of recording, the responsibility of the recorder and the power of the editorial process. *(be)longing* was the most complex project we have ever worked on in terms of making contact, asking questions and decisions around framing material and bearing witness to identities and experiences.[7]

9   Before You Go

There is a natural human propensity to want to stare into the eye of another, or by extension of oneself, a desire to see seeing itself, as if the straining to see inside the little black center of the eye will reveal not only the secrets of the other, but of the totality of human vision… Looking closely into the eye, the first thing to be seen, indeed the only thing to be seeing, is one's own self-image.

(Bill Viola in Hall and Fifer, 1999, pp. 483–4)

The desire to see is a manifestation of the desire to be seen.

(Phelan, 1993, p. 18)

Thinking on these two statements I (Helen) recall an exercise I did in the Pocha Nostra[1] workshop entitled, *The Gaze, discovering the other 'others'*. In this exercise, Guillermo Gómez-Peña instructs participants to find a partner and stand facing them, looking into each other's eyes without blinking. He asks us to try and resist nervous impulses or staging any emotions. He says: 'The goal is very simple: to be present and open, to express the basic existential message with your gaze that goes something like, "We happen to be here today, to coincide on this strange planet and it's OK. We are here together sharing a moment in life and art. It's a pleasure to be here with you"' (Gómez-Peña and Sifuentes, 2011, p. 59). The seemingly simple set-up belies the extraordinary complexities of what takes place. We stand and look at our partners, look into their eyes and let them look back at us. This is an act of seeing, of looking, of being seen, of being seen seeing. Gómez-Peña quips, 'Imagine if we had all our political leaders in the room doing this – we could change the world ¿Qué no?' He is only half joking. At the beginning of the exercise my partner and I are positioned about two feet apart, in the space of Edward T. Hall's 'close phase', where 'one can hold or grasp the other person'. We could touch, but we don't. Gómez-Peña invites us to move closer, tells us to always maintain the eye contact, not lose sight of each other even for an instant. We obey. Slowly we draw close, closer. We redraw our own rules of looking, of seeing, of closeness. We move nearer still, until we are so close that the skin of our eyeballs almost touches. Uncanny proximities. Dizzying, discombobulating. The eyeball of my partner un-anchors, detaches, floats free, suspended in some light middle-air between us. I see it as my own. I see it is my own. I look into this hanging, suspended iris as if seeing myself in a camera aperture as a picture is taken over and over and I am still not sure whose picture it is, yours? Mine? Ours? I am immobilized, hypnotized by my/our pendulum eye. We are compulsively close, too close, and yet it seems physically impossible for me to move away. I feel like Alice once she has entered the Looking Glass world. The more she tries to climb the hill in the garden the more it eludes her, the more she focuses on it the more she loses sight of it. It is like this with you now, trying not to lose sight of you by looking too close.

When it is over I think hours must have passed. I look at my watch and discover it has been ten minutes. Proximity has expanded time, seconds into hours, me into you. I have to refocus my gaze, 'pull myself together'. But I am unravelled – where do I end and you begin? I think of the addictiveness of this contact, this communication, of looking and being seen. I ponder the ethics at stake in this face-to-face encounter. What is being demanded, by whom?

There is a rich history of one-to-one and small audience performances that are participatory, immersive and intimate, such as Barbara T. Smith's *Feed Me* (1973) or Fiona Templeton's *YOU – The City* (1988). What has ignited the current desire to make and to experience this type of performance? Who is driving the desire, artist or audience? You or me? Machon describes contemporary audiences keen to attend such works as yearning 'for genuine physical connection. A need to feel sensually and imaginatively alive' (Machon, 2013, p. 25). She argues that audience responses to immersive, intimate works reflect a 'genuine wish to make *human* contact, often with another human as much as with the work itself; an enthusiasm for undergoing experiences that both replace and accentuate the live(d) existence of the everyday world' (Machon, 2013, p. 25).

Within these close encounters what lets someone in and what keeps them at a distance? Humans are very good at navigating close encounters. Hall describes the far phase of intimate distance, between 6 and 18 inches, as the distance in which 'small blood vessels in the sclera are clearly perceived'. This is a distance too close for comfort in anything but an intimate encounter, and yet a closeness all too familiar in urban settings, such as the millions of strangers jammed against each other on the London Underground each day. In this context we are experts at keeping others shut out of our compressed but still personal space, deftly pulling the shutter of that already compressed space closer, sealing ourselves off, retreating within.

And yet... 'Come closer, closer still', we entreat our audiences.

We think of the fleeting moments of contact between audience and performer: the desire to look and to be seen; the desire to pay attention and for attention to be paid; and the desire to capture and still some small moment of contact. *We are here together sharing a moment in life and art. We happen to be here today, to coincide on this strange planet and it's OK... It's a pleasure to be here with you.* This desire for connection, intimacy even, manifests at some level in all the work we have made as Curious. Across all of these moments is an unspoken acknowledgment between performer and audience of the fleetingness of the encounter. These moments of connection, transitory as they are and indeed *must be,* are perhaps enough in themselves. Ultimately, for us, there is something implicitly *political* in small audience work that pays attention to the individual, focuses on the epic in the everyday and the extraordinary in the ordinary. Proximate performances function on a political level in terms of their form, in their commitment to paying attention to face-to-face encounters, and in the physical labour it takes to perform such works – labours of love. For us, proximate performance aspires towards Dolan's vision of utopia or Turner's sense of *communitas*:

> The moments in a theatre event or a ritual in which audiences or participants feel themselves become part of the whole in an organic, nearly spiritual way; spectators' individuality becomes finely attuned to those around them, and a cohesive if fleeting feeling of belonging to the group bathes the audience.
>
> (Dolan, 2005, p. 11)

This relationship, our close-up, is marked out in the before of our encounter. Without you here, I write the things I want to say to you. I imagine how I will say them. I imagine you with me. I imagine the qualities of the what and the how of our face to face. I am looking for something in this encounter. I am looking for the give and take of it.

What do I take away from our close-up when I remove myself to the stage, me in the light and you in the dark? What trace of our encounter lingers and becomes part of me and how I perform? What lingers for you in how you let yourself watch and listen? How do we hold onto a sense of the shift in our relationship as audience and performer and how do we carry that shift with us into our future encounters? How do you feel about me when I am once more at a distance?

The close-up presents itself before we meet, before the performance is made. It is always already shaping the text I write, altering its rhythm. The timbre of how I will say it is already forming its shape in my larynx. I already hear how it might sound, sense how the words might feel in my mouth. But in this encounter what should I call you – accomplice, companion, Ishmael? From spec-actor to emancipated spectator, from attendant to guest, from participant to percipient, all these namings move closer to encompass an active, fully sensate involvement. I find myself tethered here, on the page, to the prosaic moniker 'audience member' but in my head I whisper '*you*'.

It is you that makes me return, still, to return again, and again, hundreds of performances later to continue exploring the distance between us – the how close and the too close and the not close enough. I want to keep on meeting you in the realm of performance, in its dark shadows, at its invisible borders, within its strange interiors and at its sharp edges, in close-up and in long shot, in shifting proximities and curious encounters.

Appendix Curious Selected Works and Collaborations 1997–2013

Performance and installation

Best Before End (2013) A performance that begins in the moment just before the moment that changes everything. A poetic solo that explores the power and vulnerability of language and love. Music by Graeme Miller. Commissioned by and premiered at Colchester Arts Centre.

Falling into Place (2012) By Gretchen Schiller with Johnathan McCree and Helen Paris. An intimate 15-minute guided sound and video installation, where participants are invited to touch, catch and hold the traces of place with different custom-designed audiovisual furniture environments. Supported by Université Stendhal-Grenoble, Brunel University and the France-Stanford Grant. Premiered Université Stendhal-Grenoble in 2012 and then at PSi19, Stanford and Watermans, London in 2013.

Out of Water (2012) By Helen Paris and Caroline Wright, with sound-score by acclaimed composer Jocelyn Pook and singing by Laura Wright and Oo La Lume. Stories of endeavour, of swimming, of sinking, interweave with haunting music, lifeguard drills, calls for help and struggles for breath. A LACE production.

Vanishing Point (2012) By Leslie Hill and Chris Dobrowolski, in which a video trail of vast landscapes and catastrophic incidents are screened in a series of miniature makeshift cinemas fashioned from toys and found objects, combining the epic with the pathetic. Playing with scale, distance and suspense to produce an intimate, witty and sociable encounter with film and art in the everyday world. A LACE production.

World's End (2012) An evening of strong currents, potent drinks and local legend served up by Helen Paris, Leslie Hill and Claudia Barton with support from piano man Ian Grant. Over the course of the evening, portraits of World's End residents taken by acclaimed photographer Hugo Glendinning are slowly unveiled. Performance and exhibition commissioned by Chelsea Theatre, London.

14 Lines (2011) Working with photographer Hugo Glendinning and sound artist Graeme Miller, Curious created an installation in the Swan Gallery Stratford Upon Avon incorporating 14 portraits inspired by personal stories and by the Shakespearean sonnet. Commissioned as part of a residency at the Royal Shakespeare Company.

Save for Later (2011)   Performance about the impossibility of recording archiving and saving live performance premiered at Courtyard Theatre London and then at PSi17 in Utrecht.

Slipstreaming (2011)   Audiences are taken on an evening boat cruise through past and future, fate, fact and fiction. Unmoored and adrift on the river, the Captain steers a route awash with siren songs, mythical yarns and misguided tour guiding. With a hypnotic soundtrack by Graeme Miller and songs by Claudia Barton this is a boat trip with a difference, and one where a very important choice has to be made. Commissioned as part of a residency at the Royal Shakespeare Company.

the moment I saw you I knew I could love you (2009)   About gut feelings; fight, flight and freeze reactions; impulse, love and undefended moments. Film and live action merge with sampled sound and siren song as the audience is cast adrift in life-rafts with only stories and half-remembered truths to sustain them. The Curious quest is autobiological; to expose from the inside truth and lies, biography and mythology; to probe how we compile and edit the stories of our 'selves'. Music by Graeme Miller and film with Andrew Kötting. Performance premiered Chelsea Theatre, London.

(be)longing (2007)   Camouflaged in cowboy shirts with fancy stitches made to hide broken hearts and cowboy boots custom made for the walking wounded, deflecting vulnerability with sequins and high heels, this is curious at their most personal and poignant. Beneath the neon glow of a highway road sign, their yearnings take them across vast desert landscapes in frustrated searches for fulfilment and fitting in. Leslie Hill carries the exquisite burden of newly purchased guitars she can't really play while Helen Paris exiles herself to yoga retreats and detox diets before finally giving up and retraining as a butcher. Performance premiered National Review of Live Art, Glasgow.

Dry Clean Only (2006)   An intimate one-to-one performance, set in a high street dry cleaners in Nottingham, about delicate material, sticky issues and hard to remove stains. Commissioned by NOW Festival, Nottingham.

Greenham Common (2006)   A site-specific performance and photography project set in and around the Cold War nuclear missile base and protest sites at Greenham. Commissioned by New Greenham Arts and the Corn Exchange Greenham Common.

Lost & Found (2005)   The volatile, capricious nature of change itself comes under the spotlight as Curious tugs at the seams that connect public and private transformations, linking the changes in people's neighbourhoods and cities to the sometimes subtle, sometimes dramatic, changes in their own personal lives. A live performance designed for systems of transportation specific to different cities. Performance premiered at FIERCE, Birmingham.

Dirty Laundry (2004)   Activist film and live performance in New York during the Republican convention. Franklin Furnace commission with Lois Weaver.

Et Maintenant? (2004)   Writings and performances about the US/UK special relationship made in response to the US/UK war on Iraq. Commissioned by the French Ministry of Culture, Paris, made in residence at the Couvent des Récollets, Paris.

Family Hold Back (2004)   A highly visual, darkly comic and very well mannered performance airing the perversities of politeness of the English dinner table, where no one mentions politics and everyone knows that Trotterscliffe is pronounced Trosley. It is about being shut up, talked over and con... const... constantly interrupted. Over the three courses of the evening, a leakage of repressed bad manners begins to soak the corners of the pristine white tourniquet napkins as Paris struggles to confront what really lies underneath the perfectly laid table. Performance premiered National Review of Live Art, Glasgow.

Smoking Gun (2004)   Solo performance exploring a heritage of villainy and heroism. The piece is essentially about humanness: where we come from, where we're going and why we can't seem to stop killing each other. Hill draws on current genetic research which links us all to a shared ancestry, inviting reflections on notions of 'us' and 'them', victims and perpetrators and migration and survival. Hill questions concepts of 'intelligence' in a world where the principal undertaking of our time is the preparation for war. Performance premiered National Review of Live Art, Glasgow.

Emily (Requiem for a Friend) (2003)   Film installation about the suffragette Emily Wilding Davison (11 October 1872 – 8 June 1913) shown at SITE gallery, Sheffield.

Guerrilla Performance Locator (2003)   Hill and Paris pay homage to suffragettes by recreating guerrilla performances in contemporary political contexts, and inviting audience members to likewise make spectacles of themselves for things they believe in. The resulting performances were displayed on the Guerrilla Performance Locator website. A Shooting Live Artists commission from BBCi & Arts Council England.

On the Scent (2003)   Intimate performance in a domestic setting in which scents mingle and intertwine in the living-room, kitchen and bedroom as three distinctly different performers exude haunting, darkly humorous and seductive essences throughout the house. Performance premiered at FIERCE, Birmingham.

The Seaside Towns Project (2002)   Writings and performances in and about the South East coastline. A web performance supported by South East Arts.

Deserter (2000)   A performance about desertion and the desert interweaving moments of one-to-one encounters in a confessional mode with digital imagery and live performance, heroic acts and shots of tequila. Commissioned and premiered at the Project Arts Centre, Dublin and It's Queer Up North, Manchester (retitled 'Hot').

No Absolutes (2000)   Video installation in eight parts, featuring performances by female performers (Helena Goldwater, Christine Malloy, Julie Tolentino,

Peggy Shaw, Lois Weaver) 'on location' in Arizona. Arizona State University Art Museum, Phoenix.

Resolutions (2000)   A digital video and CD-ROM project which examined personal and collective twentieth century 'resolutions', while simultaneously building an awareness, through the use of different narrative and visual styles, of the changing 'resolutions' in twentieth-century photographic-image capture. Funded by the Institute for Studies in the Arts.

BULL (1999)   A quartet for four performers; a roofless cathedral room; a 20′ × 20′ film screen; and a mechanical bull. Christine Molloy, Leslie Hill, Helen Paris and Joe Lawlor perform a quartet of highly diverse yet curiously intertwined narrative mélanges of imagery, soundtrack, live performance and bull riding. Produced by the Institute for Studies in the Arts and Live Art Platform, premiered at Ice House, Phoenix.

Vena Amoris (1999)   A journey of narcissism and self-obsession, employing both visceral and virtual means to explore the perils of self-desire: the danger of leaning too far over the black pond of the ever-present screen and slowly becoming captivated, immobilized in the quest for the perfect pixilated image. Supported by an Artsadmin bursary and performance premiered at Toynbee Studios, London.

Random Acts of Memory (1998)   (A)synchronous interplay of unreasonable facsimiles and unfaithful self-portraits rendered via circuits and synapses, RAM investigates the relationship between digital and synaptic memory, between replication and interpretation. Performance premiered Arizona State University.

I Never Go Anywhere I Can't Drive Myself (1997)   A live-art road trip through two-lane byways and information super highways, travelling Route 66 from Chicago to LA and back again whilst creating an extensive road trip web site for virtual travellers.

Left Bank Café (1997)   An on-site and on-line project dedicated to (re)creating a space for thinking, writing, reading, philosophizing and watching the world go by. Through the creation of this virtual cafe, curious.com invite an international community of artists to gather once again on the Parisian leftbank. Funded by the Institute for Studies in the Arts

The Day Don Came With the Fish (1997)   A multimedia performance juxtaposing the mortality of live performance with the immortality of film, and exploring notions of digital and analogue time in relation to pivotal moments. Commissioned by The London Filmmakers Co-op and London Electronic Arts to open their new multimedia performance space, The Lux, London.

Three Semi-Automatics Just for Fun (1997)   A dark, politically provocative and disturbingly funny piece which touches the raw nerve of current US and UK gun control debates, explores personal vigilante fantasies, and examines the new US vogue for pistol-packing wives and mothers as Family Values frontswomen for the pro-gun case. Performance premiered at the Centre for Contemporary Arts Glasgow.

Film and DVD

Landfill (2011)   A short film by Curious and Andrew Kötting, commissioned as part of a series of films, *What On Earth*, which look at the state of the species, some of the pressures on our planet, issues we face now and futures we might see as a consequence of the way we live today. *Landfill* is a Beckettian post-apocalyptic picnic. Two women slowly sink into a fissure at the edge of a cliff. Time-lapse cinematography charts their slow descent as they bravely chat on, trying to figure out what went wrong, whether it was their fault and how to keep their chins up. *What On Earth* is commissioned by Artsadmin and Xenoki Films supported by Grants for the Arts through Arts Council England and the Calouste Gulbenkian Foundation.

Gut Feelings Trilogy (2010)   A DVD which includes full-length documentation of the performance *the moment I saw you I knew I could love you*; the film *Sea Swallow'd* by Curious and Andrew Kötting; interviews on 'Autobiology' workshops – in which Curious worked with 56 artists across the UK using 'gut feelings' to generate text, performance, video and installation work – and a special bonus track on the creative process in making the performance and film. Curious and Live Art Development Agency, 93 minutes.

Sea Swallow'd (2010)   Charts the choppy waters of gut feelings, capturing the flotsam and jetsam of impulse, desire and fights to the death. A film by Andrew Kötting and Curious shot as a series of lapping and flowing, irregular chapters, which borrow their titles from Moby Dick. The film is image and urge driven, giving the viewer the feeling of beach-combing for different fragments of treasure on the shoreline. A highly experiential journey mixing 16mm B&W footage shot by filmmaker Ben Rivers with video and archival footage and a sound score by Graeme Miller. 18 mins. Premiered at Edinburgh Festival.

Fit to Survive (2009)   About plastic waste in the Pacific Ocean and its impact on the environment. Broadcast on Channel 4 on 12 February 2009 to celebrate Darwin's 200th birthday as part of the Three Minute Wonder series. Also screened at the Natural History Museum as part of their Darwin200 event. It is now online along with seven other Darwin-inspired artist films at darwinoriginals.co.uk.

(be)longing (2007)   A group of inspiring African teenagers brought illegally or trafficked into the UK overcome desperate situations and build new lives for themselves in London. Now in college, fluent in English, with dreams of going to university, the girls face deportation on their eighteenth birthdays under current Home Office rules. This film asks them what they long for and where they feel they belong. 10 mins, 35mm, colour, 2007. First Screened 24 May, Genesis Cinema, London. London: CVS. ISBN 0–9524337–5–3.

Lost & Found (2005)   A series of films exploring the volatile, capricious nature of change in three very different environments (39 minutes total). In Lost Property, an enigmatic woman whose favourite words are adhesive – 'sellotape', 'super glue' and 'safety pin' – tries to come to terms with the difference between being lost and being left. In *Lost & Found*, Black Country locals reflect on their sense of place and the breakdown of community in an area of significant regeneration. Manchester: Cornerhouse. ISBN 978–0–9551295–1–3.

Essences of London (2004)   A year-long project involving the London Boroughs of Brent, Hackney, Lambeth, Newham and Tower Hamlets, creating a composite portrait of London by capturing essences of city life through the sense of smell. Hundreds of Londoners were interviewed about their personal smell associations, including workers in 'aromatic trades' such as cobblers, fishmongers, florists, bakers and refuse collectors. London: Tribal. ISBN 0–9524337–4–5.

Red Lantern House (2004)   A recently arrived American notices a woman living in a partially demolished house on a massive development site in Shanghai. The film captures the final days of the Red Lantern House and the beginning of an unlikely friendship. Funded by the British Council.

Books

Place and Performance (2006)   Featuring a mix of both practitioners and scholars, this book explores the sites of contemporary performance and the notion of place. It examines how we experience performance's many and varied sites as part of the fabric of the art work itself, whether they are institutional or transient, real or online. Half of the chapters are by artists who speak directly from their own experience of placing performance outside of conventional spaces; half are by academics who reflect critically on place and placelessness. Published by Palgrave Macmillan.

Guerilla Guide to Performance Art: How to Make a Living as an Artist (2001)   Written by artists, for artists, the *Guerilla Guide* is designed for people engaged in creating original performance work including live art, installation, digital art and hybrids of theatre and visual art. Although there is no 'how to' for this kind of work, no clearly defined industry, this book stares unflinchingly into the headlights of the oncoming question: how do you make a living as an artist? It offers an invaluable collection of individual experiences and strategies from veteran artists and administrators, including Bobby Baker, Tim Miller, Guillermo Gómez-Peña, Stelarc, Lois Weaver and Martha Wilson. Published by Continuum, 2nd edition 2004.

Greenham Common (2006)   A limited edition artists' book, which includes writing and images from the artists' work in and around the Cold War nuclear missile base and protest sites at Greenham Common.

For further details on these and other Curious projects, see placelessness.com.

Notes

I   Introduction

1. At the time of writing: 43 Olivier Awards, 26 Critics' Circle Awards, 25 *Evening Standard* Awards, two South Bank Awards and 20 Tony Awards for Broadway transfers.
2. The 19th Performance Studies international conference, hosted by Stanford University's Department of Theatre and Performance Studies, 26–30 June 2013.

Part One   Proximity and Performance

2   Interior I: *On the Scent*

1. Sissel Tolaas (who speaks 9 languages) claims there is no existing language that accurately describes smell. She is making a language, NASALO (see Caroline Jones, 2006, p. 12).
2. Other notable olfactory performances include: Romeo Castellucci's production *On the Concept of the Face, Regarding the Son of God* (2011) about a son cleaning up after his aged father, where the smell of excrement (fabricated) fills the auditorium; Clara Ursitti's piece *Pull Up To The Bumper* (2003) where the interior of a white limo smells distinctly of semen (again a synthetic recreation); and food performances such as Bobby Baker's *Cook Dems* (1992) where the smell of dough acts as a metaphor for the female body (see Banes and Lepecki, 2007, p. 134).
3. Invited as part of ATHE's Performance Studies Focus Group's first annual Preconference, founded and organized by Josh Abrams and Jennifer Parker Starbuck, 2003.
4. Vannini, Waskul and Gotschalk,   write that, 'Together, ritual sensations and sense-making rituals situate the self within a particular place and time. Particular sensations – for example, those associated with specific toys, nature sounds, foods, beverages, even medicinal treatments such as Vaporub® – can serve as nostalgic reminders of past times, places, people, and events' (2012, p. 88).
5. Even in such proximity, however, it's impossible to always accurately read what audience members are thinking or experiencing. On one occasion when we did *On the Scent* a well-known academic was in one of the audience groups. We didn't know each other personally, though I (Leslie) knew of his work

and was pleased that he had come. During the performance, however, I was absolutely convinced that he would have paid money to be airlifted out of there – it was impossible to make eye contact with him and I worried that he was having some sort of traumatic or claustrophobic experience that might also rub off on the other three audience members. But intimate and calibrated as these pieces are, they are still performances and so I performed my part as usual, or as well as I could under the circumstances and was probably not all that discernibly different. A day or two after the performance we received a really beautiful email from the well-known academic who said that he loved the piece and I was so surprised – I suppose I normally trust my instincts on how any given performance is going, but on this occasion (and I'm sure on others) I read the signs incorrectly. I think he was creating a private cocoon for himself to experience this intimate piece and I mistook that internal energy for withdrawing from the piece whereas it seems he was drawing into it – or into himself within the piece.

6. Lois Weaver, interview during break between *On the Scent* performances, Cambridge, UK, 2009.

7. Hirsch and Spitzer write that 'Initially identified in exiles and displaced soldiers languishing for home, symptoms of nostalgia were understood to be triggered in its victims through sights, sounds, smells, tastes – any of a number of associations that might influence them to recall the homes and environments they had unwillingly left behind. Returning the "homesick," the "nostalgic," to their origins, it was believed, was the potential cure for the "disease" – its restorative ending.' See Marianne Hirsch and Leo Spitzer (2002) 'We would not have come without you': Generations of Nostalgia', in *American Imago* 59.3 (John Hopkins University Press).

8. For an alternate reading of Nostalgia, see the work of Svetlana Boym, (2001) *The Future of Nostalgia* (New York: Basic Books).

9. Vannini, Waskul and Gotschalk state that 'Interviews work well because bodily co-presence allows interviewees and interviewers to create a bond, to share common experiences, to reflect on differences, and to lean on the relational modes of dialogue typical of acquaintanceship and friendship. [...] Interviews about sensual topics can work insofar as both interviewer and interviewee are ready to scrutinize their sensations [...] It was only when we asked "difficult" questions that forced them to describe familiar places and sensations, or prompted them to narrate, that both we and our informants learned about the quality of sensations' (2012, p. 73).

3 Interior II: *the moment I saw you I knew I could love you*

1. The show premiered at Chelsea Theatre, November 2009, with original cast members Claudia Barton, Leslie Hill, Helen Paris, Joseph Young, Geoff McGarry and Rene Newby. Composer Graeme Miller. Film by Curious and Andrew Kötting. The piece was funded by the Wellcome Trust and Arts Council England and was produced by Artsadmin.

2. Margaret Morse writes that 'the theatrical tradition of the proscenium arch is itself a transformation of an actual, primordial threshold into a space dedicated to ritual transformation. To cross inside was to enter the liminal or in-between stage in a rite of passage from one mortal state or condition into another – birth, childhood, adult man- or womanhood, old age or death – while coming in contact with another realm that signifies the immortal or eternal' (Morse, 1999, p. 4).

3. See S. Johnson (2004) *Mind Wide Open: Your Brain and the Neuroscience of Everyday Life* (London: Scribner) and C. B. Pert (1997) *Molecules of Emotion: Why You Feel the Way You Feel* (London: Simon & Schuster)

4. Pool lounger/air mattress.

5. Geoff and Rene were 89 and 87 at the time of the first performance. When we toured the piece to Madison and New York we were joined by US octogenarians Don and Barbara McCrimmon and in California by Janet and John Creelman and at the City of Women festival, Ljubljana, by Ana Jovičevič, Ilije Zsabo.

6. Marvin Carlson also pointed out that at 77 he also found the unconventional seating somewhat uncomfortable, especially as he has very long legs.

7. Claudia Barton reflects: 'The life-rafts would creak and rock unsettlingly when we climbed into them. We would choose a gap between the audience members and sit down beside them. People would sometimes have to collect up their possessions and move over a little, which would send the life-rafts reeling again. Quite often there was a feeling of reluctance about allowing another person into the boat, as though a secret club had already been formed by the handful of people thrown together arbitrarily in the life-raft, as though one more person could tip the balance unfavourably in terms of their survival. This sort of quick sense of camaraderie that can be found in intimate performances was accentuated by the containment and associations of the life-raft. Midway through the whale story I untie a handkerchief filled with chalk collected from Beachy Head. Until this moment I have just been telling a story, like a fable, from the point of view of a whale. But the moment I produce genuine artefacts from the site the story takes on a tangibility, as though I was an actual witness to the event. The levity in the story evaporates, there is something foreboding about the chalk. In one hand I let the chalk fall into the palm of the other, like the few tiny crumbles of chalk that fall down the side of the cliff as the man moves closer to the edge. In this action a cloud of chalk dust rises into the air, like smoke, or little sparkly stuff, tiny dust motes, that we peer through at each other. Some of the rocks might miss my palm and bounce on the inflated rubber of the lifeboat, or land by someone's foot, creating a distraction from the story, bringing a strange significance, something incongruous you might focus on in a moment of adversity or danger' (Barton interview, 26 August, 2013).

8. In his footnotes Leder does reflect on the fact that the lived experience of the inner body may be better expressed by non-Western medicines. As part of the process of creating *the moment I saw you I knew I could love you* we

worked towards an awareness of the subtle body through daily yoga and meditation practice. See D. Leder (1990) *The Absent Body* (Chicago, IL and London: University of Chicago Press).

9. Leder adds in footnotes that there is a sense of body awareness but it is as subsiduary and secondary. See Leder, as above.

10. Claudia Barton reflects: 'Between the "swallows" of the song I gasp for breath, an inkling of the descending melody present in the gasping. It sounds like the inflating of a lilo, but inverted. These breaths continue throughout Helen's text, gradually losing pace and letting go, ending in a pause in the darkness until the first arpeggios of guitar from *Only Fools Rush In* begin. The breaths also coincide with the intermittent beeping of the spaceship orbiting in the soundtrack. I could not help thinking of a life support machine' (Barton interview, 26 August, 2013).

4 Landscape I: *Out of Water*

1. *Out of Water* is a site-specific performance made by Helen Paris and Caroline Wright, www.carolinewright.com. The original soundtrack was composed by Jocelyn Pook, www.jocelynpook.com, with singing by UK soprano Laura Wright, www.laura-wright.co.uk. A detailed description of the process Paris and Wright undertook in the making of *Out of Water* can be found in Helen Paris (forthcoming 2014) 'Still. Moving', in G. Schiller and S. Rubidge (eds), *Choreographic Dwellings, Practicing Place* (Basingstoke: Palgrave Macmillan).

   Out of Water premiered on 25–27 August 2012 at Holkham Beach, North Norfolk as part of the London 2012 Festival. It was supported using public funding by Arts Council England, Escalator Live Art, Norfolk County Council and the Women Make Music scheme through the PRS For Music Foundation with thanks to Natural England and the Holkham Estate. It was produced by Artsadmin. In 2013 *Out of Water* moved country and coast to Fort Funston Beach in San Francisco, California, where it was performed on 29 June as part of Performance Studies international 19 at Stanford University. It was supported by The British Council, Colchester Arts Centre, Stanford Arts and the Department of Theatre and Performance Studies, Stanford University.

   UK performers: Diane Archer, Claudia Barton, Jillian Buckingham, Jenny English, Annette Fry, Georgie Fuller, Sophie Gleeson, Sand Grunwald, Trudy Howson, Anne Hulse, Alan Jackson, Fiona Lawrence, Jenny Lodge, Electra May, Vanda Moye, Helen Paris, Holly Rumble, Gil Stead, Eleanor Stokes, Kayla St. Clair, Teresa Verney, Brigid Warner, Claire Whittenbury, Jane Wisbey, Caroline Wright and Laura Wright with choral group The Oo La Lume's (Jenny Minton, Ellie Showering, Verity Standen).

   US performers: Joan Berry, Juliet Brodie, Ann Carlson, Sukanya Chakrabarti, Li Cornfeld, Abbie Cunliffe, Sarah Curran, Natasha Davis, Leslie Hill, Cate Hull, Marina Kelly, Angrette McCloskey, Helen Paris, Bob Karper, Rebecca Swanson, Gretchen Schiller, Caroline Smith, Ryan Tacata, Lois Weaver, Caroline Wright, Laura Wright with Life Guard Sean Scallan.

2. Michael Peterson, San Francisco 29 June 2013.
3. Alex Hyde, Norfolk, UK, 25 August 2012.
4. In San Francisco the audience went on a 40-minute bus journey to get to the beach.
5. Michael Peterson, San Francisco, 2013.
6. Michael Peterson described the walk back at the end of the piece as 'a very effective, meditative cool-down from the piece. I felt very rested, like after a good yoga workout, by the time we reached the trail up the bluffs. Climbing up we sort of all turned back into ordinary people.'
7. Renu Cappelli, San Francisco, 2012.
8. See the vivid account by artist Sue Hill in Machon's *Immersive Theatres*, where Hill describes one performance of a piece they did where as part of the show, the company run into the sea and pull nets and harvest a catch. 'One night, when the tide was a lot further out, we ended up running for a long way and we found the audience was running with us. We reached the sea and some of them actually came into the sea... they had volunteered themselves into our world... somehow we'd created a world that was strong enough that they felt they could inhabit it without breaking any rules or without behaving in a way where they had to "perform", they were still an audience. That has become part of the journey for us; how do you create a world that's strong enough, in which the audience knows how to behave, they know what's expected of them so that they can be more interactive than they would be if they were in a conventional theatre situation' (Hill in Machon, 2013, p. 242). See also the work of UK company Punchdrunk and their strategy of masking audience members in an acknowledgement of, 'the desire for anonymity, for protection from the social risk that comes with re-staging precious and much performed social selves in the treacherous landscape of theatrical performance'. The anonymity engendered by the masks allows audience members to interact with more freedom in the work than they might do otherwise (see Gareth White's article 'Odd Anonymized Needs: Punchdrunk's Masked Spectator, in Oddey and White, 2009, p. 226).
9. Michael Peterson, San Francisco, 2013.
10. *Vena Amoris* (1999) offered possibilities of intimacy, of seeing and being seen, through the predominantly 'unmarked' presence of the performer. Close proximity between audience and performer is enabled through the *distancing* device of the mobile phone that connects the two. See full account in H. Paris (2002) 'Crossing wires/shifting boundaries in *Vena Amoris*', in *Women & Performance: A journal of feminist theory* 12.2, pp. 159–74, (Routledge).
11. One audience member commented after the Holkham performance, 'When you came towards me I started thinking "what is she going to do!" Then I saw that you were leading me to the sea. You were walking quite fast, with a purpose and you held my hand firmly and I knew that I would go with you, there was no doubt about that. I thought "I guess we are going to go right into the sea" and I thought of what I had in my backpack and would it get wet, and that in any case you would have towels, maybe cocoa.'

12. Solnit's title, *The Faraway Nearby*, is itself concerned with bringing the far close, proximate, and revealing how distance itself enables closeness. The title refers to artist Georgia O'Keeffe and is the title of one of O'Keeffe's paintings, a massive deer skull, extravagantly antlered and looming larger than life in the Arizona desert. O'Keeffe's work plays with the size, scale and perspective of an object (a flower, a skull) within a landscape, blurring distinctions between the near and the far, the large and the small.

13. Quote in full: 'Empathy means that you travel out of yourself a little or expand. It's really recognizing the reality of another's existence that constitutes the imaginative leap that is the birth of empathy, a word invented by a psychologist interested in visual art. The word is only slightly more than a century old, though the words sympathy, kindness, pity, compassion, fellow-feeling, and others covered the same general ground before Edward Titchener coined it in 1909. It was the translation of the German word *Einfühlung*, or feeling into, as though the feeling itself reached out... The root word for empathy is path, from the Greek word for passion or suffering' (Solnit, 2013, pp. 194–5)

14. brianmassumi.com/interviews/NAVIGATING%20MOVEMENTS.pdf.

15. Janet Cardiff (2004) *Her Long Black Hair*, in Janet Cardiff and George Bures Miller, Official Website, http://www.cardiffmiller.com/artworks/walks/longhair.html, audio extract/text (accessed 22 July 2013). See also E. Nedelkopoulou (2011) 'Walking Out on Our Bodies: Participation as Ecstasis in Janet Cardiff's Walks', in *Performance Research: A Journal of the Performing Arts* 16.4, pp. 117–23.

16. The San Francisco performance coincided with the city's Gay Pride march, the repeal of DOMA and Proposition 8 in California. It makes me think of the power of the simple act of walking, you and me, hand in hand.

17. Natasha Davies, an audience to the piece in the United Kingdom and a performer in it in the United States.

18. As I (Helen) wrote this chapter I felt the company of my collaborators. I heard again the soaring extraordinary voice of Laura Wright whose singing transported us, performers and audience alike. Against the wind and the ocean swell her voice a golden rope of sound, shot through with light. I felt the hauntingly powerful composition of Jocelyn Pook's music, she translated words into notes and made a poetry of sound. And most of all I felt the presence of Caroline Wright and remembered how we shared visions, memories and stories and followed water in streams, in rivers, in tidal paths till they led us to the sea.

Part Two   Proximity and Process

6   In the Lab and Incognito: Research in Profile

1. http://www.timeout.com/london/things-to-do/london-underground-lost-property.

2. Later we applied for a Wellcome Trust grant, which funded our residency at the NCBS as well as work on what would become the performance *On the Scent*.

3. Private email correspondence, Paris and Bhalla, 2002.
4. During our residency at the NCBS *New Scientist* interviewed the three of us about our collaboration. In the interview, titled 'A Sense of Wonder', Helen and I outlined our imagined future exhibition as having four chambers: Reminiscence, where the audience encounter smells that may be nostalgic for some, new to others, such as perfumes or cooking smells; False Scents, a chamber where all the sensory stimuli apart from smell will tell them they are in one environment (say an office) while the smell overwhelmingly communicates that they are in another (say the seaside); Self-Portrait, a chamber where the audience will work with a perfumer to create a 'self-portrait'; and finally an autobiographical smell memory recording booth. In a way what we produced did, in the end, have four chambers – three performances each in their own room, followed by the smell memory recording at the end. So in some ways the ideas changed radically, in other ways it was pretty true to the original concept. Hill, Paris and Bhalla (2003) *New Scientist*, p. 46.

7 In the Studio: A Case Study in Performance-Making Methods

1. Unbeknownst to us at the time, the word 'autobiology' is also used by the writer Bonnie Marranca to describe the work of Rachel Rosenthal who, according to Marranca, 'transvalues the routinely autobiographical form in to what I call the autobiological, making a performance a life science'. See B. Marranca (1993) 'A Cosmography of Herself: The Autobiology of Rachel Rosenthal', in *The Kenyon Review* n.s. 15.2, Theater Issue (Spring), p. 59.
2. Feedback was compiled anonymously for an Arts Council report. We include some of it here and are so grateful to all the amazing Autobiology artists we worked with for sharing their reflections.
3. Over the course of the workshop participants made an 'inventory' or 'table of contents' of the stories, gestured images they have accumulated, and named them in a way that marked them distinctly: 'sledging scar story' or 'body memory from the diaphragm'. As well as acting as 'aide-mémoire', particularly helpful when so much work was being generated so rapidly each day, the tables of contents also became interesting autobiological texts in their own rights.

8 In Situ: Extended Conversations

1. Over the years, people we have encountered have been surprisingly relaxed about being recorded and signing release forms. Only about 5 per cent of the people we have interviewed for projects have declined to sign, despite the somewhat intimidating legal language of British broadcasting permissions. In general it seems that people are happy to share thoughts and stories within the context of art projects, or at least that has been our experience.
2. See L. Hill and H. Paris (1998) 'I never go anywhere I can't drive myself', in *Performance Research* 3.2, 102–8 (London and New York: Routledge).

3. As per our usual Curious process, we asked ourselves the same two questions and from our musing on these twin themes of longing and belonging we created a live performance piece which was also called *(be)longing* – entirely personal and unrelated to sex work. This piece premiered at the National Review of Live Art in 2007 and toured the United Kingdom in the same year.

4. The Providence Row group wasn't identified as a sex-worker support group, though they state that 55 per cent of the women they support are involved in sex work and that 90 per cent of the women have been sex workers at some point in their lives.

5. When children are trafficked into the United Kingdom they are considered 'unaccompanied minors' by the state and if they are able to get away from the people who trafficked them and get help, they come under state protection until they turn 18. Once they turn 18, they no longer have asylum status as unaccompanied minors and are deported to their country of origin, even if they have no living family there. This is extremely traumatic, especially as many of these young women have been in the United Kingdom for seven or eight years at this point and many of them are mothers.

6. The women at Open Doors fell in with the project simply because they got to know and like us through our work on the night shifts with their outreach workers and having lunch with them once a week at their NHS drop-in centre. They would dip in and out of the activities we offered as part of the project, depending on what we were doing that week and how they were doing physically – it wasn't uncommon for them to show up having been beaten and needing medical attention more than participatory art. On weeks when they had the ability to participate, they did so simply because they enjoyed it.

7. See also L. Hill (2012) '(be)longing: A Case Study of Recording and Representation', in S. Broadhurst and J. Machon (eds), *Identity, Performance and Technology* 145-159 (Basingstoke: Palgrave Macmillan).

9 Before You Go

1. Since 1993, Guillermo Gómez-Peña and members of the Pocha Nostra performance troupe have conducted cross-cultural/cross-disciplinary/cross-generational workshops involving performance artists, actors, dancers and students from diverse ethnic communities, generations and artistic backgrounds, see http://www.pochanostra.com.

Bibliography

Alrutz, M., Listengarten, J. and Van Duyn Wood, M. (eds) (2012) *Playing with Theory in Theatre Practice* (Basingstoke: Palgrave Macmillan).

Anker, S. and Nelkin, D. (2004) *Molecular Gaze: Art in the Genetic Age* (Cold Spring Harbor, NY: Cold Spring Harbor Laboratory Press Series on Genomics, Bioethics, and Public Policy).

Arends, B. and Slater, V. (eds) (2004) *Talking Back to Science: Art, Science and the Personal* (London: Wellcome Trust).

Auslander, P. (1999) *Liveness* (London and New York: Routledge).

Bachelard, G. (1969) *The Poetics of Space*. Trans. Maria Jolas (Boston, MA: Beacon Press).

Banes, S. and Lepecki, A. (eds) (2007) *The Senses in Performance* (London and New York: Routledge).

Barba, E. and Savares, N. (2006) *A Dictionary of Theatre Anthropology: The Secret Art of the Performer* (London and New York: Routledge).

Barthes, R. (1981) *Camera Lucida; Reflections on Photography*. Trans. Richard Howard (New York: Hill & Wang).

Baumol, William J. and Bowen, William G. (1966) *Performing Arts – The Economic Dilemma: A Study of Problems Common to Theater, Opera, Music and Dance* (New York: Twentieth Century Fund).

Ben Chaim, D. (1984) *Distance in the Theatre: The Aesthetics of Audience Response* (Ann Arbor, MI: UMI Research Press).

Benjamin, W. (1968) *Illuminations, Essays and Reflections*. Trans. Harry Zohn (New York: Schocken).

Bennett, S. (1996) *Performing Nostalgia: Shifting Shakespeare and the Contemporary Past* (London and New York: Routledge).

——. (1997) *Theatre Audiences: A Theory of Production and Reception* (London and New York: Routledge).

Blackadder, N. M. (2003) *Performing Opposition: Modern Theater and the Scandalized Audience* (Westport, CT: Praeger).

Blau, H. (1982) *Blooded Thought: Occasions of Theatre* (New York: Performing Arts Journal Publications).

——. (1990) *The Audience* (Baltimore, MD: Johns Hopkins University Press).

——. (1992) *To all Appearances: Ideology and Performance* (London and New York: Routledge).

Bleeker, M. (2008) *Visuality in the Theatre: The Locus of Looking* (Basingstoke: Palgrave Macmillan).

Bishop, C. (2006) *Participation* (London: Whitechapel).

Bourriaud, P. (1998) *Relational Aesthetics* (Paris: Les Presses Du Réel).

Boym, S. (2001) *The Future of Nostalgia* (New York: Basic Books).

Brecht, B. and Willett, J. (1964) *Brecht On Theatre: The Development of an Aesthetic* (New York: Hill & Wang).

Broadhurst, S. and Machon, J. (eds) (2012) *Identity, Performance and Technology* (Basingstoke: Palgrave Macmillan).

Brook, P. (1972) *The Empty Space* (London: Penguin Books).

Canton, U. (2011) *Biographical Theatre: Re-Presenting Real People* (Basingstoke: Palgrave Macmillan).

Carr, C. (1994) *On Edge: Performance at the End of the 20th Century* (Middletown, CT: Wesleyan University Press).

Chalmers, J. and Chaudhuri, U. (2004) 'Sniff Art', *TDR: The Drama Review* 48.2 (T 182) (Summer), 76–80 (Cambridge, MA: MIT Press).

Chandler, A. and Neumark, N. (eds) (2005) *At a Distance: Precursors to Art and Activism on the Internet* (Cambridge, MA: MIT press).

Chatzichristodoulou, M. and Zeriham, R. (eds) (2012) *Intimacy across Visceral and Digital Performance* (Basingstoke: Palgrave Macmillan).

Classen, C. (1993) *Worlds of Sense: Exploring the Senses in History and across Cultures* (London and New York: Routledge).

Classen, C., Howes, D. and Synnott, A. (eds) (1995) *Aroma: The Cultural History of Smell* (London and New York: Routledge).

Corbin, A. (1994) *The Foul and The Fragrant: Odour and the Social Imagination* (London: Picador).

Davis, Tracy C. and McConachie, B. (1998) 'Introduction', *Theatre Survey* 39.2, 1–5 (Cambridge: Cambridge University Press).

de Marinis, M. (1993) *The Semiotics of Performance* (Bloomington, IN: Indiana University Press).

de Marinis, M. and Dwyer, P. (1987) 'Dramaturgy of the Spectator', *The Drama Review: TDR* 31.2 (Summer), 100–14, 15 (Cambridge, MA: MIT Press).

Deluze, G. and Guattari, F. (2004) *A Thousand Plateaus* (London and New York: Continuum).

Dewey, J. (1932) *Art As Experience* (New York: Minton, Balch).

Diamond, E. (ed.) (1996) *Performance and Cultural Politics* (London and New York: Routledge).

——. (1997) *Unmaking Mimesis: Essays on Feminism and Theatre* (London and New York: Routledge).

Doane, M. (2003) 'The Close-Up: Scale and Detail in the Cinema', *differences: A Journal of Feminist Cultural Studies* 14.3 (Fall), 89–111 (Durham, NC: Duke University Press).

Dolan, J. (2005) *Utopia in Performance: Finding Hope at the Theatre* (Ann Arbor, MI: University of Michigan Press).

Drobnick, J. (2006) *The Smell Culture Reader* (New York: Berg Publishing).

——. (due 2014) 'Smell: The Hybrid Art', in Chantal Jaquet (ed.), *L'Art Olfactif Contemporain* (Paris: Sorbonne).

Ekman, P. and Rosenberg, E. (2005) *What the Face Reveals: Basic and Applied Studies of Spontaneous Expression Using the Facial Action Coding System* (Oxford: Oxford University Press).

Engen, T. (1991) *Odor Sensation and Memory* (New York: Praeger Publishers).

Fischer-Lichte, E. (2008) *The Transformative Power of Performance: A New Aesthetics.* Trans. Saskya Iris Jain (London and New York: Routledge).

Freshwater, H. (2009) *Theatre & Audience* (Basingstoke: Palgrave Macmillan).

Frieling, R. (2008) *The Art of Participation, 1950 to Now* (San Francisco, CA: San Francisco Museum of Modern Art).

Fuchs, E. and Chaudhuri, U. (eds) (2002) *Land/Scape/Theatre* (Ann Arbor, MI: University of Michigan Press).

Garner, S. B. Jr (1994) *Bodies Spaces: Phenomenology and Performance in Contemporary Drama* (Ithaca, NY, and London: Cornell University Press).

Gershon, M. D. (1999) *The Second Brain* (New York: Quill).

Giannachi. G., Kaye, N. and Shanks, M. (eds) (2012) *Archaeologies of Presence Art Performance and the Persistence of Being* (London and New York: Routledge).

Gigerenzer, G. (2007) *Gut Feelings: The Intelligence of the Unconscious* (London: Penguin).

Gladwell, M. (2005) *Blink: The Power of Thinking Without Thinking* (London: Penguin).

Goffman, E. (1959) *The Presentation of Self in Everyday Life* (Garden City, NY: Anchor).

——. (1986) *Frame Analysis* (Harmondsworth: Penguin).

Gómez-Peña, G. and Sifuentes, R. (2011) *Exercises for Rebel Artists: Radical Performance Pedagogy* (London and New York: Routledge).

Goulish, M. (2000) *39 Microlectures in Proximity of Performance* (London and New York: Routledge).

Grehan, H. (2009) *Performance, Ethics and Spectatorship In a Global Age* (Basingstoke: Palgrave Macmillan).

Grotowski, J. (1969) *Towards a Poor Theatre* (London: Methuen).

Hall, D. and Fifer, S. J, (eds) (1991) *Illuminating Video: An Essential Guide to Video Art* (New York: Aperture in association with the Bay Area Video Collective).

Hall, E. T. (1966) *The Hidden Dimension* (Garden City, NY: Anchor Books, Random House).

Hennion, A. (2004) 'Pragmatics of Taste', in M. Jacobs and N. Weiss Hanrahan (eds), *The Blackwell Companion to the Sociology of Culture* (Oxford: Blackwell Press), 131–44.

——. (2007) 'Those things that Hold us Together: Taste and Sociology', *Cultural Sociology* 1, 97–114 (Thousand Oaks, CA: Sage).

Henshaw, J. (2012) *A Tour of the Senses: How your Brain Interprets the World* (Baltimore, MD: Johns Hopkins University Press).

Herrschaft, F. (2008) 'Performing Proximity – "Learning To Fly"' *Forum Qualitative Sozialforschung/Forum: Qualitative Social Research* 9.2, 1–15.

Hill, J. (2002) *Stages and Playgoers: From Guild Plays to Shakespeare* (Montreal: McGill-Queen's University Press).

Hill, L. and Paris, H. (1998) 'I Never Go Anywhere I Can't Drive Myself', *Performance Research* 3.2, 102–8 (London and New York: Routledge).

Hill, L. and Paris, H. (eds) (2006) *Performance and Place* ((Basingstoke: Palgrave Macmillan).

Hill, L., Paris, H. and Bhalla, U. (2003) 'A Sense of Wonder' interview, *New Scientist* (1 March), 44–7.

Hirsch, M. and Spitzer, L. (2002) '"We would not have come without you": Generations of Nostalgia', *American Imago* 59.3, 253–76 (Baltimore, MD: The Johns Hopkins University Press).

Hopkins, D. J., Orr, S. and Solga, K. (eds) (2009) *Performance and the City* (Basingstoke: Palgrave Macmillan).

Howes, D. (2003) *Sensual Relations: Engaging the Senses in Culture and Social Theory* (Ann Arbor, MI: University of Michigan).

——. (2005) *Empire of the Senses: The Sensual Cultural Reader* (New York: Berg Publishing).

Hurley, E. (2010) *Theatre & Feeling* (Basingstoke: Palgrave Macmillan).

Jackson, S. (2011) *Social Works, Performing Art, Supporting Publics* (London and New York: Routledge).

Johnson, S. (2004) *Mind Wide Open: Your Brain and the Neuroscience of Everyday Life* (London: Scribner).

Jones, A. (1998) *Body Art: Performing the Subject* (Minneapolis, MN: University of Minnesota).

——. 'The "Eternal Return": Self-Portrait Photography as a Technology of Embodiment', *Signs*, 27.4 (Summer 2002), 947–78 (Chicago, IL: University of Chicago Press).

——. (2012) *Seeing Differently: A History and Theory of Identification and the Visual Arts* (London and New York: Routledge).

Jones, C. (ed.) (2006) *Sensorium: Embodied Experience, Technology and Contemporary Art* (Cambridge, MA: MIT press).

Kattwinkel, S. (ed.) (2003) *Audience Participation: Essays on Inclusion in Performance* (Westport, CT, and London: Praeger).

Kawash, S. (1999) 'Interactivity and Vulnerability', *Performing Arts Journal* 21.1 (January), 46–52 (Baltimore, MD: Johns Hopkins University Press).

Kaye, N. (2000) *Site-Specific Art Performance: Place and Documentation* (London and New York: Routledge).

Latour, B. (2005) *Reassembling the Social: An Introduction to Actor-Network-Theory* (Oxford: Oxford University Press).

Leder, D. (1990) *The Absent Body* (Chicago, IL, and London: University of Chicago Press).

Lefebvre, H. (1991) *The Production of Space* (Oxford: Blackwell Press).

Levinas, E. (1969) *Totality and Infinity: An Essay on Exteriority*. Trans. Alphonso Lingis (Pittsburgh, PA: Duquesne University Press).

——. (1987) *Time and the Other*. Trans. Richard A. Cohen (Pittsburgh, PA: Duquesne University Press).

——. (1998) *Entre Nous: On Thinking of the Other*. Trans. Michael B. Smith and Barbara Harshaw (New York: Columbia University Press).

——. (2011) *Otherwise Than Being or Beyond Essence* (Pittsburgh, PA: Duquesne University Press).

Lorraine, T. (1999) *Irigaray and Deluze: Experiments in Visceral Philosophy* (Ithaca, NY, and London: Cornell University Press).

Low, K. E. Y. (2005) 'Ruminations on Smell as a Sociocultural Phenomenon', *Current Sociology* 53, 397 (Thousand Oaks, CA: Sage).

McAuley, G. (2000) *Space in Performance: Making Meaning in the Theatre* (Ann Arbor, MI: University of Michigan Press).

McConachie, B. (2008) *Engaging Audiences: A Cognitive Approach to Spectating in the Theatre* (Basingstoke: Palgrave Macmillan).

McConachie, B. and Hart, E. (eds) (2006) *Performance and Cognition: Theatre Studies and the Cognitive Turn* (London and New York: Routledge).

Machon, J. (2009) *(Syn)aesthetics: Redefining Visceral Performance* (Basingstoke: Palgrave Macmillan).

——. (2013) *Immersive Theatres: Intimacy and Immediacy in Contemporary Performance* (Basingstoke: Palgrave Macmillan).

Mackintosh, I. (1993) *Architecture, Actor and Audience* (London: Routledge).

Massey, D. (2005*) For Space* (Los Angeles, London, New Delhi, Singapore and Washington DC: Sage).

Merleau-Ponty, M. (1968) *The Visible and the Invisible*. Trans. Alphonso Lingis (Evanston, IL: Northwestern University Press).

——. (1989) *Phenomenology of Perception*. Trans. Colin Smith (London and New York: Routledge).

Mock, R. (ed.) (2009) *Walking, Writing and Performance* (Bristol and Chicago: Intellect).

Morse, M. (1999) 'Body and Screen', *Wide Angle* 21.1, 63–75 (Birmingham, AL: Samford University).

Oddey, A. (2007) *Re-Framing the Theatrical: Interdisciplinary Landscapes for Performance* (Basingstoke: Palgrave Macmillan).

Oddey, A. and White, C. (eds) (2006) *The Potentials of Spaces: The Theory and Practice of Scenography and Performance* (Bristol and Chicago, IL: Intellect).

——. (eds) (2009) *Modes of Spectating* (Bristol and Chicago, IL: Intellect).

Paris, H. (2002) 'Crossing Wires/Shifting Boundaries in Vena Amoris', *Women & Performance* 12.2, 159–74 (London and New York: Routledge).

Pearson, M. (2010) *Site Specific Performance* (Basingstoke: Palgrave Macmillan).

Pearson, M. and Shanks, M. (2001) *Theatre/Archeology* (London and New York: Routledge).

Performance Research: On Philosophy and Participation (2011) 16.4 (London and New York: Routledge).

Pert, C. B. (1997) *Molecules of Emotion: Why You Feel the Way You Feel* (London: Simon & Schuster).

Phelan, P. (1993) *Unmarked: The Politics of Performance* (London and New York: Routledge).

——. (1997) *Mourning Sex; Performing Public Memories* (London and New York: Routledge).

Phelan, P. and Lane, J. (eds) (1998) *The Ends Of Performance* (New York and London: New York University Press).

Pitches, J. and Popat, S. (eds) (2011) *Performance Perspectives: A Critical Introduction* (Basingstoke: Palgrave Macmillan).

Powers, S. (2008) *Insight Yoga* (Boston, MA: Shambhala Publications).

Rancière, J. (2009) *The Emancipated Spectator* (London and New York: Verso).

Radosavljević, D. (2013) *Theatre-Making: Interplay Between Text and Performance in the 21st Century* (Basingstoke: Palgrave Macmillan).

Read, A. (1993) *Theatre and Everyday Life and Ethics of Performance* (London and New York: Routledge).

——. (2008) *Theatre, Intimacy & Engagement: The Last Human Venue* (Basingstoke: Palgrave Macmillan).

Ridout, N. (2009) *Theatre & Ethics* (Basingstoke: Palgrave Macmillan).

Scarry, E. (1985) *The Body in Pain: The Making and Unmaking of the World* (New York and Oxford: Oxford University Press).

Schechner, R. (1968) '6 Axioms for Environmental Theatre', *The Drama Review: TDR* 12.3, Architecture/Environment (Spring), 41–64 (Cambridge, MA: MIT Press).

——. (1988) *Performance Theory* (London and New York: Routledge).

——. (1994) *Environmental Theatre* (New York: Applause Theatre Books).

Schneider, R. (1997) *The Explicit Body in Performance* (London and New York: Routledge).

Shepherd, S. (2006) *Theatre, Body and Pleasure* (London: Routledge).

Sherman, J. F. (2011) 'Plural Intimacy in Micropublic Performances', *Performance Research: A Journal of the Performing Arts* 16.4, 52–61 (London and New York: Routledge).

Sidiropoulou, A. (2011) *Authoring Performance: The Director in Contemporary Theatre* (Basingstoke: Palgrave Macmillan).

Sobchack, V. (1992) *The Address of the Eye: A Phenomonology of Film Experience* (Princeton, NJ: Princeton University Press).

Solnit, R. (2000) *Wanderlust: A History of Walking* (London: Penguin).

——. (2013) *The Faraway Nearby* (New York: Viking).

Stewart, S. (1993) *On Longing: Narratives of the Miniature, the Gigantic, the Souvenir, the Collection* (Durham, NC, and London: Duke University Press).

Stoller, P. (1997) *Sensuous Scholarship* (Philadelphia, PA: University of Pennsylvania Press).

Straus, E. (1963) *The Primary World of Senses: A Vindication of Sensory Experience* (London: The Free Press of Glencoe, Collier-Macmillan).

Strindberg, A. (1955) 'Author's Foreword'. *Miss Julie*. Trans. Elizabeth Sprigge (New York: Doubleday).

Tan, E. (1982) 'Cognitive Processes in Reception', in *Multimedial Communication*, Volume 11: *Theatre Semiotics*. Ed. Ernest W. B. Hess-Lüttich (Tübingen: Gunter Narr Verlag).

Thompson, J. (2009) *Performance Affects: Applied Theatre and the End of Effect* (Basingstoke: Palgrave Macmillan).

Tuan, Y. F. (1993) *Passing Strange and Wonderful: Aesthetics, Nature and Culture* (Washington, DC: Island Press; Covelo, CA: Shearwater Books).

——. (2001) *Space and Place: The Perspective of Experience* (Minneapolis, MN: University of Minnesota Press).

Turner, V. (1988) *The Anthropology of Performance* (New York: PAJ Publications).

Vannini, P., Waskul, D. and Gotschalk, S. (eds) (2012) *The Senses in Self, Society, and Culture: A Sociology of the Senses* (London and New York: Routledge).

Vroon, P. (1997) *Smell: The Secret Seducer*. Trans. Paul Vincent (New York: Farrar, Straus & Giroux).

Welton, M. (2013) *Feeling Theatre* (Basingstoke: Palgrave Macmillan).

White, G. (2013) *Audience Participation in Theatre: Aesthetics of the Invitation* (Basingstoke: Palgrave Macmillan).

Wilkie, F. (2002), 'Mapping the Terrain: A Survey of Site-Specific Performance in Britain', *New Theatre Quarterly* 18.2, 154 (Cambridge: Cambridge University Press).

Online

Brianmassumi.com.

Cardiffmiller.com.

Pocha Nostra.com

Index